D1784042

EPHEMERIS OF
CHIRON
1890-2000

In 1977, the discovery of a celestial body in orbit between Saturn and Uranus took everyone by surprise. Chiron, as it was named, reminded both astronomers and astrologers that the structure of the solar system is far more complex than we often assume it to be.

This is the original record-breaking ephemeris by Phenomena Publications, released only months after the discovery of Chiron. There is no more accurate, complete and extensive information on Chiron available anywhere. It's all here: geocentric as well as heliocentric positions; right ascension in addition to longitude. Not to mention stations and complete orbital data.

And more! In this second edition, we have added longitudes of Chiron back to 1686 A.D., giving you unparalleled coverage in one compact, convenient volume.

EPHEMERIS OF
CHIRON
1890-2000

by

James Neely
Eric Tarkington

with additional longitudes
1890-1889
by
Mark Pottenger

EDP Support
Michael Campbell

Introduction
Tony Joseph, M.A.

Edited by
Malcolm Dean

PHENOMENA PUBLICATIONS ● MONOGRAPH SERIES

First edition published December 1978,
limited to 500 numbered copies.

Second edition, revised, published 1982 by
Phenomena Publications
P.O. Box 6299
Toronto, Ontario M5W 1P7
Canada

Second printing 1983

Distributed by
Samuel Weiser, Inc.
P.O. Box 612
York Beach, Maine 03910

Copyright © by Phenomena Publications, 1980.
All rights reserved. No part of this publication
may be reproduced whatsoever, including photocopy,
xerography, or any information storage system,
without written permission from the publisher.

ISBN 0-920654-01-0

Canadian Cataloguing in Publication Data:

Neely, James
Ephemeris of Chiron, 1890-2000

(Monograph Series/Phenomena Publications)

1. Planets, Minor - Ephemerides. 2. Astrology
3. Chiron (Planet). I. Tarkington, Eric,
II. Dean, Malcolm, 1948-   III. Pottenger, Mark.
IV. Title

BF1715.N44 1980   133.5'5   C81-094054-X

Designed by Jean Vartan

The publication of this ephemeris was generously
supported by Wim van Dam, Don Weiser, and others.

Printed in the U.S.A. by
Maple-Vail Book Manufacturing Group
Binghamton, NY 13902

Preface
to the revised edition

The publication of this ephemeris, so soon after the discovery of a new celestial body, is an event of interest to contemporary observers as well as future historians of astrology. Never before has such an extended, complete and accurate ephemeris been available, just a few months after the initial observations were made.

Primarily responsible for this breakthrough is the development of digital computers, and their widespread availability. This ephemeris was prepared and printed by an IBM 3033, taking less than twelve minutes to calculate and print the data - a timespan which does not reflect the months of frustrating development which went into creating a program specifically for the calculation of ephemerides for a distant minor planet such as Chiron.

In 1978, a computer program such as this had to be invented. Once prepared, its usefulness was limited in time, and it could not handle bodies much nearer to the Sun, such as main-belt asteroids. Yet, only two years later, programs were developed which could generate upon request ephemerides for most minor planets over considerably longer periods of time, with great accuracy, on a home computer!

Taking advantage of these developments, Mark Pottenger has contributed additional longitudes for this revised edition, so as to increase the usefulness of this ephemeris. We opted to publish only the longitudes in the addendum, since these positions take little additional space and satisfy the

requirements of the vast majority of astrological techniques. Those who may desire more specialized data will find their way to the programs and computer facilities they require.

Secondly, we are fortunate in living long enough *after* the discovery of photography that early plates of Chiron taken (unwittingly) by the U.S. Naval Observatory have provided us with an accurate checkpoint in 1895. Additional photographic observations in the 1940's permitted the rapid calculation of accurate orbital elements in December, 1977. Although we have no earlier positions of Chiron against which to check the new program which generated the additional longitudes of Chiron, a test with other asteroids showed that the positions given are accurate at least as far back as 1800.

The discovery of Chiron, and subsequent determinations of its physical nature and astronomical implications, were documented in various issues of **PHENOMENA** and many science journals. The emerging astrology of Chiron, however, is quite another story.

Astrologers have always had difficulty in dealing with celestial phenomena which are not found in the astrological canon of the Greek era. While asteroids were experimentally employed in astrology soon after their discovery in the early 19th century, they did not begin to attain common usage in horoscopes until Eleanor Bach published her ephemeris of Ceres, Pallas, Juno and Vesta in 1973. Astrologers most often attempt to discern the influence of a new body by comparing events with transits of angles and rapidly-forming aspects. Events most easily used for this purpose are of short duration and striking in nature. Thus, the earliest interpretations of the first four asteroids concentrated on accidents and calamities - just as nearly every other "new" celestial body has initially been given a negative interpretation by astrologers. Only through the steady growth of

Humanistic astrological philosophy have more psychological interpretations of the outer planets and the asteroids overtaken the doom-and-calamity approach.

Chiron, in contrast not only to this pattern, but also to the pessimistic tone of the times, has enjoyed largely positive reviews from most observers. One happily commented, "At last, a new benefic!" Although a small number of researchers are actively promoting their own specific interpretations, it is far too early to expect any definitive understanding of Chiron. Indeed, recent research by Drs. Michel and Francoise Gauquelin demonstrates that astrologers still have a good deal of homework to do on the major planets, especially Jupiter.(1)

Astrologers have a strong tradition of bickering amongst themselves. And it should come as no surprise that Chiron's discovery was accompanied by the usual name-calling and jealousy which children reserve for a newly-found and much-coveted toy. Certain astrologers railed against this ephemeris, believing (incorrectly) that theirs was more accurate. Others were influenced to choose an alternate symbol, which was then held forth as the "official" symbol of Chiron. There were charges that the symbol given in this ephemeris for Chiron looked suspiciously like the Marxist hammer-and-sickle. One year later, rumours were being deliberately spread that our symbol for Chiron was an old witch-symbol capable of dooming anyone who foolishly uses it.(2)

History, not committees, chooses symbols. The simple fact is that symbols become agents of destructive powers only when their multi-faceted natures are restricted to "party-lines", "official" interpretations and demagoguery. While it is true that symbols apparently similar to that presented here for Chiron were used in past centuries (one was a short-form for "hundredweight" - far from a witch-symbol!)

the Chiron glyph presented on the title page of the main ephemeris was simply developed spontaneously and intuitively as a convenience during the earliest stages of our Chiron project. My initial sketch was given the more precise form shown herein by Eric Tarkington. Subsequently, it was realized that the symbol incorporates some interesting features which run strongly parallel to the symbolism of Chiron, and which therefore strengthen the case for its adoption:

> The component letters "ch" for the hard "k" sound of Chiron are only the most obvious features of this symbol. We find also a lunar crescent which is closely linked to the mythical Chiron's role as a Teacher, guru or hierophant. Chiron taught the Greek heroes not only to sharpen and clarify their minds through the arts and philosophy. He also taught that the spirit must rise through the habitual and animalistic realm which the Moon often symbolizes, into a higher synthesis, just as he himself was half-human, half-animal, and divine in origin. There is, therefore, a curious parallel between Chiron's symbol and the Hierophant key of the Tarot (BOTA version), where the Teacher sits between two columns, his neck adorned with a lunar crescent. According to Paul Foster Case, the Hierophant is linked with the words *aid*, *furtherance*, and *ministry*. His teaching is " 'union,' and this is the exact English translation of the Sanskrit noun 'yoga.' "(3)
>
> The pillars in the Hierophant card, and in the symbol of Chiron, represent the polar absolutes of duality, which mind (the crescent) must bridge to achieve transcendant union. Both Chiron

and the Hierophant teach that the powers of the subconscious, the lower and lunar nature which is symbolized by Chiron's animal half, are a key to the energies involved in this process. Case relates the Hierophant to Taurus, in which the Moon is exalted. And by an interesting synchronism, Chiron was discovered while transitting Taurus.

Current astronomical opinion holds that tiny bodies such as Chiron may sometimes be ejected from one orbit to another by the gravitational influences of the major planets. Many small celestial bodies thus enter orbits which reflect the specific influences of one or more larger bodies, just as our Moon's orbit is clearly related to that of the Earth. Chiron's orbit carries it across Saturn's, and occasionally across the orbit of Uranus as well. These passages may be symbolized where the crescent crosses the two vertical lines in our symbol.

Taken as a whole, one can see in this symbol the outlines of the Centaur himself, as he is often pictured, his human half rising up from his standing horselike body, stretching his bow. Following this theme even further, we see that the circle begins at the right, descends into the realm of duality, symbolized by the two pillars or feet, then ascends to the zenith just as a planet rises through the houses or diurnal circle. Yet it returns towards its origin, to carry forward the experience it gained in the lower realm. The circle is not perfect because Chiron is not entirely divine. Finally, we notice that the crescent is large enough to encompass the pillars: thus,

mind must *encompass* duality, and pass beyond to larger spheres.

These comments are made clear through Tony Joseph's valuable paper on Chiron, which follows. It is obvious that no other symbol which has been proposed for Chiron is so closely linked with the deeper ramifications of his mythology, despite what its critics have vehemently maintained. Readers may therefore independently choose to adopt it or deprecate it as they wish.

Repeating a pattern established since the discovery of Uranus, other astrologers have expressed surprise at the eagerness of their colleagues to experiment with Chiron. Similarly, there are those who still refuse to accept the validity of the outer planets in horoscopes, as well as those who heap not a few undiscovered, hypothetical and even astronomically impossible celestial bodies into the symbolic circus of horoscopy.

As I have pointed out elsewhere, the publication of this ephemeris affords a unique opportunity to observe the astrological process in action. While it has been a major problem, until now, to obtain data in astrological form for bodies such as asteroids and comets, astrologers have been presented for the first time with a complete, extensive and accurate ephemeris of a new celestial body, just a few months after discovery. Experiments may now be performed in a variety of positional systems over a considerable period of time. The data is now available for practically any horoscope one might choose.

Previously, astrologers were forced to employ only the few positions which might have been translated out of astronomical sources. The astrology which emerged was sometimes based on poor or inaccurate data. But with this Ephemeris of Chiron, the database is for the first time presented substantially *before* the astrological consensus emerges. It is clearly now the responsibility of serious researchers to determine

what, if anything, is the astrology of Chiron, and what the process of "astrologizing" a new astronomical discovery reveals about Astrology itself.

Only when this process is properly understood will the scientific aspects of astrology emerge into the light of modern day. Just as there are those who actively deny astrology any possible scientific basis, there are those who will continue to refuse to test Chiron by any method - horoscopic or statistical. Neither group, in my opinion, has a strong desire (if any) to see a scientific astrology develop out of the traditions we have inherited.

We might recall that the mythical Chiron taught that out of the arts, traditions and mysteries of the past, new heroes must emerge to forge out new quests, and eventually to conquer. Astrology is clearly in a period of heroic trials - a period which will demand heroic efforts from those determined to expose the true scientific basis of its mysteries. As the Initiate, the Teacher, the Healer, Chiron may lead us to discover more than most today suspect.

Malcolm Dean
November 1980
Toronto

Notes

1. See *The Astrology Game*, Chapter 10, Beaufort Books, NY, 1980.
2. All candidates for the position of "official symbol" were presented in **PHENOMENA** 2.2, 1978. To my knowledge, those who opposed our choice never returned the favour in their publications. As of this writing, at least one

computer service has adopted this symbol for Chiron, and it is in common usage in many countries throughout the world where **PHENOMENA** and this ephemeris have been received.

3. Case, Paul Foster, *The Tarot, A Key to the Wisdom of the Ages*, Macoy, 1947.

Introduction

CHIRON: ARCHETYPAL IMAGE OF TEACHER AND HEALER

© Copyright by Tony Joseph, 1978.

The discovery of the planetoid Chiron (1) in late 1977 by Charles Kowal of the Hale Observatories introduces a new factor to the related complex of astrology, mythology, and psychology. Mythological figures and the planetary bodies named after them symbolize living forces that operate within human consciousness both at the collective level and in our personal lives (2). Accordingly, accounts of the Greek mythological figure after whom the new celestial body was named contribute to our understanding of the nature of human psychological experience. It is not too soon to begin introducing Chiron into astrological symbolism.

Historically, the astronomical discovery of a planetary body has reflected significant cultural developments, particularly within Western societies. The discovery of Uranus in 1781 has been linked symbolically to the revolutionary movements occurring at that time in France and elsewhere. The discovery of Neptune in 1846 marked the quest for ideals and a belief in the transcendental so characteristic of the Romantic Age, which reached its peak in the middle of the nineteenth century. Concordant with Pluto's discovery in the 1930s, civilization braced itself for the threat of mass destruction in an age of totalitarianism and the nuclear arms race. The sighting of a new planet in our solar system, then, provides a metaphorical key to crucial trends arising from within the collective psyche. If Chiron is similarly linked to themes emerging in society, his mythological descriptions would offer insight into the changes currently unfolding in the fields of education and medicine.

Chiron was the son of Chronos (Saturn) and Philyra, a daughter of Oceanus. The first of the centaurs, Chiron was conceived when his father took the form of a stallion to conceal his extramarital sexual union with Philyra from his wife. As a result, Chiron was born a creature with the lower and hind portions of a horse and the upper torso and head of a man (3). This unusual birth took place in a cave -- later named the Chironian -- situated on Mt. Pelion. Here Chiron lived most of his life. In his mountaintop grotto Chiron devoted his time to teaching music, ethics, astrology, and the arts of healing, riding, hunting, and war (4). Occasionally, he would cavort with his fellow centaurs in the surrounding forests and meadows of Thessaly. His wife was the Naiad Charicles, and his daughter, the prophetess Thea. When Thea prophesied that her father would long to give up his immortality, she was transformed into a mare by Poseidon, who placed her image in the heavens as the constellation, the Horse. And, upon Chiron's death, his Olympian brother, Zeus, set him up in the heavens as the constellation Sagittarius, the Archer (6).

Of Chiron's diverse activities, he is most typically depicted as foster parent and teacher to many of the greatest Greek heroes. He instructed Achilles, Jason, Acktaeon, and Peleus in the skills of riding, hunting, and war (7). To Aristaeus he taught music (8). To his most renowned pupils, Achilles and Asclepios Chiron gave the art of healing through the use of medicinal herbs and surgery (9). "Surgery" originates from the word "chirurgery," after Chiron, and arises from the same Greek word for "handiwork" (10). Astrology, too, was introduced by Chiron and considered an essential part of the hero's training. According to one legend (11) Chiron was credited with teaching Heracles the art of astrology. The individual parts of the body, its organs and their diseases, and critical days on which patients were susceptible to illness, were brought into definite relation to astrology through the teachings of Chiron's famous pupil, Asclepios. Later, this relationship between astrology and medicine was further promoted in the medical treatises of Galen (12) and Hippocrates. The original Hippocratic Oath held that astrology was essential to physicians for both diagnostic and therapeutic purposes (13).

Chiron's tutelary role was to provide apprentices with the necessary cultural and ethical values as well as survival skills that enabled them to embark prepared on their heroic quests. Chiron's nature and its embodiment in his teachings parallel the individuation process, the movement toward psychological wholeness. Individuation of the self, according to Carl Jung (14), is not to be merely thought of as the ego's mastery of the environment, or the drive for power and rationality. Individuation inevitably embraces paradox and the conflicting and irrational forces revealed in Nature and in the human psyche.

Significantly, Chiron represents our reaction to and our relation with Nature. As G. S. Kirk puts it, the centaur expresses "a general feeling of Nature itself that we all share: that it can be either hostile and repellent, or sympathetic, uncomplicated and desirable (15)." Centaurs symbolize the dark and destructive forces of Nature and serve as a metaphor for these same irrational forces seen in human activity. This is conveyed in the story of Chiron's fellow centaurs who, in attending the marriage ceremony of Hippodameia, become intoxicated and carry off the women in an orgy. Or, they can symbolize the wisdom, restraint, and compassion of Chiron, who stands aloof from such bestial behavior to occupy himself with the cultural pursuits of education and healing. Boticelli's fifteenth-century painting. "Minerva Subduing the Centaur" (16), depicts Pallas Athena (Minerva) touching Chiron on the forehead, thereby bestowing on him reason and wisdom. Primitive elements in Nature give way to law and ethics and education in the arts.

Closer inspection of the myths reveals the integration of instinct and intellect in Chiron's teaching activities. This union is essential in the skills of hunting, war, and healing. Instinct is not used here simply in the biological sense of inherited release mechanisms, but more completely in the sense of man's psychological capacity for the irrational so characteristically expressed through emotions, and the faculties of intuition and feeling. Chiron's image reminds us that human culture rests on the integration of the irrational with the rational, of instinct with intelligence, of body with mind, of soul with spirit. We see in the discovery of the planetoid Chiron a parallel to the awareness

that education in its higher function is a movement toward psychological wholeness. This is not a new awareness but one reflecting the concern that modern society tends frequently to view man as outside Nature. This separation leads man to strive for intellectual achievements geared to the rational control and domination of Nature.

Chiron's instruction is elevated to the level of an ethical or religious function. It is as if the heroes are being initiated into a cultural consciousness. As Bachofen states: "It is the distinction between a lower and a higher conception of the divine as revealed in Nature, between a primordial and a more highly developed stage of Culture. The religious development of the human race follows the same law that is disclosed in the education of a person. It progresses from the lower to the higher, from the material to the psychic and spiritual . . . from the impure to the pure, from darkness to light (17)." Stated psychologically, it is the integration of the irrational with the rational, of the emotions with the intellect.

Contemporary society inherits the high value placed on education by the Greeks. Education's aim has been to direct our primitive side upward, to sublimate instinct into cultural activity enhancing both the individual and the collective. This is stated in Freud's theory of sublimation. But unlike the pre-Aristotelian Greeks, we have split consciousness from the body. Historically, Christianity and the dualistic thinking of Descartes and the rationalists, which led to the philosophy of materialism, have contributed to establishing the misconception that matter and body are without soul. Nature is no longer animated but is *merely* matter to be manipulated by man's will. From a Greek perspective, today's education is a one-sided activity; but there is now an increasing recognition that most schools and academic settings are not meeting the individual's need to become more psychologically and spiritually integrated. Rather than stressing a split between Nature and Culture, the irrational and the rational, body and mind, true education creates a natural bridge between these fundamental expressions of human activity.

Nowhere is this dilemma within education more evident than in the archetypal significance of Chiron's role as physician and

in the confrontation with his own death. Chiron is not only a surgeon but he also introduces the use of medicinal herbs in healing (18). Modern surgery frequently seeks the removal of diseased tissue without addressing the role the whole organism plays in shaping illness. The Simontons' work with cancer patients (19) reveals the crucial part a person's attitudes and emotions take in contributing to the prognosis of the disease. This kind of investigation in the field of medicine just within the past ten years reflects the growing concern for a more "holistic" medicine. Chiron's discovery symbolizes the recent upsurge of interest in holistic health, naturopathic healing, the body therapies, and the use of various symbolic languages such as astrology and dreams, all of which reveal that one's state of health depends in large part on one's state of consciousness. Chirognomy (20), chiropody (21), and chiropractics (22), which have their etymological origins in the Greek root, *chir,* "hand" (23), are further outgrowths of Chiron's activities as naturopathic healer and holistic educator.

Chiron's accidental wounding and the nature of his death provide interesting possibilities for illustrating his symbolic relationship to the human psyche. While attending the wedding feast of Hippodameia, during which several of the heroes enter into battle with the drunken centaurs, Chiron sustains a serious wound from his friend Heracles, whose poison arrow accidently pierces Chiron's ankle (24). Though Chiron is credited with devising herbal remedies, particularly for snake bites and poison arrow wounds, he cannot heal himself. Because of his immortality he continually suffers. Kerenyi writes about this tragic view of Chiron: "Chiron's world with its inexhaustible possibilities of cure, remained a world of sickness (25)." He willingly offers up his life in place of Prometheus (26) who is forced to undergo eternal torture in punishment for stealing fire from the gods and bringing it to man. Chiron's motivation for accepting death in Prometheus' stead is unclear. One story suggests that Chiron chose death not so much because of the pain he suffered from his incurable wound, but because he had grown weary of his long life. (27) Or, he may have expressed compassion for Prometheus's suffering which was greater than his own. Whatever his motivation, all accounts portray Chiron

as willingly embracing death, a necessary human experience (28). The reversal is evident. While many heroic figures seek to attain immortality, here is an immortal who accepts the plight of man. Chiron is the wise and just centaur not merely for his vast knowledge and wide-ranging education. He enacts a noble drama linking us to our humanity.

Elizabeth Kubler-Ross's monumental work over the past ten years with the acceptance of the experience of death (29) points to the archetypal significance of Chiron's confrontation with his own fate. There is a revealing contrast between Chiron's acceptance of suffering and death and the objectives of conventional medicine which seeks to eradicate illness, to extend and prolong life at any cost, and, like the hero-physician Asclepios, to eliminate death and suffering altogether. We are reminded that the frightening aspects of death and dying can be accepted nobly, and that the more we struggle to deny suffering and death, the less truly human we become.

Chiron's function in astrology seems clear. His image as the sagacious and kindly centaur is conveyed in the zodiacal figure of Sagittarius. The upward directed arrow of the Archer symbolizes the upward movement one's values and attitudes take in shaping society today, just as for the ancient Greeks, Chiron embodied the transmission of such integrated cultural activities as ethics, education and learning, healing, and training in survival skills. But the arrow can also symbolize the capacity for woundedness and the ultimate confrontation with death. This latter function seems to be conveyed also by the zodiacal sign Scorpio. So, too, is the healing function of Chiron contained within the figure of Scorpio, symbolic of death and renewal. Chiron, then, is connected to Scorpio as well (30). Another suggestion that Chiron may have affinity with Scorpio as well as Sagittarius is signified by the similar glyphs for the two zodiacal signs which both contain the symbolism of the arrow: the tail of Scorpio and the arrow-like glyph of Sagittarius.

But though Chiron can be connected primarily with Sagittarius, he must share this rulership with Jupiter (Zeus). It has been argued (31) that Chiron (the planetoid) has been misnamed, for the centaur used in representations of the

constellation Sagittarius is actually Chiron. It should be noted that in mythology Chiron shared a sanctuary on the summit of Mt. Pelion with his brother Zeus. As brothers, Chiron and Zeus are associated with mountain-tops; Chiron is king of the centaurs, Zeus is sovereign over all the gods and goddesses on Mt. Olympus. Kerenyi tells us that the shared sanctuary atop Mt. Pelion was divided into two parts: "In the southern part stood the temple of Zeus facing the sun and looking as it were toward the diurnal side of the world. In the northern half lies a cave that can only be the Chironian, the cave of Chiron. This division bears witness not only to the nocturnal character of Chiron but also to his high rank in the Thessalian hierarchy of the gods . . . Chiron is brother to Zeus and shares the world with him (32)." Chiron is also brother to Hades (Pluto), mythologically supporting in yet another way the link to zodiacal Scorpio.

Viewing Chiron's myths psychologically reveals a way of understanding the use of this new celestial discovery in astrology. It is a further illustration that mythological symbolism can disclose insights into the forces that shape our lives and alter society. If the discovery of a new celestial body heralds a change in consciousness within society, then the knowledge of Chiron's presence in the solar system at this time directs us to consider transforming and renewing the attitudes and values currently held in education and medicine, cornerstone activities of human culture.

Tony Joseph
San Francisco

NOTES & REFERENCES

(1)   There is considerable disagreement over whether to designate Chiron a planet or an asteroid, owing to its small size -- no more than 400 miles in diameter -- and rather

eccentric orbit which at times crosses the paths of Saturn and Uranus. Although most known asteroids are found between the orbits of Mars and Jupiter, there is speculation that Chiron may be the first of numerous other smaller bodies between the orbits of the outer planets. For further details, see: **PHENOMENA, especially Vol. 1.9, Dec. 1977; 2.1, Jan-Feb. 1978 and 2.3/2.4, May-Aug. 1978.**

(2)   Jung spoke of these forces as the "archetypes" of the collective unconscious. See his *The Archetypes Of The Collective Unconscious,* the Collected Works, Bollingen Series XX, Volume 9. Princeton, N.J.: Princeton University Press: 1969.

(3)   Graves, Robert. *Greek Myths,* Volume 2. Harmondsworth, Middlesex: Penguin Books, Ltd., 1974, p. 235.

(4)   Grimal, Pierre. *Dictionnaire De La Mythologie Greque Et Romain.* Paris: Presses Universitaires de France, 1951, p. 90.

(5)   Graves, Robert. *Greek Myths,* Volume 1. Harmondsworth, Middlesex: Penguin Books, Ltd., 1974, p. 158.

(6)   Allen, Richard. *Star Names: Their Lore And Meaning.* New York: Dover Publications, Inc., 1963, pp. 351-360.

(7)   For individual myths of the heroes, see: Graves, *Greek Myths,* Volumes 1 and 2; and, Carl Kerenyi, *Heroes Of The Greeks.* London: Thames and Hudson, 1952.

(8)   Graves, Robert. *Greek Myths,* Volume 1. Harmondsworth, Middlesex: Penguin Books, Ltd., 1974, pp. 276-280.

(9)   Kerenyi, Carl. *Asclepios: Archetypal Image Of The Physician's Existence,* Bollingen Series LXV, Volume 3. New York: Pantheon Books, Inc., 1959, pp. 78-79.

(10) Liddel and Scott. *Greek-English Lexicon.* Oxford: Clarendon Press, 1975, p. 885.

(11) A. Bouché-Leclercq. *Histoire De La Divination Dans L'Antiquité,* Volume 1. Brussels: Culture et civilization, 1967, p. 63.

(12) Cramer, Frederick. *Astrology In Roman Law And Politics.* Philadelphia: The American Philosophical Society, 1954, p. 45.

(13) Hippocrates. *The Medical Works Of Hippocrates.* Oxford: Blackwell, 1950.

(14) "But again and again I note that the individuation process is confused with the coming of the ego into consciousness and that the ego is in consequence identified with the self, which naturally produces a hopeless conceptual muddle. Individuation is then nothing but ego-centredness and autoeroticism. But the self comprises infinitely more than a mere ego . . . Individuation does not shut one out from the world, but gathers the world to oneself." Carl Jung. *The Structure And Dynamics Of The Psyche,* the Collected Works, Volume 8. Princeton, N.J.: Princeton University Press, 1969, p. 226.

(15) Kirk, G. S. *The Nature Of Greek Myths.* Woodstock, New York: The Overlook Press, 1975, p. 208.

(16) National Gallery, London.

(17) Bachofen, J. J. *Myth, Religion And Mother Right,* Bollingen Series LXXXIV, Princeton, N.J.: Princeton University Press, 1967, p. 63.

(18) Chiron's use of medicinal herbs serves as a precursor to the development of pharmocognosy, the study of drugs originating from plants. Digitalis extracted from foxglove, atropine from delphinium, and bella donna from deadly nightshade are characteristic examples.

(19) Simonton, Carl, M.D. and Stephanie Simonton, R.N. "Belief systems and management of the emotional aspects of malignancy," **Journal Of Transpersonal Psychology,** Volume 7:1, 1975, pp. 29-48.

(20) "The art of estimating character by the hand." *Oxford English Dictionary* (Compact Edition; Volume 1) Oxford: Oxford University Press, 1971, p. 358.

(21) "Originally refers to the treatment of the diseases of the hands and feet and from which podiatry arose." *Oxford English Dictionary,* p. 358.

(22) "A system of healing holding that disease results from a lack of normal nerve function and employing manipulation (by the hands) and specific adjustments of body structures." *Webster's Seventh New Collegiate Dictionary,* Springfield Massachusetts: G. & C. Merriam Co., 1963, p. 145.

(23) *Oxford English Dictionary* (Compact Edition, Volume 1). Oxford: Oxford University Press, 1971, p. 357.

(24) A similar wound was fatal to Achilles, Chiron's pupil. James Hillman points out that woundedness, particularly to the hands and feet is characteristic of the **puer aeternus,** the archetype of Eternal Youth. See his, "Pothos: The Nostalgia of the Puer Eternus," *Loose Ends.* Zurich: Spring Publications, 1975.

(25) Kerenyi, Carl. *Asclepios: Archetypal Image Of The Physician's Existence,* Bollingen Series LXV, Volume 3. New York: Pantheon Books, Inc., 1959, p. 99.

(26) See Kerenyi, *Prometheus,* where the hero is depicted as the archetypal image of human consciousness and human ingenuity.

(27) Graves, Robert. *Greek Myths,* Volume 2. Harmondsworth, Middlesex: Penguin Books, Ltd., 1974, p. 113.

(28) The hero-physician Asclepios, Apollo's son, who was entrusted into Chiron's care and tutelage, carries the image of the "wounded healer" further. His activities as physician are distinctely more exalted than Chiron's. Asclepios is credited with ending plagues, founding medical academies, and instituting the first healing centers that utilized dream incubation for diagnostic and healing purposes. He was hailed throughout ancient Greece and Rome as the "divine physician." Yet, Asclepios, too, was wounded. When he attempted the hubristic feat of raising the dead, Zeus struck him down with a thunderbolt. Asclepios had transgressed his mortal limits.

(29) See Elizabeth Kubler-Ross, *On Death And Dying.* New York: MacMillan Publishing, 1969.

(30) Similarly, Jupiter is said to "rule" Sagittarius and Pisces; Saturn rules Capricorn and Aquarius; Mars rules Aries and Scorpio; Venus rules Taurus and Libra; and Mercury rules Gemini and Virgo. Contrary to the attempts to neatly fit each of the major celestial bodies with each of the zodiacal signs, there seems to be emerging a system of planetary rulership which allows for each planet/celestial body to correspond to two of the twelve zodiacal signs. The Sun and Moon are the exceptions, "ruling" Leo and Cancer, respectively. In personal correspondence, Malcolm Dean suggests "that the major asteroids have so far been connected to Virgo-Libra. And, if Chiron is substantiated as 'ruler' of Scorpio-Sagittarius, then a clear progression emerges." He suggests that the Apollo and Amor asteroids might then be found linked with Cancer-Leo, but he goes on to warn that the real problem here is what is "rulership" *per se?*

(31) **PHENOMENA** 2.3/2.4, May-Aug. 1978, "Letters" p.9.

(32) Kerenyi, Carl. *Asclepios: Archetypal Image of the Physician's Existence,* Bollingen Series, LXV, Volume 3, New York: Pantheon Books, Inc., 1959. pp. 88-89.

Foreword

The calculation of ephemerides has been a challenge crucial to the development of human consciousness and scientific thought. Mankind learned the basic techniques of acquiring true knowledge about the universe primarily through centuries of attempts to understand the movements of celestial objects. The point in history at which these efforts became fully scientific is a matter of dispute, but there is a clear line through Copernicus and Kepler to Newton, and the first **coherent** view of physics. Some of the most valuable tools of mathematics were originally developed to solve problems of orbital mechanics.

Modern methods of orbital calculations can be exceedingly precise, and exceedingly complicated - it is tremendously impressive to discover that a single individual, working to satisfy his own desire for knowledge, has mastered the methods of celestial mechanics to the point of writing a computer program capable of generating an accurate ephemeris of a newly-discovered body covering a period of more than a century. Beyond its clear display of deep understanding, James Neely's ephemeris program is a small miracle of detail, and working with it has been a pleasure for his co-authors here at the other side of the American Continent.

The accuracy of the Chiron ephemeris should be allowed to speak for itself:

	Observed Values		Computed Values	
DATE	R.A.	DEC.	R.A.	DEC.
1895 Apr 24. 1475	12h 09m 25s	- 4o 11ʹ 29ʺ	12h 09m 33s	- 4o 12ʹ 06ʺ
1941 Jan 23. 8627	7 54 23	13 03 40	7 54 24	13 03 36
1943 Mar 08. 8034	9 38 42	6 54 25	9 38 44	6 54 17
1948 Aug 04. 7580	15 08 22	-14 22 24	15 08 23	-14 22 33
1952 Aug 23. 16736	18 28 26	-16 18 30	18 28 27	-16 18 30
1969 Sep 10. 36875	0 14 51	4 55 53	0 14 51	4 55 54
1976 Nov 17. 09557	1 45 50	10 50 06	1 45 50	10 50 06
1977 Nov 18. 30069	2 01 36	11 45 33	2 01 36	11 45 35

Table 1

Clearly, the agreement with observation is quite adequate for astrological purposes, and more than adequate for most astronomical applications. Only the most superficial of changes have been made to Neely's original program in order to generate the ephemeris presently in your hands.

A quick survey of the methods used would go something as follows. First, orbital elements were taken from Brian Marsden's results published in the International Astronomical Union Circulars. Out of several sets of elements published by Marsden, the set chosen was the one which matched observations dating back to 1895. These elements were put through a procedure designed in the 1960's by Lloyd Carpenter to produce a new data set that could be used to calculate heliocentric rectangular co-ordinates of Chiron, with perturbations, for the epoch of 1950. (Carpenter's procedure is explained in a 1967 NASA technical note.) James Neely's program uses this new data set to generate the heliocentric rectangular co-ordinates, finds corresponding positions of the Sun using the well-known methods of Newcomb, combines these data to produce geo-centric co-ordinates, rotates the co-ordinate system to get positions for the mean equinox of date, and performs trans-lations to produce positions expressed for the different co-ordinate systems used.

The Chiron ephemeris is markedly astrological in that it includes stations: a feature that is ordinarily of no interest to astronomers. We have chosen to calculate a precise approximation of the time and position of station by fitting a parabola to a graph of geocentric longitude versus time, and using some very basic calculus to determine the time and position at which the curve "turns" from positive-going to negative-going, or vice-versa. This technique has proven highly reliable for known planets other than Chiron, but the testing to prove the method uncovered a startling fact about station calculations in general.

The calculation of stations is tremendously insensitive to time in amounts on the order of a few minutes or hours. For example, a typical station of Chiron:

Time	Longitude
Station time plus 0.00 days	112.350020480
Station time plus 0.01 days	112.350020401
Station time plus 0.10 days	112.350012570

In 1/100 of a day immediately after station, Chiron typically moves about 8/100,000,000 of a degree. This means that we must know Chiron's position to the nearest 8×10^{-8} degree in order to specify the actual time of station to within .01 of a day, and .01 day equals about 15 minutes! We urge that users of this ephemeris and those of all other bodies keep in mind this point regarding the time of station. The demand for positional precision makes calculation of stations to the nearest minute of time impractical. It is probably best to regard stations as correct to within a few hours. These arguments will apply to other bodies, and stations calculated by other techniques.

To conclude with a personal note, I am extremely pleased with the quality of the *Chiron Ephemeris,* and the effort put forward by all those involved in its production. Special thanks are owed to Michael Campbell, who guided us successfully through a fabulously complex computer installation. May everyone who applies this ephemeris display a similar level of energy and intelligence!

Eric Tarkington
8 December 1978
Toronto

Ephemeris of Chiron
1890-2000

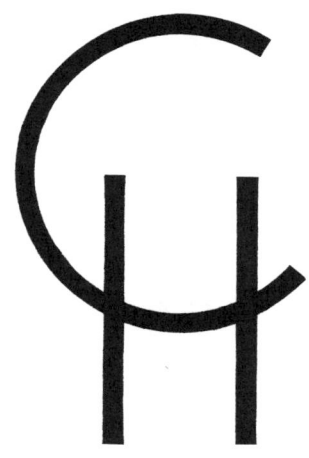

Oh Ephemeris Time
Equinox of Date

1890

Date	Long.	Lat.	R.A.		Dec.	HLong.	HLat.
1/ 3	19CN41	7S35	110	11	14N30	19CN 2	6S54
1/13	18CN58	7S36	109	27	14N35	19CN20	6S54
1/23	18CN16	7S35	108	44	14N41	19CN38	6S54
2/ 2	17CN37	7S33	108	4	14N48	19CN56	6S55
2/12	17CN 2	7S30	107	30	14N56	20CN15	6S55
2/22	16CN35	7S25	107	3	15N 4	20CN33	6S55
3/ 4	16CN16	7S20	106	44	15N11	20CN51	6S56
3/14	16CN 6	7S13	106	34	15N18	21CN10	6S56
3/24	16CN 5	7S 7	106	34	15N25	21CN28	6S56
4/ 3	16CN15	7S 1	106	45	15N30	21CN47	6S57
4/13	16CN33	6S54	107	5	15N34	22CN 5	6S57
4/23	17CN 1	6S48	107	34	15N37	22CN24	6S57
5/ 3	17CN37	6S42	108	11	15N38	22CN43	6S57
5/13	18CN20	6S37	108	56	15N38	23CN 1	6S58
5/23	19CN11	6S33	109	48	15N36	23CN20	6S58
6/ 2	20CN 6	6S29	110	46	15N32	23CN39	6S58
6/12	21CN 7	6S26	111	48	15N26	23CN58	6S58
6/22	22CN11	6S24	112	54	15N19	24CN17	6S58
7/ 2	23CN18	6S22	114	2	15N10	24CN36	6S59
7/12	24CN26	6S21	115	12	14N59	24CN56	6S59
7/22	25CN36	6S21	116	22	14N47	25CN15	6S59
8/ 1	26CN45	6S22	117	32	14N34	25CN34	6S59
8/11	27CN53	6S24	118	40	14N19	25CN54	6S59
8/21	28CN59	6S26	119	46	14N 4	26CN13	6S59
8/31	0LE 2	6S30	120	48	13N48	26CN33	6S59
9/10	1LE 0	6S34	121	46	13N32	26CN52	7S 0
9/20	1LE54	6S38	122	38	13N16	27CN12	7S 0
9/30	2LE40	6S44	123	23	13N 1	27CN32	7S 0
10/10	3LE20	6S50	124	1	12N46	27CN52	7S 0
10/20	3LE51	6S57	124	30	12N33	28CN11	7S 0
10/30	4LE13	7S 4	124	51	12N21	28CN31	7S 0
11/ 9	4LE26	7S11	125	1	12N11	28CN51	7S 0
11/19	4LE28	7S18	125	2	12N 4	29CN12	7S 0
11/29	4LE20	7S25	124	52	11N59	29CN32	7S 0
12/ 9	4LE 2	7S31	124	33	11N57	29CN52	7S 0
12/19	3LE35	7S37	124	6	11N57	0LE12	7S 0
12/29	3LE 1	7S41	123	31	12N 1	0LE33	7S 0

Stations	Date	Long.	Lat.
DIRECT	3/19.45	16CN 4	7S10
RETROGRADE	11/16.18	4LE28	7S16

Date	Long.	Lat.	R.A.	Dec.	HLong.	HLat.
1/ 8	2LE21	7S44	122 50	12N 6	0LE53	7S 0
1/18	1LF37	7S45	122 7	12N14	1LE14	6S59
1/28	0LE52	7S45	121 22	12N24	1LE34	6S59
2/ 7	0LE 9	7S43	120 40	12N35	1LE55	6S59
2/17	29CN30	7S40	120 1	12N46	2LE16	6S59
2/27	28CN56	7S35	119 29	12N57	2LE36	6S59
3/ 9	28CN30	7S29	119 4	13N 8	2LE57	6S59
3/19	28CN14	7S23	118 49	13N18	3LE18	6S59
3/29	28CN 7	7S16	118 44	13N26	3LE39	6S58
4/ 8	28CN11	7S 8	118 49	13N32	4LE 0	6S58
4/18	28CN25	7S 1	119 4	13N37	4LE21	6S58
4/28	28CN48	6S54	119 30	13N40	4LE43	6S58
5/ 8	29CN21	6S47	120 4	13N40	5LE 4	6S57
5/18	0LE 3	6S40	120 47	13N38	5LE25	6S57
5/28	0LF52	6S34	121 37	13N33	5LE47	6S57
6/ 7	1LE48	6S29	122 34	13N26	6LE 8	6S57
6/17	2LF49	6S25	123 36	13N17	6LE30	6S56
6/27	3LF55	6S21	124 43	13N 6	6LE51	6S56
7/ 7	5LE 5	6S18	125 53	12N53	7LE13	6S56
7/17	6LE18	6S16	127 5	12N38	7LE35	6S55
7/27	7LF32	6S15	128 19	12N21	7LE57	6S55
8/ 6	8LE47	6S15	129 33	12N 2	8LE19	6S54
8/16	10LF 2	6S15	130 46	11N43	8LE41	6S54
8/26	11LF15	6S17	131 57	11N22	9LE 3	6S53
9/ 5	12LE26	6S19	133 6	11N 1	9LE25	6S53
9/15	13LF34	6S22	134 11	10N40	9LE47	6S52
9/25	14LE37	6S25	135 11	10N18	10LE10	6S52
10/ 5	15LF34	6S30	136 5	9N58	10LE32	6S51
10/15	16LE24	6S35	136 52	9N38	10LE54	6S51
10/25	17LE 7	6S41	137 31	9N20	11LE17	6S50
11/ 4	17LE41	6S47	138 2	9N 4	11LE39	6S50
11/14	18LE 5	6S54	138 23	8N51	12LE 2	6S49
11/24	18LF19	7S 1	138 34	8N40	12LE25	6S48
12/ 4	18LE21	7S 7	138 35	8N33	12LE48	6S48
12/14	18LE13	7S14	138 25	8N29	13LE11	6S47
12/24	17LF55	7S20	138 6	8N29	13LE34	6S46

Stations	Date	Long.	Lat.
DIRECT	3/30.47	28CN 7	7S15
RETROGRADE	12/ 1.56	18LE22	7S 6

1892

Date	Long.	Lat.	R.A.		Dec.	HLong.	HLat.
1/ 3	17LE27	7S24	137	37	8N33	13LE57	6S46
1/13	16LE51	7S28	137	2	8N40	14LE20	6S45
1/23	16LE 9	7S30	136	21	8N50	14LE43	6S44
2/ 2	15LE24	7S31	135	37	9N 2	15LE 6	6S43
2/12	14LE37	7S30	134	53	9N17	15LE29	6S43
2/22	13LE53	7S27	134	11	9N32	15LE53	6S42
3/ 3	13LE13	7S23	133	33	9N47	16LE16	6S41
3/13	12LE39	7S17	133	3	10N 1	16LE40	6S40
3/23	12LE15	7S10	132	40	10N15	17LE 3	6S39
4/ 2	12LE 0	7S 3	132	28	10N26	17LE27	6S38
4/12	11LE55	6S55	132	26	10N35	17LE51	6S37
4/22	12LE 1	6S46	132	34	10N41	18LE15	6S36
5/ 2	12LE18	6S38	132	53	10N45	18LE38	6S36
5/12	12LE45	6S30	133	21	10N45	19LE 2	6S35
5/22	13LE22	6S23	133	59	10N42	19LE26	6S34
6/ 1	14LE 8	6S16	134	45	10N36	19LE51	6S32
6/11	15LE 1	6S 9	135	39	10N27	20LE15	6S31
6/21	16LE 1	6S 3	136	39	10N15	20LE39	6S30
7/ 1	17LE 8	5S58	137	45	10N 1	21LE 3	6S29
7/11	18LE19	5S54	138	55	9N44	21LE28	6S28
7/21	19LE34	5S51	140	8	9N24	21LE52	6S27
7/31	20LE52	5S48	141	23	9N 3	22LE17	6S26
8/10	22LE11	5S46	142	40	8N40	22LE41	6S25
8/20	23LE32	5S45	143	57	8N15	23LE 6	6S23
8/30	24LE52	5S45	145	13	7N49	23LE30	6S22
9/ 9	26LE11	5S45	146	28	7N23	23LE55	6S21
9/19	27LE27	5S46	147	40	6N56	24LE20	6S20
9/29	28LE40	5S49	148	47	6N29	24LE45	6S18
10/ 9	29LE48	5S51	149	51	6N 3	25LE10	6S17
10/19	0VI51	5S55	150	48	5N39	25LE35	6S16
10/29	1VI46	5S59	151	38	5N16	26LE 0	6S14
11/ 8	2VI33	6S 4	152	20	4N55	26LE25	6S13
11/18	3VI11	6S 9	152	54	4N36	26LE51	6S11
11/28	3VI38	6S14	153	17	4N22	27LE16	6S10
12/ 8	3VI55	6S20	153	31	4N10	27LE41	6S 9
12/18	4VI 0	6S25	153	34	4N 3	28LE 7	6S 7
12/28	3VI54	6S31	153	26	4N 1	28LE32	6S 6

Stations	Date	Long.	Lat.
DIRECT	4/11.23	11LE55	6S55
RETROGRADE	12/17.50	4VI 0	6S25

Date	Long.	Lat.	R.A.	Dec.	HLong.	HLat.
1/ 7	3VI36	6S35	153 8	4N 3	28LE58	6S 4
1/17	3VI 9	6S39	152 41	4N 9	29LE23	6S 2
1/27	2VI33	6S42	152 7	4N19	29LE49	6S 1
2/ 6	1VI50	6S43	151 27	4N33	0VI15	5S59
2/16	1VI 4	6S42	150 44	4N49	0VI41	5S58
2/26	0VI17	6S40	150 0	5N 8	1VI 7	5S56
3/ 8	29LE31	6S37	149 19	5N27	1VI33	5S54
3/18	28LE50	6S32	148 42	5N45	1VI59	5S53
3/28	28LE16	6S26	148 12	6N 3	2VI25	5S51
4/ 7	27LE50	6S18	147 50	6N18	2VI51	5S49
4/17	27LE35	6S11	147 39	6N31	3VI17	5S47
4/27	27LE31	6S 2	147 37	6N40	3VI43	5S45
5/ 7	27LE37	5S54	147 46	6N46	4VI 9	5S44
5/17	27LE55	5S45	148 6	6N48	4VI36	5S42
5/27	28LE24	5S37	148 36	6N46	5VI 2	5S40
6/ 6	29LE 2	5S29	149 15	6N40	5VI29	5S38
6/16	29LE50	5S22	150 2	6N30	5VI55	5S36
6/26	0VI46	5S15	150 57	6N17	6VI22	5S34
7/ 6	1VI49	5S 9	151 59	6N 1	6VI48	5S32
7/16	2VI59	5S 4	153 6	5N42	7VI15	5S30
7/26	4VI13	4S59	154 17	5N20	7VI42	5S28
8/ 5	5VI32	4S55	155 32	4N55	8VI 8	5S26
8/15	6VI54	4S51	156 50	4N28	8VI35	5S24
8/25	8VI18	4S48	158 9	4N 0	9VI 2	5S22
9/ 4	9VI43	4S46	159 28	3N30	9VI29	5S20
9/14	11VI 8	4S45	160 47	3N 0	9VI56	5S18
9/24	12VI31	4S44	162 5	2N29	10VI23	5S15
10/ 4	13VI53	4S44	163 20	1N58	10VI50	5S13
10/14	15VI11	4S45	164 31	1N28	11VI17	5S11
10/24	16VI24	4S46	165 38	0N58	11VI45	5S 9
11/ 3	17VI31	4S48	166 39	0N31	12VI12	5S 7
11/13	18VI32	4S50	167 34	0N 5	12VI39	5S 4
11/23	19VI24	4S53	168 20	0S18	13VI 6	5S 2
12/ 3	20VI 6	4S56	168 58	0S37	13VI34	5S 0
12/13	20VI38	5S 0	169 26	0S53	14VI 1	4S57
12/23	20VI59	5S 3	169 44	1S 4	14VI28	4S55

Stations	Date	Long.	Lat.
DIRECT	4/25.96	27LE30	6S 3

1894

Date	Long.	Lat.	R.A.	Dec.	HLong.	HLat.
1/ 2	21VI 8	5S 7	169 51	1S11	14VI56	4S53
1/12	21VI 5	5S10	169 47	1S13	15VI23	4S50
1/22	20VI51	5S13	169 32	1S10	15VI51	4S48
2/ 1	20VI26	5S15	169 9	1S 2	16VI19	4S45
2/11	19VI51	5S16	168 37	0S49	16VI46	4S43
2/21	19VI 9	5S15	167 59	0S33	17VI14	4S40
3/ 3	18VI23	5S14	167 17	0S13	17VI42	4S38
3/13	17VI35	5S11	166 34	0N 8	18VI 9	4S35
3/23	16VI49	5S 7	165 53	0N29	18VI37	4S33
4/ 2	16VI 6	5S 2	165 15	0N50	19VI 5	4S30
4/12	15VI30	4S56	164 45	1N10	19VI33	4S27
4/22	15VI 2	4S49	164 22	1N27	20VI 1	4S25
5/ 2	14VI45	4S42	164 9	1N40	20VI28	4S22
5/12	14VI39	4S34	164 6	1N50	20VI56	4S19
5/22	14VI44	4S26	164 13	1N55	21VI24	4S17
6/ 1	15VI 0	4S18	164 31	1N56	21VI52	4S14
6/11	15VI27	4S11	165 0	1N53	22VI20	4S11
6/21	16VI 5	4S 3	165 37	1N45	22VI48	4S 9
7/ 1	16VI52	3S56	166 23	1N33	23VI16	4S 6
7/11	17VI48	3S50	167 17	1N18	23VI45	4S 3
7/21	18VI52	3S44	168 18	0N58	24VI13	4S 0
7/31	20VI 2	3S39	169 24	0N36	24VI41	3S57
8/10	21VI18	3S34	170 36	0N11	25VI 9	3S54
8/20	22VI38	3S29	171 51	0S17	25VI37	3S52
8/30	24VI 2	3S25	173 10	0S46	26VI 5	3S49
9/ 9	25VI28	3S22	174 30	1S17	26VI33	3S46
9/19	26VI55	3S19	175 51	1S49	27VI 2	3S43
9/29	28VI23	3S17	177 13	2S22	27VI30	3S40
10/ 9	29VI50	3S15	178 33	2S55	27VI58	3S37
10/19	1LI14	3S13	179 51	3S27	28VI26	3S34
10/29	2LI36	3S12	181 6	3S59	28VI55	3S31
11/ 8	3LI53	3S12	182 17	4S29	29VI23	3S28
11/18	5LI 4	3S12	183 23	4S57	29VI51	3S25
11/28	6LI 9	3S12	184 22	5S22	0LI20	3S22
12/ 8	7LI 5	3S12	185 14	5S45	0LI48	3S19
12/18	7LI51	3S13	185 57	6S 4	1LI16	3S16
12/28	8LI28	3S13	186 30	6S19	1LI45	3S13

Stations	Date	Long.	Lat.
RETROGRADE	1/ 4.55	21VI 9	5S 8
DIRECT	5/12.65	14VI39	4S34

Date	Long.	Lat.	R.A.	Dec.	HLong.	HLat.
1/ 7	8LI53	3S14	186 53	6S30	2LI13	3S10
1/17	9LI 6	3S15	187 5	6S36	2LI41	3S 7
1/27	9LI 7	3S15	187 5	6S36	3LI10	3S 4
2/ 6	8LI57	3S15	186 55	6S32	3LI38	3S 0
2/16	8LI35	3S15	186 35	6S23	4LI 6	2S57
2/26	8LI 3	3S14	186 7	6S10	4LI35	2S54
3/ 8	7LI24	3S12	185 31	5S53	5LI 3	2S51
3/18	6LI39	3S10	184 50	5S33	5LI31	2S48
3/28	5LI51	3S 7	184 8	5S11	6LI 0	2S45
4/ 7	5LI 4	3S 3	183 26	4S49	6LI28	2S41
4/17	4LI20	2S58	182 48	4S27	6LI57	2S38
4/27	3LI42	2S53	182 14	4S 7	7LI25	2S35
5/ 7	3LI11	2S47	181 49	3S49	7LI53	2S32
5/17	2LI50	2S41	181 32	3S35	8LI22	2S29
5/27	2LI40	2S35	181 26	3S26	8LI50	2S25
6/ 6	2LI42	2S28	181 29	3S21	9LI18	2S22
6/16	2LI54	2S22	181 43	3S20	9LI46	2S19
6/26	3LI18	2S16	182 7	3S24	10LI15	2S15
7/ 6	3LI52	2S10	182 41	3S32	10LI43	2S12
7/16	4LI37	2S 5	183 24	3S45	11LI11	2S 9
7/26	5LI30	2S 0	184 15	4S 1	11LI40	2S 6
8/ 5	6LI31	1S55	185 13	4S21	12LI 8	2S 2
8/15	7LI39	1S50	186 18	4S44	12LI36	1S59
8/25	8LI54	1S46	187 28	5S 9	13LI 4	1S56
9/ 4	10LI13	1S42	188 43	5S36	13LI32	1S52
9/14	11LI36	1S38	190 1	6S 6	14LI 1	1S49
9/24	13LI 1	1S35	191 22	6S36	14LI29	1S46
10/ 4	14LI29	1S32	192 44	7S 7	14LI57	1S42
10/14	15LI56	1S29	194 7	7S38	15LI25	1S39
10/24	17LI24	1S26	195 29	8S 9	15LI53	1S36
11/ 3	18LI49	1S23	196 50	8S40	16LI21	1S32
11/13	20LI12	1S21	198 8	9S 9	16LI49	1S29
11/23	21LI30	1S19	199 22	9S36	17LI17	1S26
12/ 3	22LI43	1S17	200 31	10S 1	17LI45	1S22
12/13	23LI49	1S15	201 35	10S24	18LI13	1S19
12/23	24LI47	1S13	202 30	10S44	18LI41	1S16

Stations	Date	Long.	Lat.
RETROGRADE	1/22.95	9LI 8	3S15
DIRECT	5/30.89	2LI40	2S32

1896

Date	Long.	Lat.	R.A.	Dec.	HLong.	HLat.
1/ 2	25LI36	1S11	203 18	11S 0	19LI 9	1S12
1/12	26LI15	1S 9	203 55	11S12	19LI37	1S 9
1/22	26LI43	1S 7	204 23	11S20	20LI 4	1S 5
2/ 1	26LI59	1S 4	204 39	11S24	20LI32	1S 2
2/11	27LI 4	1S 2	204 44	11S24	21LI 0	0S59
2/21	26LI56	1S 0	204 38	11S19	21LI28	0S55
3/ 2	26LI38	0S57	204 21	11S10	21LI55	0S52
3/12	26LI 9	0S54	203 55	10S56	22LI23	0S49
3/22	25LI32	0S51	203 21	10S40	22LI51	0S45
4/ 1	24LI49	0S47	202 42	10S21	23LI18	0S42
4/11	24LI 3	0S44	202 0	10S 1	23LI46	0S39
4/21	23LI16	0S40	201 17	9S40	24LI13	0S35
5/ 1	22LI31	0S36	200 36	9S19	24LI41	0S32
5/11	21LI52	0S32	200 0	9S 1	25LI 8	0S28
5/21	21LI19	0S28	199 31	8S45	25LI36	0S25
5/31	20LI55	0S24	199 10	8S32	26LI 3	0S22
6/10	20LI41	0S20	198 58	8S23	26LI30	0S18
6/20	20LI37	0S16	198 57	8S18	26LI58	0S15
6/30	20LI45	0S12	199 6	8S18	27LI25	0S12
7/10	21LI 4	0S 9	199 25	8S22	27LI52	0S 8
7/20	21LI34	0S 5	199 54	8S29	28LI19	0S 5
7/30	22LI13	0S 2	200 32	8S41	28LI46	0S 2
8/ 9	23LI 2	0N 1	201 19	8S56	29LI13	0N 2
8/19	23LI59	0N 5	202 14	9S14	29LI40	0N 5
8/29	25LI 3	0N 8	203 15	9S35	0SC 7	0N 8
9/ 8	26LI14	0N11	204 23	9S58	0SC34	0N11
9/18	27LI29	0N13	205 36	10S23	1SC 1	0N15
9/28	28LI49	0N16	206 53	10S48	1SC28	0N18
10/ 8	0SC12	0N19	208 13	11S15	1SC54	0N21
10/18	1SC36	0N22	209 35	11S42	2SC21	0N25
10/28	3SC 2	0N25	210 57	12S 8	2SC48	0N28
11/ 7	4SC27	0N28	212 20	12S34	3SC14	0N31
11/17	5SC50	0N31	213 42	12S59	3SC41	0N34
11/27	7SC11	0N34	215 1	13S23	4SC 7	0N38
12/ 7	8SC28	0N37	216 17	13S44	4SC34	0N41
12/17	9SC39	0N41	217 28	14S 4	5SC 0	0N44
12/27	10SC44	0N44	218 33	14S21	5SC26	0N47

Stations	Date	Long.	Lat.
RETROGRADE	2/ 9.73	27LI 4	1S 2
DIRECT	6/17.84	20LI37	0S17

Date	Long.	Lat.	R.A.	Dec.	HLong.	HLat.
1/ 6	11SC42	0N48	219 31	14S35	5SC52	0N50
1/16	12SC30	0N52	220 20	14S46	6SC19	0N54
1/26	13SC 9	0N56	221 0	14S54	6SC45	0N57
2/ 5	13SC38	1N 1	221 29	14S59	7SC11	1N 0
2/15	13SC55	1N 5	221 48	14S59	7SC37	1N 3
2/25	14SC 1	1N10	221 55	14S57	8SC 3	1N 6
3/ 7	13SC55	1N14	221 51	14S51	8SC29	1N 9
3/17	13SC39	1N19	221 36	14S42	8SC55	1N12
3/27	13SC13	1N23	221 11	14S29	9SC20	1N16
4/ 6	12SC38	1N28	220 39	14S15	9SC46	1N19
4/16	11SC57	1N32	220 0	13S58	10SC12	1N22
4/26	11SC13	1N36	219 17	13S41	10SC37	1N25
5/ 6	10SC27	1N39	218 34	13S24	11SC 3	1N28
5/16	9SC43	1N42	217 51	13S 7	11SC28	1N31
5/26	9SC 2	1N45	217 13	12S52	11SC54	1N34
6/ 5	8SC28	1N47	216 40	12S39	12SC19	1N37
6/15	8SC 1	1N49	216 15	12S28	12SC44	1N40
6/25	7SC44	1N50	215 59	12S21	13SC 9	1N43
7/ 5	7SC38	1N52	215 53	12S18	13SC35	1N46
7/15	7SC41	1N53	215 57	12S18	14SC 0	1N49
7/25	7SC56	1N54	216 11	12S22	14SC25	1N52
8/ 4	8SC21	1N55	216 36	12S29	14SC50	1N55
8/14	8SC55	1N56	217 10	12S39	15SC15	1N58
8/24	9SC39	1N56	217 52	12S52	15SC39	2N 1
9/ 3	10SC31	1N57	218 43	13S 7	16SC 4	2N 4
9/13	11SC30	1N59	219 42	13S25	16SC29	2N 6
9/23	12SC36	2N 0	220 46	13S43	16SC53	2N 9
10/ 3	13SC47	2N 1	221 56	14S 3	17SC18	2N12
10/13	15SC 2	2N 3	223 11	14S24	17SC43	2N15
10/23	16SC20	2N 5	224 29	14S44	18SC 7	2N18
11/ 2	17SC40	2N 7	225 49	15S 5	18SC31	2N21
11/12	19SC 1	2N 9	227 11	15S25	18SC56	2N23
11/22	20SC22	2N12	228 32	15S44	19SC20	2N26
12/ 2	21SC42	2N15	229 53	16S 1	19SC44	2N29
12/12	22SC58	2N19	231 11	16S17	20SC 8	2N32
12/22	24SC11	2N22	232 25	16S32	20SC32	2N34

Stations	Date	Long.	Lat.
RETROGRADE	2/25.08	14SC 1	1N10
DIRECT	7/ 6.43	7SC37	1N52

1898

Date	Long.	Lat.	R.A.	Dec.	HLong.	HLat.
1/ 1	25SC19	2N27	233 35	16S44	20SC56	2N37
1/11	26SC21	2N31	234 39	16S54	21SC20	2N40
1/21	27SC15	2N36	235 35	17S 2	21SC44	2N43
1/31	28SC 1	2N41	236 23	17S 7	22SC 7	2N45
2/10	28SC37	2N47	237 1	17S 9	22SC31	2N48
2/20	29SC 4	2N52	237 30	17S 9	22SC55	2N50
3/ 2	29SC20	2N58	237 47	17S 7	23SC18	2N53
3/12	29SC25	3N 4	237 54	17S 2	23SC42	2N56
3/22	29SC19	3N10	237 49	16S55	24SC 5	2N58
4/ 1	29SC 3	3N16	237 34	16S46	24SC28	3N 1
4/11	28SC38	3N21	237 10	16S36	24SC52	3N 3
4/21	28SC 5	3N26	236 37	16S24	25SC15	3N 6
5/ 1	27SC25	3N30	235 58	16S11	25SC38	3N 8
5/11	26SC43	3N34	235 16	15S58	26SC 1	3N11
5/21	25SC58	3N37	234 32	15S45	26SC24	3N13
5/31	25SC15	3N39	233 49	15S33	26SC47	3N16
6/10	24SC35	3N40	233 9	15S22	27SC10	3N18
6/20	24SC 1	3N41	232 35	15S13	27SC32	3N21
6/30	23SC34	3N41	232 8	15S 6	27SC55	3N23
7/10	23SC15	3N40	231 49	15S 2	28SC18	3N26
7/20	23SC 7	3N39	231 40	15S 1	28SC40	3N28
7/30	23SC 8	3N38	231 41	15S 3	29SC 3	3N30
8/ 9	23SC19	3N37	231 52	15S 7	29SC25	3N33
8/19	23SC40	3N35	232 13	15S13	29SC47	3N35
8/29	24SC11	3N34	232 43	15S22	0SA10	3N37
9/ 8	24SC50	3N33	233 23	15S33	0SA32	3N40
9/18	25SC38	3N32	234 10	15S45	0SA54	3N42
9/28	26SC33	3N31	235 5	15S58	1SA16	3N44
10/ 8	27SC34	3N31	236 7	16S12	1SA38	3N47
10/18	28SC40	3N31	237 14	16S26	2SA 0	3N49
10/28	29SC50	3N32	238 26	16S41	2SA22	3N51
11/ 7	1SA 3	3N32	239 41	16S55	2SA44	3N53
11/17	2SA19	3N34	240 58	17S 8	3SA 5	3N55
11/27	3SA34	3N36	242 16	17S21	3SA27	3N58
12/ 7	4SA50	3N38	243 34	17S32	3SA48	4N 0
12/17	6SA 4	3N41	244 51	17S42	4SA10	4N 2
12/27	7SA16	3N44	246 6	17S51	4SA31	4N 4

Stations	Date	Long.	Lat.
RETROGRADE	3/11.65	29SC25	3N 4
DIRECT	7/23.84	23SC 6	3N39

Date	Long.	Lat.	R.A.	Dec.	HLong.	HLat.
1/ 6	8SA23	3N48	247 16	17S58	4SA53	4N 6
1/16	9SA26	3N53	248 22	18S 3	5SA14	4N 8
1/26	10SA22	3N58	249 21	18S 6	5SA35	4N10
2/ 5	11SA12	4N 3	250 13	18S 7	5SA56	4N12
2/15	11SA53	4N 9	250 57	18S 7	6SA17	4N14
2/25	12SA25	4N15	251 31	18S 5	6SA38	4N16
3/ 7	12SA48	4N21	251 56	18S 1	6SA59	4N18
3/17	13SA 0	4N28	252 10	17S56	7SA20	4N20
3/27	13SA 3	4N35	252 13	17S50	7SA41	4N22
4/ 6	12SA55	4N41	252 6	17S43	8SA 2	4N24
4/16	12SA38	4N47	251 49	17S35	8SA22	4N26
4/26	12SA12	4N53	251 23	17S26	8SA43	4N28
5/ 6	11SA40	4N58	250 50	17S17	9SA 4	4N30
5/16	11SA 1	5N 2	250 11	17S 8	9SA24	4N32
5/26	10SA20	5N 5	249 29	16S59	9SA44	4N34
6/ 5	9SA37	5N 7	248 45	16S51	10SA 5	4N36
6/15	8SA56	5N 8	248 3	16S44	10SA25	4N38
6/25	8SA18	5N 8	247 24	16S38	10SA45	4N39
7/ 5	7SA45	5N 7	246 50	16S33	11SA 5	4N41
7/15	7SA19	5N 6	246 23	16S31	11SA25	4N43
7/25	7SA 1	5N 3	246 4	16S30	11SA45	4N45
8/ 4	6SA52	5N 1	245 54	16S31	12SA 5	4N47
8/14	6SA52	4N58	245 54	16S34	12SA25	4N48
8/24	7SA 2	4N55	246 4	16S39	12SA45	4N50
9/ 3	7SA21	4N52	246 23	16S45	13SA 5	4N52
9/13	7SA50	4N49	246 52	16S52	13SA24	4N53
9/23	8SA26	4N46	247 29	17S 1	13SA44	4N55
10/ 3	9SA11	4N44	248 14	17S10	14SA 3	4N57
10/13	10SA 2	4N42	249 7	17S19	14SA23	4N58
10/23	10SA59	4N40	250 6	17S29	14SA42	5N 0
11/ 2	12SA 1	4N39	251 10	17S38	15SA 1	5N 2
11/12	13SA 7	4N39	252 18	17S46	15SA21	5N 3
11/22	14SA15	4N39	253 29	17S54	15SA40	5N 5
12/ 2	15SA26	4N40	254 43	18S 1	15SA59	5N 7
12/12	16SA36	4N41	255 57	18S 7	16SA18	5N 8
12/22	17SA46	4N43	257 10	18S11	16SA37	5N10

Stations	Date	Long.	Lat.
RETROGRADE	3/24.38	13SA 3	4N33
DIRECT	8/ 8.60	6SA51	5N 0

1900

Date	Long.	Lat.	R.A.	Dec.	HLong.	HLat.
1/ 1	18SA55	4N46	258 22	18S14	16SA56	5N11
1/11	20SA 0	4N49	259 30	18S16	17SA15	5N13
1/21	21SA 2	4N53	260 35	18S16	17SA34	5N14
1/31	21SA58	4N58	261 34	18S15	17SA52	5N16
2/10	22SA49	5N 3	262 27	18S13	18SA11	5N17
2/20	23SA32	5N 9	263 13	18S 9	18SA30	5N19
3/ 2	24SA 7	5N15	263 50	18S 5	18SA48	5N20
3/12	24SA34	5N21	264 19	18S 0	19SA 7	5N21
3/22	24SA52	5N28	264 37	17S54	19SA25	5N23
4/ 1	25SA 0	5N34	264 46	17S47	19SA44	5N24
4/11	24SA58	5N41	264 45	17S41	20SA 2	5N26
4/21	24SA48	5N47	264 34	17S34	20SA20	5N27
5/ 1	24SA28	5N53	264 14	17S27	20SA38	5N28
5/11	24SA 2	5N58	263 46	17S21	20SA56	5N30
5/21	23SA28	6N 3	263 12	17S15	21SA14	5N31
5/31	22SA51	6N 6	262 33	17S10	21SA32	5N32
6/10	22SA11	6N 9	261 52	17S 5	21SA50	5N34
6/20	21SA30	6N10	261 9	17S 2	22SA 8	5N35
6/30	20SA51	6N10	260 29	16S59	22SA26	5N36
7/10	20SA15	6N 9	259 51	16S58	22SA44	5N37
7/20	19SA44	6N 7	259 19	16S57	23SA 1	5N39
7/30	19SA20	6N 4	258 54	16S58	23SA19	5N40
8/ 9	19SA 4	6N 1	258 37	17S 0	23SA37	5N41
8/19	18SA56	5N57	258 29	17S 4	23SA54	5N42
8/29	18SA57	5N53	258 30	17S 8	24SA12	5N44
9/ 8	19SA 8	5N49	258 40	17S13	24SA29	5N45
9/18	19SA27	5N44	259 0	17S19	24SA46	5N46
9/28	19SA54	5N41	259 28	17S25	25SA 4	5N47
10/ 8	20SA30	5N37	260 5	17S31	25SA21	5N48
10/18	21SA13	5N34	260 49	17S37	25SA38	5N49
10/28	22SA 1	5N31	261 40	17S42	25SA55	5N50
11/ 7	22SA56	5N29	262 36	17S47	26SA12	5N51
11/17	23SA54	5N27	263 38	17S52	26SA29	5N53
11/27	24SA56	5N26	264 42	17S55	26SA46	5N54
12/ 7	26SA 1	5N26	265 50	17S57	27SA 3	5N55
12/17	27SA 6	5N27	266 58	17S59	27SA20	5N56
12/27	28SA12	5N28	268 7	17S59	27SA36	5N57

Stations	Date	Long.	Lat.
RETROGRADE	4/ 4.49	25SA 0	5N37
DIRECT	8/22.61	18SA56	5N55

Date	Long.	Lat.	R.A.	Dec.	HLong.	HLat.
1/ 6	29SA17	5N30	269 15	17S57	27SA53	5N58
1/16	0CP19	5N32	270 20	17S55	28SA10	5N59
1/26	1CP18	5N36	271 22	17S51	28SA26	6N 0
2/ 5	2CP14	5N40	272 20	17S46	28SA43	6N 1
2/15	3CP 3	5N44	273 12	17S41	28SA59	6N 2
2/25	3CP47	5N49	273 57	17S35	29SA16	6N 3
3/ 7	4CP24	5N55	274 35	17S28	29SA32	6N 4
3/17	4CP53	6N 1	275 5	17S21	29SA48	6N 5
3/27	5CP13	6N 7	275 26	17S14	0CP 5	6N 6
4/ 6	5CP25	6N14	275 38	17S 7	0CP21	6N 7
4/16	5CP28	6N20	275 41	17S 0	0CP37	6N 7
4/26	5CP22	6N27	275 35	16S54	0CP53	6N 8
5/ 6	5CP 8	6N33	275 19	16S49	1CP 9	6N 9
5/16	4CP46	6N38	274 57	16S44	1CP25	6N10
5/26	4CP17	6N42	274 27	16S41	1CP41	6N11
6/ 5	3CP44	6N46	273 52	16S38	1CP57	6N12
6/15	3CP 6	6N49	273 13	16S36	2CP13	6N13
6/25	2CP27	6N50	272 33	16S36	2CP29	6N14
7/ 5	1CP48	6N50	271 52	16S36	2CP44	6N14
7/15	1CP12	6N49	271 14	16S37	3CP 0	6N15
7/25	0CP39	6N47	270 40	16S40	3CP16	6N16
8/ 4	0CP11	6N45	270 12	16S43	3CP31	6N17
8/14	29SA50	6N41	269 50	16S46	3CP47	6N18
8/24	29SA37	6N37	269 36	16S50	4CP 2	6N18
9/ 3	29SA32	6N32	269 31	16S55	4CP18	6N19
9/13	29SA35	6N27	269 34	17S 0	4CP33	6N20
9/23	29SA47	6N22	269 47	17S 5	4CP48	6N21
10/ 3	0CP 8	6N18	270 8	17S10	5CP 4	6N21
10/13	0CP36	6N13	270 37	17S14	5CP19	6N22
10/23	1CP11	6N 9	271 14	17S18	5CP34	6N23
11/ 2	1CP53	6N 6	271 58	17S21	5CP49	6N23
11/12	2CP41	6N 2	272 47	17S23	6CP 4	6N24
11/22	3CP33	6N 0	273 42	17S24	6CP19	6N25
12/ 2	4CP29	5N58	274 41	17S24	6CP34	6N25
12/12	5CP28	5N57	275 42	17S23	6CP49	6N26
12/22	6CP29	5N57	276 45	17S21	7CP 4	6N27

Stations	Date	Long.	Lat.
RETROGRADE	4/14.28	5CP28	6N19
DIRECT	9/ 3.97	29SA32	6N32

1902

Date	Long.	Lat.	R.A.	Dec.	HLong.	HLat.
1/ 1	7CP30	5N58	277 49	17S17	7CP19	6N27
1/11	8CP31	5N59	278 52	17S13	7CP34	6N28
1/21	9CP30	6N 1	279 53	17S 7	7CP48	6N29
1/31	10CP27	6N 3	280 52	17S 0	8CP 3	6N29
2/10	11CP20	6N 7	281 47	16S53	8CP18	6N30
2/20	12CP 9	6N11	282 37	16S45	8CP32	6N30
3/ 2	12CP52	6N15	283 21	16S36	8CP47	6N31
3/12	13CP29	6N20	283 59	16S28	9CP 2	6N32
3/22	13CP58	6N26	284 29	16S19	9CP16	6N32
4/ 1	14CP21	6N32	284 51	16S11	9CP30	6N33
4/11	14CP35	6N38	285 5	16S 4	9CP45	6N33
4/21	14CP40	6N44	285 10	15S57	9CP59	6N34
5/ 1	14CP38	6N50	285 7	15S51	10CP13	6N34
5/11	14CP27	6N56	284 55	15S46	10CP28	6N35
5/21	14CP 9	7N 1	284 36	15S43	10CP42	6N35
5/31	13CP44	7N 6	284 10	15S41	10CP56	6N36
6/10	13CP14	7N 9	283 38	15S40	11CP10	6N36
6/20	12CP39	7N12	283 3	15S41	11CP24	6N37
6/30	12CP 2	7N14	282 25	15S42	11CP38	6N37
7/10	11CP25	7N14	281 46	15S45	11CP52	6N38
7/20	10CP48	7N13	281 9	15S49	12CP 6	6N38
7/30	10CP15	7N12	280 34	15S53	12CP20	6N39
8/ 9	9CP45	7N 9	280 4	15S58	12CP34	6N39
8/19	9CP21	7N 5	279 40	16S 3	12CP48	6N40
8/29	9CP 4	7N 1	279 23	16S 9	13CP 1	6N40
9/ 8	8CP55	6N56	279 13	16S14	13CP15	6N41
9/18	8CP53	6N51	279 12	16S19	13CP29	6N41
9/28	9CP 0	6N46	279 19	16S24	13CP42	6N41
10/ 8	9CP15	6N41	279 35	16S28	13CP56	6N42
10/18	9CP37	6N36	279 58	16S31	14CP 9	6N42
10/28	10CP 6	6N31	280 29	16S34	14CP23	6N43
11/ 7	10CP43	6N27	281 7	16S35	14CP36	6N43
11/17	11CP25	6N23	281 50	16S36	14CP50	6N43
11/27	12CP12	6N21	282 39	16S35	15CP 3	6N44
12/ 7	13CP 3	6N18	283 32	16S32	15CP17	6N44
12/17	13CP57	6N17	284 28	16S29	15CP30	6N45
12/27	14CP53	6N16	285 26	16S24	15CP43	6N45

Stations	Date	Long.	Lat.
RETROGRADE	4/22.88	14CP40	6N45
DIRECT	9/14.90	8CP53	6N53

Date	Long.	Lat.	R.A.	Dec.	HLong.	HLat.
1/ 6	15CP50	6N16	286 25	16S18	15CP56	6N45
1/16	16CP47	6N16	287 23	16S10	16CP 9	6N46
1/26	17CP43	6N18	288 21	16S 2	16CP23	6N46
2/ 5	18CP37	6N20	289 16	15S53	16CP36	6N46
2/15	19CP28	6N22	290 8	15S44	16CP49	6N47
2/25	20CP15	6N26	290 55	15S34	17CP 2	6N47
3/ 7	20CP57	6N30	291 38	15S24	17CP15	6N47
3/17	21CP34	6N35	292 14	15S14	17CP28	6N47
3/27	22CP 4	6N40	292 43	15S 4	17CP41	6N48
4/ 6	22CP26	6N45	293 6	14S55	17CP54	6N48
4/16	22CP42	6N51	293 20	14S47	18CP 6	6N48
4/26	22CP49	6N57	293 27	14S40	18CP19	6N49
5/ 6	22CP49	7N 2	293 26	14S35	18CP32	6N49
5/16	22CP41	7N 8	293 17	14S30	18CP45	6N49
5/26	22CP25	7N13	293 0	14S28	18CP57	6N49
6/ 5	22CP 3	7N17	292 37	14S27	19CP10	6N50
6/15	21CP36	7N21	292 9	14S28	19CP23	6N50
6/25	21CP 4	7N24	291 36	14S30	19CP35	6N50
7/ 5	20CP29	7N25	291 1	14S33	19CP48	6N50
7/15	19CP53	7N26	290 24	14S37	20CP 0	6N50
7/25	19CP17	7N25	289 48	14S43	20CP13	6N51
8/ 4	18CP44	7N24	289 14	14S49	20CP25	6N51
8/14	18CP14	7N21	288 43	14S56	20CP37	6N51
8/24	17CP48	7N17	288 18	15S 2	20CP50	6N51
9/ 3	17CP29	7N13	287 59	15S 9	21CP 2	6N51
9/13	17CP16	7N 8	287 47	15S15	21CP14	6N52
9/23	17CP11	7N 3	287 42	15S21	21CP27	6N52
10/ 3	17CP14	6N58	287 46	15S26	21CP39	6N52
10/13	17CP24	6N53	287 57	15S30	21CP51	6N52
10/23	17CP42	6N48	288 16	15S32	22CP 3	6N52
11/ 2	18CP 7	6N43	288 42	15S34	22CP15	6N53
11/12	18CP39	6N39	289 15	15S34	22CP27	6N53
11/22	19CP16	6N35	289 54	15S33	22CP39	6N53
12/ 2	19CP59	6N31	290 37	15S31	22CP51	6N53
12/12	20CP45	6N29	291 26	15S27	23CP 3	6N53
12/22	21CP35	6N27	292 17	15S21	23CP15	6N53

Stations	Date	Long.	Lat.
RETROGRADE	4/30.52	22CP50	6N59
DIRECT	9/24.59	17CP11	7N 3

1904

Date	Long.	Lat.	R.A.		Dec.	HLong.	HLat.
1/ 1	22CP27	6N25	293	10	15S14	23CP27	6N53
1/11	23CP21	6N25	294	5	15S 6	23CP39	6N53
1/21	24CP15	6N25	294	59	14S57	23CP51	6N54
1/31	25CP 8	6N26	295	53	14S47	24CP 3	6N54
2/10	25CP59	6N27	296	45	14S37	24CP15	6N54
2/20	26CP48	6N30	297	33	14S26	24CP26	6N54
3/ 1	27CP33	6N33	298	18	14S14	24CP38	6N54
3/11	28CP14	6N36	298	58	14S 3	24CP50	6N54
3/21	28CP49	6N41	299	33	13S52	25CP 1	6N54
3/31	29CP19	6N45	300	2	13S42	25CP13	6N54
4/10	29CP42	6N50	300	24	13S32	25CP24	6N54
4/20	29CP58	6N55	300	39	13S24	25CP36	6N54
4/30	0AQ 6	7N 1	300	46	13S17	25CP48	6N54
5/10	0AQ 7	7N 6	300	46	13S11	25CP59	6N54
5/20	0AQ 1	7N11	300	39	13S 8	26CP10	6N55
5/30	29CP48	7N16	300	24	13S 6	26CP22	6N55
6/ 9	29CP28	7N20	300	4	13S 6	26CP33	6N55
6/19	29CP 3	7N24	299	38	13S 7	26CP45	6N55
6/29	28CP33	7N26	299	8	13S10	26CP56	6N55
7/ 9	28CP 0	7N28	298	34	13S15	27CP 7	6N55
7/19	27CP26	7N29	298	0	13S21	27CP19	6N55
7/29	26CP51	7N28	297	25	13S28	27CP30	6N55
8/ 8	26CP18	7N27	296	52	13S35	27CP41	6N55
8/18	25CP47	7N24	296	22	13S43	27CP52	6N55
8/28	25CP21	7N21	295	56	13S51	28CP 3	6N55
9/ 7	25CP 0	7N17	295	36	13S59	28CP14	6N55
9/17	24CP46	7N12	295	22	14S 6	28CP26	6N55
9/27	24CP38	7N 7	295	16	14S12	28CP37	6N55
10/ 7	24CP38	7N 2	295	16	14S17	28CP48	6N55
10/17	24CP45	6N57	295	25	14S21	28CP59	6N55
10/27	25CP 0	6N52	295	40	14S23	29CP10	6N55
11/ 6	25CP21	6N47	296	3	14S24	29CP21	6N55
11/16	25CP49	6N42	296	32	14S24	29CP32	6N55
11/26	26CP23	6N38	297	6	14S22	29CP42	6N55
12/ 6	27CP 2	6N35	297	46	14S18	29CP53	6N55
12/16	27CP45	6N32	298	30	14S13	0AQ 4	6N55
12/26	28CP31	6N30	299	17	14S 6	0AQ15	6N55

Stations	Date	Long.	Lat.
RETROGRADE	5/ 6.49	0AQ 8	7N 4
DIRECT	10/ 2.32	24CP37	7N 4

Date	Long.	Lat.	R.A.	Dec.	HLong.	HLat.
1/ 5	29CP20	6N28	300 7	13S58	0AQ26	6N55
1/15	0AQ11	6N27	300 57	13S49	0AQ36	6N55
1/25	1AQ 2	6N27	301 48	13S38	0AQ47	6N55
2/ 4	1AQ52	6N28	302 39	13S27	0AQ58	6N54
2/14	2AQ41	6N29	303 27	13S15	1AQ 9	6N54
2/24	3AQ28	6N31	304 13	13S 3	1AQ19	6N54
3/ 6	4AQ11	6N33	304 56	12S51	1AQ30	6N54
3/16	4AQ50	6N37	305 34	12S39	1AQ40	6N54
3/26	5AQ25	6N40	306 7	12S27	1AQ51	6N54
4/ 5	5AQ53	6N44	306 34	12S16	2AQ 2	6N54
4/15	6AQ16	6N49	306 55	12S 6	2AQ12	6N54
4/25	6AQ32	6N54	307 10	11S58	2AQ23	6N54
5/ 5	6AQ41	6N59	307 18	11S51	2AQ33	6N54
5/15	6AQ43	7N 4	307 18	11S46	2AQ43	6N54
5/25	6AQ38	7N 8	307 12	11S42	2AQ54	6N54
6/ 4	6AQ26	7N13	307 0	11S41	3AQ 4	6N54
6/14	6AQ 8	7N17	306 41	11S41	3AQ15	6N53
6/24	5AQ45	7N20	306 17	11S44	3AQ25	6N53
7/ 4	5AQ17	7N23	305 49	11S48	3AQ35	6N53
7/14	4AQ45	7N24	305 18	11S53	3AQ45	6N53
7/24	4AQ12	7N25	304 45	12S 0	3AQ56	6N53
8/ 3	3AQ39	7N24	304 11	12S 8	4AQ 6	6N53
8/13	3AQ 6	7N23	303 39	12S17	4AQ16	6N53
8/23	2AQ36	7N21	303 10	12S26	4AQ26	6N53
9/ 2	2AQ 9	7N18	302 45	12S34	4AQ37	6N52
9/12	1AQ48	7N14	302 24	12S43	4AQ47	6N52
9/22	1AQ32	7N10	302 10	12S50	4AQ57	6N52
10/ 2	1AQ23	7N 5	302 1	12S57	5AQ 7	6N52
10/12	1AQ21	7N 0	302 0	13S 2	5AQ17	6N52
10/22	1AQ26	6N55	302 6	13S 6	5AQ27	6N52
11/ 1	1AQ38	6N49	302 19	13S 9	5AQ37	6N52
11/11	1AQ56	6N45	302 39	13S10	5AQ47	6N51
11/21	2AQ21	6N40	303 5	13S 8	5AQ57	6N51
12/ 1	2AQ52	6N36	303 37	13S 6	6AQ 7	6N51
12/11	3AQ28	6N33	304 13	13S 1	6AQ17	6N51
12/21	4AQ 8	6N30	304 54	12S55	6AQ27	6N51
12/31	4AQ52	6N27	305 38	12S47	6AQ37	6N51

Stations	Date	Long.	Lat.
RETROGRADE	5/12.79	6AQ43	7N 2
DIRECT	10/10.10	1AQ21	7N 1

1906

Date	Long.	Lat.	R.A.	Dec.	HLong.	HLat.
1/10	5AQ38	6N25	306 24	12S38	6AQ46	6N50
1/20	6AQ26	6N24	307 11	12S28	6AQ56	6N50
1/30	7AQ14	6N24	307 59	12S17	7AQ 6	6N50
2/ 9	8AQ 2	6N24	308 46	12S 4	7AQ16	6N50
2/19	8AQ49	6N25	309 32	11S52	7AQ26	6N50
3/ 1	9AQ34	6N27	310 15	11S39	7AQ35	6N50
3/11	10AQ15	6N29	310 55	11S26	7AQ45	6N49
3/21	10AQ53	6N32	311 31	11S13	7AQ55	6N49
3/31	11AQ26	6N35	312 3	11S 1	8AQ 4	6N49
4/10	11AQ54	6N39	312 29	10S50	8AQ14	6N49
4/20	12AQ16	6N43	312 50	10S40	8AQ24	6N49
4/30	12AQ32	6N48	313 4	10S32	8AQ33	6N48
5/10	12AQ41	6N52	313 11	10S25	8AQ43	6N48
5/20	12AQ44	6N57	313 13	10S20	8AQ52	6N48
5/30	12AQ39	7N 1	313 7	10S17	9AQ 2	6N48
6/ 9	12AQ29	7N 5	312 56	10S16	9AQ11	6N48
6/19	12AQ12	7N 9	312 38	10S17	9AQ21	6N47
6/29	11AQ50	7N12	312 16	10S20	9AQ30	6N47
7/ 9	11AQ23	7N14	311 49	10S24	9AQ40	6N47
7/19	10AQ53	7N16	311 20	10S31	9AQ49	6N47
7/29	10AQ21	7N16	310 48	10S39	9AQ59	6N47
8/ 8	9AQ48	7N16	310 17	10S47	10AQ 8	6N46
8/18	9AQ17	7N15	309 46	10S57	10AQ17	6N46
8/28	8AQ47	7N13	309 17	11S 6	10AQ27	6N46
9/ 7	8AQ20	7N10	308 52	11S16	10AQ36	6N46
9/17	7AQ59	7N 6	308 32	11S25	10AQ45	6N45
9/27	7AQ42	7N 2	308 17	11S33	10AQ55	6N45
10/ 7	7AQ32	6N57	308 8	11S40	11AQ 4	6N45
10/17	7AQ28	6N53	308 6	11S45	11AQ13	6N45
10/27	7AQ32	6N48	308 10	11S49	11AQ22	6N44
11/ 6	7AQ42	6N43	308 21	11S52	11AQ32	6N44
11/16	7AQ59	6N38	308 39	11S52	11AQ41	6N44
11/26	8AQ21	6N34	309 3	11S51	11AQ50	6N44
12/ 6	8AQ50	6N30	309 32	11S47	11AQ59	6N43
12/16	9AQ24	6N26	310 6	11S42	12AQ 8	6N43
12/26	10AQ 1	6N23	310 43	11S35	12AQ17	6N43

Stations	Date	Long.	Lat.
RETROGRADE	5/18.63	12AQ44	6N56
DIRECT	10/17.21	7AQ28	6N52

Date	Long.	Lat.	R.A.	Dec.	HLong.	HLat.
1/ 5	10AQ43	6N21	311 24	11S27	12AQ27	6N43
1/15	11AQ26	6N19	312 8	11S17	12AQ36	6N42
1/25	12AQ12	6N18	312 52	11S 6	12AQ45	6N42
2/ 4	12AQ58	6N17	313 37	10S54	12AQ54	6N42
2/14	13AQ44	6N17	314 22	10S41	13AQ 3	6N42
2/24	14AQ29	6N18	315 5	10S28	13AQ12	6N41
3/ 6	15AQ12	6N19	315 46	10S14	13AQ21	6N41
3/16	15AQ52	6N21	316 24	10S 1	13AQ30	6N41
3/26	16AQ28	6N24	316 59	9S48	13AQ39	6N40
4/ 5	17AQ 0	6N27	317 29	9S36	13AQ48	6N40
4/15	17AQ27	6N30	317 54	9S24	13AQ56	6N40
4/25	17AQ48	6N34	318 13	9S15	14AQ 5	6N40
5/ 5	18AQ 4	6N38	318 27	9S 6	14AQ14	6N39
5/15	18AQ13	6N42	318 34	9S 0	14AQ23	6N39
5/25	18AQ16	6N46	318 36	8S55	14AQ32	6N39
6/ 4	18AQ12	6N50	318 31	8S52	14AQ41	6N38
6/14	18AQ 2	6N54	318 20	8S52	14AQ49	6N38
6/24	17AQ46	6N57	318 3	8S53	14AQ58	6N38
7/ 4	17AQ24	7N 0	317 42	8S57	15AQ 7	6N38
7/14	16AQ59	7N 2	317 17	9S 2	15AQ16	6N37
7/24	16AQ30	7N 4	316 49	9S 9	15AQ25	6N37
8/ 3	15AQ59	7N 5	316 19	9S17	15AQ33	6N37
8/13	15AQ27	7N 4	315 48	9S27	15AQ42	6N36
8/23	14AQ56	7N 3	315 19	9S37	15AQ51	6N36
9/ 2	14AQ27	7N 1	314 51	9S47	15AQ59	6N36
9/12	14AQ 1	6N58	314 27	9S57	16AQ 8	6N35
9/22	13AQ39	6N55	314 6	10S 6	16AQ17	6N35
10/ 2	13AQ22	6N51	313 51	10S15	16AQ25	6N35
10/12	13AQ11	6N46	313 42	10S22	16AQ34	6N34
10/22	13AQ 7	6N42	313 39	10S27	16AQ42	6N34
11/ 1	13AQ 9	6N37	313 43	10S31	16AQ51	6N34
11/11	13AQ18	6N32	313 53	10S34	16AQ59	6N33
11/21	13AQ33	6N28	314 9	10S34	17AQ 8	6N33
12/ 1	13AQ54	6N24	314 30	10S32	17AQ16	6N33
12/11	14AQ21	6N20	314 58	10S28	17AQ25	6N32
12/21	14AQ53	6N16	315 29	10S22	17AQ33	6N32
12/31	15AQ29	6N13	316 5	10S15	17AQ42	6N32

Stations	Date	Long.	Lat.
RETROGRADE	5/24.02	18AQ16	6N46
DIRECT	10/23.71	13AQ 7	6N41

1908

Date	Long.	Lat.	R.A.	Dec.	HLong.	HLat.
1/10	16AQ 8	6N11	316 44	10S 6	17AQ50	6N31
1/20	16AQ50	6N 9	317 24	9S56	17AQ59	6N31
1/30	17AQ33	6N 8	318 7	9S44	18AQ 7	6N31
2/ 9	18AQ18	6N 7	318 49	9S31	18AQ16	6N30
2/19	19AQ 2	6N 7	319 32	9S18	18AQ24	6N30
2/29	19AQ45	6N 8	320 13	9S 4	18AQ32	6N30
3/10	20AQ26	6N 9	320 52	8S51	18AQ41	6N29
3/20	21AQ 5	6N11	321 28	8S37	18AQ49	6N29
3/30	21AQ40	6N13	322 1	8S24	18AQ57	6N29
4/ 9	22AQ10	6N16	322 30	8S12	19AQ 6	6N28
4/19	22AQ36	6N19	322 53	8S 1	19AQ14	6N28
4/29	22AQ57	6N22	323 12	7S51	19AQ22	6N28
5/ 9	23AQ12	6N26	323 25	7S43	19AQ30	6N27
5/19	23AQ21	6N30	323 32	7S36	19AQ39	6N27
5/29	23AQ24	6N33	323 33	7S32	19AQ47	6N27
6/ 8	23AQ20	6N37	323 29	7S29	19AQ55	6N26
6/18	23AQ10	6N41	323 18	7S29	20AQ 3	6N26
6/28	22AQ55	6N44	323 3	7S31	20AQ11	6N25
7/ 8	22AQ34	6N46	322 42	7S35	20AQ20	6N25
7/18	22AQ10	6N48	322 18	7S41	20AQ28	6N25
7/28	21AQ42	6N50	321 51	7S49	20AQ36	6N24
8/ 7	21AQ12	6N50	321 22	7S58	20AQ44	6N24
8/17	20AQ41	6N50	320 53	8S 7	20AQ52	6N24
8/27	20AQ10	6N49	320 24	8S18	21AQ 0	6N23
9/ 6	19AQ41	6N47	319 58	8S28	21AQ 8	6N23
9/16	19AQ16	6N44	319 34	8S39	21AQ16	6N23
9/26	18AQ54	6N41	319 14	8S48	21AQ25	6N22
10/ 6	18AQ37	6N37	318 59	8S57	21AQ33	6N22
10/16	18AQ26	6N33	318 50	9S 4	21AQ41	6N21
10/26	18AQ21	6N28	318 46	9S10	21AQ49	6N21
11/ 5	18AQ23	6N24	318 49	9S14	21AQ57	6N21
11/15	18AQ31	6N19	318 58	9S16	22AQ 5	6N20
11/25	18AQ45	6N15	319 13	9S16	22AQ13	6N20
12/ 5	19AQ 5	6N11	319 34	9S14	22AQ21	6N19
12/15	19AQ30	6N 7	319 59	9S 9	22AQ28	6N19
12/25	20AQ 1	6N 4	320 29	9S 3	22AQ36	6N19

Stations	Date	Long.	Lat.
RETROGRADE	5/28.12	23AQ24	6N33
DIRECT	10/28.71	18AQ21	6N27

Date	Long.	Lat.	R.A.	Dec.	HLong.	HLat.
1/ 4	20AQ35	6N 1	321 3	8S55	22AQ44	6N18
1/14	21AQ13	5N59	321 40	8S46	22AQ52	6N18
1/24	21AQ53	5N57	322 19	8S35	23AQ 0	6N18
2/ 3	22AQ35	5N56	322 59	8S23	23AQ 8	6N17
2/13	23AQ17	5N55	323 40	8S10	23AQ16	6N17
2/23	24AQ 0	5N55	324 20	7S56	23AQ24	6N16
3/ 5	24AQ41	5N55	324 59	7S43	23AQ32	6N16
3/15	25AQ21	5N56	325 37	7S29	23AQ39	6N16
3/25	25AQ58	5N58	326 11	7S15	23AQ47	6N15
4/ 4	26AQ32	6N 0	326 43	7S 2	23AQ55	6N15
4/14	27AQ 2	6N 2	327 10	6S50	24AQ 3	6N14
4/24	27AQ27	6N 5	327 33	6S39	24AQ11	6N14
5/ 4	27AQ47	6N 8	327 50	6S29	24AQ18	6N14
5/14	28AQ 1	6N12	328 3	6S21	24AQ26	6N13
5/24	28AQ 9	6N15	328 9	6S15	24AQ34	6N13
6/ 3	28AQ12	6N19	328 10	6S11	24AQ42	6N12
6/13	28AQ 8	6N22	328 6	6S 9	24AQ49	6N12
6/23	27AQ59	6N25	327 56	6S 9	24AQ57	6N11
7/ 3	27AQ44	6N28	327 41	6S12	25AQ 5	6N11
7/13	27AQ24	6N30	327 21	6S16	25AQ12	6N11
7/23	27AQ 0	6N32	326 58	6S22	25AQ20	6N10
8/ 2	26AQ32	6N33	326 32	6S30	25AQ28	6N10
8/12	26AQ 3	6N34	326 4	6S40	25AQ35	6N 9
8/22	25AQ33	6N33	325 36	6S50	25AQ43	6N 9
9/ 1	25AQ 3	6N32	325 8	7S 1	25AQ51	6N 9
9/11	24AQ35	6N30	324 42	7S12	25AQ58	6N 8
9/21	24AQ10	6N28	324 19	7S22	26AQ 6	6N 8
10/ 1	23AQ48	6N25	324 0	7S32	26AQ13	6N 7
10/11	23AQ32	6N21	323 45	7S41	26AQ21	6N 7
10/21	23AQ20	6N17	323 36	7S48	26AQ28	6N 6
10/31	23AQ15	6N13	323 32	7S54	26AQ36	6N 6
11/10	23AQ16	6N 9	323 34	7S57	26AQ44	6N 6
11/20	23AQ24	6N 4	323 43	7S59	26AQ51	6N 5
11/30	23AQ37	6N 0	323 57	7S59	26AQ59	6N 5
12/10	23AQ56	5N56	324 16	7S56	27AQ 6	6N 4
12/20	24AQ21	5N53	324 41	7S52	27AQ14	6N 4
12/30	24AQ50	5N50	325 10	7S45	27AQ21	6N 3

Stations	Date	Long.	Lat.
RETROGRADE	6/ 1.93	28AQ12	6N18
DIRECT	11/ 3.32	23AQ15	6N12

1910

Date	Long.	Lat.	R.A.	Dec.	HLong.	HLat.
1/ 9	25AQ23	5N47	325 42	7S37	27AQ29	6N 3
1/19	26AQ 0	5N45	326 17	7S27	27AQ36	6N 3
1/29	26AQ38	5N43	326 54	7S16	27AQ43	6N 2
2/ 8	27AQ19	5N42	327 33	7S 3	27AQ51	6N 2
2/18	28AQ 0	5N41	328 12	6S50	27AQ58	6N 1
2/28	28AQ41	5N41	328 51	6S36	28AQ 6	6N 1
3/10	29AQ21	5N41	329 29	6S22	28AQ13	6N 0
3/20	0PI 0	5N42	330 4	6S 8	28AQ20	6N 0
3/30	0PI35	5N43	330 37	5S55	28AQ28	5N59
4/ 9	1PI 8	5N45	331 7	5S42	28AQ35	5N59
4/19	1PI37	5N47	331 33	5S29	28AQ43	5N59
4/29	2PI 1	5N50	331 55	5S19	28AQ50	5N58
5/ 9	2PI20	5N53	332 12	5S 9	28AQ57	5N58
5/19	2PI34	5N56	332 24	5S 2	29AQ 5	5N57
5/29	2PI42	5N59	332 30	4S56	29AQ12	5N57
6/ 8	2PI44	6N 2	332 31	4S52	29AQ19	5N56
6/18	2PI40	6N 5	332 26	4S51	29AQ27	5N56
6/28	2PI30	6N 8	332 16	4S51	29AQ34	5N55
7/ 8	2PI16	6N11	332 2	4S54	29AQ41	5N55
7/18	1PI56	6N13	331 42	4S59	29AQ48	5N54
7/28	1PI32	6N14	331 20	5S 6	29AQ56	5N54
8/ 7	1PI 6	6N15	330 55	5S14	0PI 3	5N54
8/17	0PI37	6N16	330 28	5S24	0PI10	5N53
8/27	0PI 7	6N15	330 0	5S34	0PI17	5N53
9/ 6	29AQ38	6N14	329 33	5S46	0PI25	5N52
9/16	29AQ11	6N12	329 8	5S57	0PI32	5N52
9/26	28AQ46	6N10	328 45	6S 7	0PI39	5N51
10/ 6	28AQ25	6N 7	328 27	6S17	0PI46	5N51
10/16	28AQ 9	6N 4	328 12	6S26	0PI53	5N50
10/26	27AQ58	6N 0	328 3	6S33	1PI 0	5N50
11/ 5	27AQ52	5N56	328 0	6S39	1PI 8	5N49
11/15	27AQ53	5N52	328 2	6S42	1PI15	5N49
11/25	28AQ 0	5N48	328 10	6S44	1PI22	5N49
12/ 5	28AQ13	5N44	328 24	6S43	1PI29	5N48
12/15	28AQ32	5N40	328 42	6S40	1PI36	5N48
12/25	28AQ55	5N37	329 6	6S35	1PI43	5N47

Stations	Date	Long.	Lat.
RETROGRADE	6/ 6.53	2PI44	6N 2
DIRECT	11/ 8.54	27AQ52	5N54

Date	Long.	Lat.	R.A.	Dec.	HLong.	HLat.
1/ 4	29AQ24	5N34	329 34	6S28	1PI50	5N47
1/14	29AQ56	5N31	330 5	6S20	1PI57	5N46
1/24	0PI31	5N29	330 39	6S10	2PI 5	5N46
2/ 3	1PI 9	5N27	331 15	5S58	2PI12	5N45
2/13	1PI48	5N26	331 52	5S45	2PI19	5N45
2/23	2PI28	5N25	332 30	5S32	2PI26	5N44
3/ 5	3PI 8	5N25	333 7	5S18	2PI33	5N44
3/15	3PI47	5N25	333 43	5S 4	2PI40	5N43
3/25	4PI24	5N26	334 18	4S50	2PI47	5N43
4/ 4	4PI59	5N27	334 50	4S36	2PI54	5N42
4/14	5PI31	5N29	335 18	4S23	3PI 1	5N42
4/24	5PI58	5N31	335 43	4S11	3PI 8	5N41
5/ 4	6PI22	5N33	336 4	4S 1	3PI15	5N41
5/14	6PI40	5N36	336 20	3S52	3PI22	5N40
5/24	6PI53	5N39	336 31	3S44	3PI29	5N40
6/ 3	7PI 0	5N42	336 37	3S39	3PI36	5N39
6/13	7PI 2	5N44	336 37	3S36	3PI43	5N39
6/23	6PI58	5N47	336 33	3S35	3PI50	5N39
7/ 3	6PI48	5N50	336 23	3S36	3PI57	5N38
7/13	6PI34	5N52	336 8	3S39	4PI 4	5N38
7/23	6PI14	5N54	335 50	3S44	4PI10	5N37
8/ 2	5PI51	5N55	335 28	3S51	4PI17	5N37
8/12	5PI25	5N56	335 3	4S 0	4PI24	5N36
8/22	4PI56	5N56	334 37	4S10	4PI31	5N36
9/ 1	4PI27	5N56	334 10	4S21	4PI38	5N35
9/11	3PI59	5N55	333 43	4S32	4PI45	5N35
9/21	3PI32	5N53	333 19	4S43	4PI52	5N34
10/ 1	3PI 8	5N51	332 57	4S54	4PI59	5N34
10/11	2PI47	5N48	332 39	5S 4	5PI 6	5N33
10/21	2PI31	5N45	332 25	5S13	5PI12	5N33
10/31	2PI20	5N41	332 16	5S20	5PI19	5N32
11/10	2PI15	5N37	332 13	5S25	5PI26	5N32
11/20	2PI16	5N34	332 15	5S29	5PI33	5N31
11/30	2PI23	5N30	332 23	5S30	5PI40	5N31
12/10	2PI36	5N26	332 36	5S29	5PI46	5N30
12/20	2PI54	5N23	332 54	5S25	5PI53	5N30
12/30	3PI17	5N19	333 17	5S20	6PI 0	5N29

Stations	Date	Long.	Lat.
RETROGRADE	6/10.94	7PI 2	5N44
DIRECT	11/13.51	2PI15	5N36

1912

Date	Long.	Lat.	R.A.		Dec.	HLong.	HLat.
1/ 9	3PI45	5N17	333	44	5S13	6PI 7	5N29
1/19	4PI16	5N14	334	15	5S 4	6PI14	5N28
1/29	4PI51	5N12	334	48	4S54	6PI20	5N28
2/ 8	5PI28	5N10	335	22	4S42	6PI27	5N27
2/18	6PI 6	5N 9	335	59	4S29	6PI34	5N27
2/28	6PI45	5N 9	336	35	4S15	6PI41	5N26
3/ 9	7PI24	5N 8	337	11	4S 1	6PI47	5N26
3/19	8PI 2	5N 9	337	46	3S47	6PI54	5N25
3/29	8PI38	5N 9	338	19	3S33	7PI 1	5N25
4/ 8	9PI12	5N10	338	50	3S20	7PI 8	5N24
4/18	9PI42	5N12	339	18	3S 7	7PI14	5N24
4/28	10PI 9	5N14	339	42	2S55	7PI21	5N23
5/ 8	10PI31	5N16	340	2	2S45	7PI28	5N23
5/18	10PI49	5N18	340	17	2S36	7PI34	5N22
5/28	11PI 1	5N21	340	27	2S29	7PI41	5N22
6/ 7	11PI 8	5N23	340	33	2S24	7PI48	5N21
6/17	11PI 9	5N26	340	33	2S22	7PI54	5N21
6/27	11PI 5	5N28	340	28	2S21	8PI 1	5N20
7/ 7	10PI55	5N31	340	18	2S22	8PI 8	5N20
7/17	10PI40	5N33	340	4	2S26	8PI14	5N19
7/27	10PI21	5N34	339	45	2S32	8PI21	5N19
8/ 6	9PI58	5N36	339	23	2S39	8PI28	5N18
8/16	9PI32	5N36	338	59	2S48	8PI34	5N18
8/26	9PI 4	5N36	338	33	2S59	8PI41	5N17
9/ 5	8PI35	5N36	338	7	3S10	8PI47	5N17
9/15	8PI 7	5N35	337	42	3S21	8PI54	5N16
9/25	7PI41	5N33	337	18	3S32	9PI 1	5N16
10/ 5	7PI17	5N31	336	56	3S43	9PI 7	5N15
10/15	6PI57	5N28	336	39	3S53	9PI14	5N14
10/25	6PI41	5N25	336	26	4S 1	9PI20	5N14
11/ 4	6PI31	5N22	336	17	4S 8	9PI27	5N13
11/14	6PI26	5N18	336	14	4S13	9PI34	5N13
11/24	6PI27	5N14	336	16	4S16	9PI40	5N12
12/ 4	6PI34	5N11	336	24	4S17	9PI47	5N12
12/14	6PI47	5N 7	336	37	4S16	9PI53	5N11
12/24	7PI 5	5N 4	336	55	4S12	10PI 0	5N11

Stations	Date	Long.	Lat.
RETROGRADE	6/14.21	11PI 9	5N25
DIRECT	11/17.18	6PI26	5N17

Date	Long.	Lat.	R.A.	Dec.	HLong.	HLat.
1/ 3	7PI28	5N 1	337 17	4S 7	10PI 6	5N10
1/13	7PI55	4N58	337 44	3S59	10PI13	5N10
1/23	8PI26	4N56	338 13	3S50	10PI19	5N 9
2/ 2	9PI 0	4N54	338 46	3S39	10PI26	5N 9
2/12	9PI36	4N53	339 20	3S27	10PI32	5N 8
2/22	10PI14	4N52	339 55	3S14	10PI39	5N 8
3/ 4	10PI52	4N51	340 30	3S 0	10PI45	5N 7
3/14	11PI30	4N51	341 5	2S46	10PI52	5N 7
3/24	12PI 7	4N51	341 39	2S32	10PI58	5N 6
4/ 3	12PI42	4N51	342 12	2S18	11PI 5	5N 6
4/13	13PI15	4N52	342 41	2S 5	11PI11	5N 5
4/23	13PI44	4N54	343 8	1S53	11PI18	5N 5
5/ 3	14PI10	4N55	343 31	1S41	11PI24	5N 4
5/13	14PI32	4N57	343 50	1S31	11PI31	5N 3
5/23	14PI48	4N59	344 5	1S23	11PI37	5N 3
6/ 2	15PI 0	5N 2	344 15	1S16	11PI43	5N 2
6/12	15PI 6	5N 4	344 20	1S12	11PI50	5N 2
6/22	15PI 7	5N 6	344 19	1S 9	11PI56	5N 1
7/ 2	15PI 2	5N 9	344 14	1S 9	12PI 3	5N 1
7/12	14PI52	5N11	344 4	1S11	12PI 9	5N 0
7/22	14PI37	5N12	343 50	1S15	12PI15	5N 0
8/ 1	14PI18	5N14	343 31	1S21	12PI22	4N59
8/11	13PI55	5N15	343 10	1S29	12PI28	4N59
8/21	13PI29	5N15	342 46	1S38	12PI35	4N58
8/31	13PI 2	5N15	342 21	1S49	12PI41	4N58
9/10	12PI33	5N15	341 55	2S 0	12PI47	4N57
9/20	12PI 6	5N14	341 30	2S11	12PI54	4N57
9/30	11PI40	5N12	341 7	2S23	13PI 0	4N56
10/10	11PI17	5N10	340 46	2S34	13PI 7	4N56
10/20	10PI57	5N 7	340 29	2S43	13PI13	4N55
10/30	10PI42	5N 4	340 16	2S52	13PI19	4N54
11/ 9	10PI32	5N 1	340 8	2S58	13PI26	4N54
11/19	10PI27	4N58	340 5	3S 3	13PI32	4N53
11/29	10PI29	4N54	340 8	3S 6	13PI38	4N53
12/ 9	10PI36	4N51	340 15	3S 6	13PI45	4N52
12/19	10PI49	4N48	340 28	3S 4	13PI51	4N52
12/29	11PI 7	4N45	340 46	3S 0	13PI57	4N51

Stations		Date	Long.	Lat.
RETROGRADE		6/18.35	15PI 7	5N 5
DIRECT		11/21.70	10PI27	4N57

1914

Date	Long.	Lat.	R.A.		Dec.	HLong.	HLat.
1/ 8	11PI29	4N42	341	8	2S55	14PI 4	4N51
1/18	11PI56	4N39	341	34	2S47	14PI10	4N50
1/28	12PI27	4N37	342	3	2S37	14PI16	4N50
2/ 7	13PI 1	4N35	342	35	2S26	14PI22	4N49
2/17	13PI36	4N34	343	8	2S14	14PI29	4N48
2/27	14PI13	4N33	343	43	2S 1	14PI35	4N48
3/ 9	14PI50	4N32	344	17	1S47	14PI41	4N47
3/19	15PI28	4N32	344	52	1S33	14PI48	4N47
3/29	16PI 4	4N32	345	25	1S19	14PI54	4N46
4/ 8	16PI38	4N33	345	56	1S 5	15PI 0	4N46
4/18	17PI10	4N34	346	25	0S52	15PI 6	4N45
4/28	17PI39	4N35	346	51	0S40	15PI13	4N45
5/ 8	18PI 3	4N36	347	13	0S29	15PI19	4N44
5/18	18PI24	4N38	347	32	0S19	15PI25	4N44
5/28	18PI40	4N40	347	46	0S11	15PI31	4N43
6/ 7	18PI51	4N42	347	55	0S 5	15PI38	4N42
6/17	18PI57	4N44	347	59	0S 1	15PI44	4N42
6/27	18PI57	4N46	347	59	0N 1	15PI50	4N41
7/ 7	18PI52	4N48	347	53	0N 1	15PI56	4N41
7/17	18PI41	4N50	347	43	0S 2	16PI 2	4N40
7/27	18PI26	4N51	347	28	0S 6	16PI 9	4N40
8/ 6	18PI 7	4N53	347	10	0S13	16PI15	4N39
8/16	17PI44	4N54	346	49	0S21	16PI21	4N39
8/26	17PI18	4N54	346	25	0S30	16PI27	4N38
9/ 5	16PI51	4N54	346	0	0S41	16PI33	4N38
9/15	16PI23	4N53	345	35	0S52	16PI40	4N37
9/25	15PI56	4N52	345	10	1S 4	16PI46	4N36
10/ 5	15PI30	4N50	344	47	1S15	16PI52	4N36
10/15	15PI 8	4N48	344	27	1S26	16PI58	4N35
10/25	14PI49	4N46	344	10	1S35	17PI 4	4N35
11/ 4	14PI34	4N43	343	58	1S43	17PI10	4N34
11/14	14PI25	4N40	343	51	1S50	17PI17	4N34
11/24	14PI21	4N37	343	48	1S54	17PI23	4N33
12/ 4	14PI22	4N34	343	51	1S56	17PI29	4N33
12/14	14PI30	4N31	343	59	1S57	17PI35	4N32
12/24	14PI43	4N28	344	12	1S54	17PI41	4N31

Stations	Date	Long.	Lat.
RETROGRADE	6/22.40	18PI58	4N45
DIRECT	11/26.00	14PI20	4N36

Date	Long.	Lat.	R.A.	Dec.	HLong.	HLat.
1/ 3	15PI 1	4N25	344 30	1S50	17PI47	4N31
1/13	15PI23	4N22	344 52	1S44	17PI53	4N30
1/23	15PI50	4N20	345 17	1S36	18PI 0	4N30
2/ 2	16PI21	4N18	345 46	1S26	18PI 6	4N29
2/12	16PI54	4N16	346 17	1S15	18PI12	4N29
2/22	17PI29	4N15	346 50	1S 2	18PI18	4N28
3/ 4	18PI 5	4N14	347 24	0S49	18PI24	4N28
3/14	18PI42	4N13	347 58	0S35	18PI30	4N27
3/24	19PI19	4N13	348 31	0S21	18PI36	4N26
4/ 3	19PI54	4N13	349 4	0S 7	18PI42	4N26
4/13	20PI28	4N14	349 34	0N 6	18PI48	4N25
4/23	20PI59	4N14	350 3	0N19	18PI55	4N25
5/ 3	21PI26	4N15	350 28	0N31	19PI 1	4N24
5/13	21PI51	4N17	350 49	0N42	19PI 7	4N24
5/23	22PI11	4N18	351 7	0N51	19PI13	4N23
6/ 2	22PI26	4N20	351 20	0N58	19PI19	4N22
6/12	22PI36	4N22	351 29	1N 4	19PI25	4N22
6/22	22PI41	4N23	351 33	1N 8	19PI31	4N21
7/ 2	22PI41	4N25	351 32	1N 9	19PI37	4N21
7/12	22PI35	4N27	351 26	1N 9	19PI43	4N20
7/22	22PI24	4N29	351 16	1N 6	19PI49	4N20
8/ 1	22PI 9	4N30	351 1	1N 1	19PI55	4N19
8/11	21PI49	4N31	350 43	0N54	20PI 1	4N18
8/21	21PI26	4N32	350 21	0N46	20PI 7	4N18
8/31	21PI 1	4N32	349 58	0N36	20PI13	4N17
9/10	20PI34	4N32	349 33	0N25	20PI19	4N17
9/20	20PI 6	4N31	349 8	0N14	20PI25	4N16
9/30	19PI39	4N30	348 44	0N 2	20PI31	4N16
10/10	19PI14	4N28	348 21	0S 9	20PI37	4N15
10/20	18PI52	4N26	348 2	0S19	20PI43	4N14
10/30	18PI33	4N24	347 46	0S29	20PI49	4N14
11/ 9	18PI19	4N21	347 34	0S37	20PI56	4N13
11/19	18PI10	4N18	347 27	0S43	21PI 2	4N13
11/29	18PI 7	4N16	347 25	0S47	21PI 8	4N12
12/ 9	18PI 9	4N13	347 28	0S49	21PI14	4N12
12/19	18PI17	4N10	347 36	0S48	21PI20	4N11
12/29	18PI30	4N 7	347 49	0S46	21PI26	4N10

Stations	Date	Long.	Lat.
RETROGRADE	6/26.37	22PI42	4N24
DIRECT	11/30.20	18PI 7	4N15

1916

Date	Long.	Lat.	R.A.	Dec.	HLong.	HLat.
1/ 8	18PI48	4N 4	348 7	0S41	21PI31	4N10
1/18	19PI11	4N 2	348 29	0S34	21PI37	4N 9
1/28	19PI38	4N 0	348 54	0S26	21PI43	4N 9
2/ 7	20PI 8	3N58	349 23	0S16	21PI49	4N 8
2/17	20PI41	3N56	349 54	0S 4	21PI55	4N 8
2/27	21PI16	3N55	350 26	0N 8	22PI 1	4N 7
3/ 8	21PI52	3N54	351 0	0N21	22PI 7	4N 6
3/18	22PI28	3N53	351 33	0N35	22PI13	4N 6
3/28	23PI 4	3N53	352 6	0N49	22PI19	4N 5
4/ 7	23PI39	3N53	352 38	1N 3	22PI25	4N 5
4/17	24PI12	3N54	353 8	1N16	22PI31	4N 4
4/27	24PI42	3N54	353 35	1N29	22PI37	4N 4
5/ 7	25PI 9	3N55	354 0	1N40	22PI43	4N 3
5/17	25PI33	3N56	354 21	1N51	22PI49	4N 2
5/27	25PI52	3N58	354 38	1N59	22PI55	4N 2
6/ 6	26PI 7	3N59	354 51	2N 7	23PI 1	4N 1
6/16	26PI16	4N 1	354 59	2N12	23PI 7	4N 1
6/26	26PI21	4N 2	355 2	2N15	23PI13	4N 0
7/ 6	26PI20	4N 4	355 1	2N16	23PI19	4N 0
7/16	26PI14	4N 5	354 55	2N15	23PI25	3N59
7/26	26PI 2	4N 7	354 44	2N12	23PI31	3N58
8/ 5	25PI47	4N 8	354 29	2N 7	23PI36	3N58
8/15	25PI27	4N 9	354 11	2N 0	23PI42	3N57
8/25	25PI 4	4N 9	353 49	1N51	23PI48	3N57
9/ 4	24PI38	4N 9	353 26	1N41	23PI54	3N56
9/14	24PI11	4N 9	353 1	1N30	24PI 0	3N55
9/24	23PI44	4N 8	352 36	1N18	24PI 6	3N55
10/ 4	23PI17	4N 7	352 12	1N 7	24PI12	3N54
10/14	22PI52	4N 5	351 50	0N56	24PI18	3N54
10/24	22PI31	4N 4	351 31	0N45	24PI24	3N53
11/ 3	22PI13	4N 1	351 16	0N36	24PI30	3N53
11/13	21PI59	3N59	351 4	0N29	24PI35	3N52
11/23	21PI51	3N56	350 58	0N23	24PI41	3N51
12/ 3	21PI48	3N53	350 56	0N19	24PI47	3N51
12/13	21PI50	3N51	350 59	0N18	24PI53	3N50
12/23	21PI59	3N48	351 8	0N19	24PI59	3N50

Stations	Date	Long.	Lat.
RETROGRADE	6/29.27	26PI21	4N 3
DIRECT	12/ 3.25	21PI48	3N53

Date	Long.	Lat.	R.A.	Dec.	HLong.	HLat.
1/ 2	22PI12	3N45	351 22	0N21	25PI 5	3N49
1/12	22PI31	3N43	351 39	0N27	25PI11	3N48
1/22	22PI54	3N41	352 2	0N34	25PI17	3N48
2/ 1	23PI21	3N39	352 27	0N42	25PI23	3N47
2/11	23PI51	3N37	352 55	0N53	25PI28	3N47
2/21	24PI24	3N36	353 26	1N 4	25PI34	3N46
3/ 3	24PI58	3N34	353 58	1N17	25PI40	3N45
3/13	25PI34	3N33	354 31	1N30	25PI46	3N45
3/23	26PI10	3N33	355 4	1N44	25PI52	3N44
4/ 2	26PI45	3N33	355 37	1N58	25PI58	3N44
4/12	27PI20	3N33	356 8	2N11	26PI 3	3N43
4/22	27PI52	3N33	356 38	2N24	26PI 9	3N42
5/ 2	28PI22	3N34	357 5	2N37	26PI15	3N42
5/12	28PI48	3N34	357 29	2N48	26PI21	3N41
5/22	29PI11	3N35	357 49	2N58	26PI27	3N41
6/ 1	29PI29	3N36	358 6	3N 6	26PI33	3N40
6/11	29PI43	3N38	358 18	3N13	26PI39	3N40
6/21	29PI52	3N39	358 26	3N18	26PI44	3N39
7/ 1	29PI56	3N40	358 28	3N21	26PI50	3N38
7/11	29PI55	3N42	358 27	3N21	26PI56	3N38
7/21	29PI48	3N43	358 20	3N20	27PI 2	3N37
7/31	29PI36	3N44	358 9	3N16	27PI 8	3N37
8/10	29PI20	3N45	357 54	3N11	27PI13	3N36
8/20	29PI 0	3N46	357 35	3N 3	27PI19	3N35
8/30	28PI37	3N46	357 14	2N54	27PI25	3N35
9/ 9	28PI11	3N46	356 50	2N44	27PI31	3N34
9/19	27PI44	3N46	356 25	2N33	27PI37	3N34
9/29	27PI17	3N45	356 1	2N21	27PI43	3N33
10/ 9	26PI51	3N44	355 37	2N10	27PI48	3N32
10/19	26PI26	3N42	355 16	1N59	27PI54	3N32
10/29	26PI 5	3N40	354 57	1N49	28PI 0	3N31
11/ 8	25PI47	3N38	354 42	1N40	28PI 6	3N31
11/18	25PI35	3N36	354 31	1N33	28PI12	3N30
11/28	25PI27	3N34	354 25	1N27	28PI17	3N29
12/ 8	25PI24	3N31	354 23	1N24	28PI23	3N29
12/18	25PI28	3N28	354 27	1N23	28PI29	3N28
12/28	25PI36	3N26	354 36	1N24	28PI35	3N28

Stations	Date	Long.	Lat.
RETROGRADE	7/ 3.15	29PI56	3N41
DIRECT	12/ 7.24	25PI24	3N31

1918

Date	Long.	Lat.	R.A.		Dec.	HLong.	HLat.
1/ 7	25PI50	3N24	354	50	1N28	28PI40	3N27
1/17	26PI 9	3N21	355	8	1N33	28PI46	3N26
1/27	26PI33	3N19	355	31	1N40	28PI52	3N26
2/ 6	27PI 0	3N17	355	56	1N49	28PI58	3N25
2/16	27PI30	3N16	356	25	2N 0	29PI 4	3N25
2/26	28PI 3	3N14	356	55	2N12	29PI 9	3N24
3/ 8	28PI37	3N13	357	27	2N24	29PI15	3N23
3/18	29PI13	3N13	358	0	2N38	29PI21	3N23
3/28	29PI48	3N12	358	33	2N51	29PI27	3N22
4/ 7	0AR23	3N12	359	5	3N 5	29PI32	3N22
4/17	0AR57	3N12	359	36	3N18	29PI38	3N21
4/27	1AR29	3N12	0	5	3N31	29PI44	3N20
5/ 7	1AR58	3N12	0	32	3N43	29PI50	3N20
5/17	2AR24	3N13	0	55	3N54	29PI56	3N19
5/27	2AR46	3N14	1	15	4N 4	0AR 1	3N18
6/ 6	3AR 4	3N15	1	31	4N12	0AR 7	3N18
6/16	3AR17	3N16	1	43	4N18	0AR13	3N17
6/26	3AR25	3N17	1	50	4N22	0AR19	3N17
7/ 6	3AR29	3N18	1	52	4N25	0AR24	3N16
7/16	3AR26	3N19	1	50	4N25	0AR30	3N15
7/26	3AR19	3N20	1	43	4N23	0AR36	3N15
8/ 5	3AR 7	3N21	1	31	4N19	0AR42	3N14
8/15	2AR50	3N22	1	16	4N13	0AR47	3N14
8/25	2AR30	3N22	0	57	4N 5	0AR53	3N13
9/ 4	2AR 7	3N23	0	35	3N56	0AR59	3N12
9/14	1AR41	3N22	0	12	3N46	1AR 5	3N12
9/24	1AR14	3N22	359	47	3N35	1AR10	3N11
10/ 4	0AR47	3N21	359	23	3N23	1AR16	3N11
10/14	0AR21	3N20	358	59	3N12	1AR22	3N10
10/24	29PI57	3N18	358	38	3N 1	1AR27	3N 9
11/ 3	29PI36	3N17	358	19	2N51	1AR33	3N 9
11/13	29PI19	3N15	358	5	2N42	1AR39	3N 8
11/23	29PI 7	3N13	357	54	2N35	1AR45	3N 7
12/ 3	28PI59	3N10	357	49	2N30	1AR50	3N 7
12/13	28PI58	3N 8	357	48	2N28	1AR56	3N 6
12/23	29PI 2	3N 6	357	52	2N27	2AR 2	3N 6

Stations	Date	Long.	Lat.
RETROGRADE	7/ 6.98	3AR29	3N18
DIRECT	12/11.11	28PI58	3N 8

Date	Long.	Lat.	R.A.	Dec.	HLong.	HLat.
1/ 2	29PI11	3N 3	358 2	2N29	2AR 8	3N 5
1/12	29PI25	3N 1	358 16	2N32	2AR13	3N 4
1/22	29PI45	2N59	358 35	2N38	2AR19	3N 4
2/ 1	0AR 8	2N57	358 57	2N46	2AR25	3N 3
2/11	0AR36	2N55	359 23	2N55	2AR30	3N 3
2/21	1AR 6	2N54	359 51	3N 6	2AR36	3N 2
3/ 3	1AR39	2N53	0 22	3N18	2AR42	3N 1
3/13	2AR13	2N52	0 54	3N31	2AR48	3N 1
3/23	2AR49	2N51	1 27	3N44	2AR53	3N 0
4/ 2	3AR24	2N50	1 59	3N57	2AR59	2N59
4/12	3AR59	2N50	2 31	4N11	3AR 5	2N59
4/22	4AR32	2N50	3 2	4N24	3AR10	2N58
5/ 2	5AR 3	2N50	3 31	4N37	3AR16	2N58
5/12	5AR32	2N51	3 57	4N48	3AR22	2N57
5/22	5AR57	2N51	4 20	4N59	3AR28	2N56
6/ 1	6AR19	2N52	4 40	5N 8	3AR33	2N56
6/11	6AR36	2N52	4 55	5N16	3AR39	2N55
6/21	6AR49	2N53	5 7	5N22	3AR45	2N54
7/ 1	6AR57	2N54	5 13	5N25	3AR50	2N54
7/11	6AR59	2N55	5 15	5N27	3AR56	2N53
7/21	6AR56	2N56	5 12	5N27	4AR 2	2N53
7/31	6AR49	2N57	5 5	5N25	4AR 8	2N52
8/10	6AR36	2N58	4 53	5N20	4AR13	2N51
8/20	6AR19	2N58	4 37	5N14	4AR19	2N51
8/30	5AR58	2N58	4 18	5N 6	4AR25	2N50
9/ 9	5AR34	2N58	3 56	4N57	4AR30	2N49
9/19	5AR 8	2N58	3 32	4N46	4AR36	2N49
9/29	4AR41	2N58	3 8	4N35	4AR42	2N48
10/ 9	4AR14	2N57	2 43	4N23	4AR47	2N48
10/19	3AR49	2N56	2 20	4N12	4AR53	2N47
10/29	3AR25	2N54	1 59	4N 1	4AR59	2N46
11/ 8	3AR 5	2N53	1 41	3N52	5AR 5	2N46
11/18	2AR48	2N51	1 26	3N44	5AR10	2N45
11/28	2AR36	2N49	1 16	3N37	5AR16	2N44
12/ 8	2AR30	2N47	1 11	3N32	5AR22	2N44
12/18	2AR29	2N44	1 11	3N30	5AR27	2N43
12/28	2AR33	2N42	1 16	3N30	5AR33	2N43

Stations		Date	Long.	Lat.
RETROGRADE		7/10.81	6AR59	2N55
DIRECT		12/14.94	2AR29	2N45

1920

Date	Long.	Lat.	R.A.	Dec.	HLong.	HLat.
1/ 7	2AR43	2N40	1 26	3N32	5AR39	2N42
1/17	2AR58	2N38	1 41	3N36	5AR44	2N41
1/27	3AR18	2N36	2 0	3N42	5AR50	2N41
2/ 6	3AR42	2N35	2 22	3N50	5AR56	2N40
2/16	4AR10	2N33	2 48	4N 0	6AR 1	2N39
2/26	4AR41	2N32	3 17	4N11	6AR 7	2N39
3/ 7	5AR13	2N31	3 48	4N23	6AR13	2N38
3/17	5AR48	2N30	4 20	4N36	6AR19	2N37
3/27	6AR23	2N29	4 53	4N49	6AR24	2N37
4/ 6	6AR58	2N28	5 25	5N 2	6AR30	2N36
4/16	7AR33	2N28	5 57	5N16	6AR36	2N36
4/26	8AR 6	2N28	6 28	5N29	6AR41	2N35
5/ 6	8AR37	2N28	6 56	5N41	6AR47	2N34
5/16	9AR 5	2N28	7 22	5N52	6AR53	2N34
5/26	9AR30	2N29	7 45	6N 2	6AR58	2N33
6/ 5	9AR51	2N29	8 4	6N11	7AR 4	2N32
6/15	10AR 8	2N30	8 19	6N18	7AR10	2N32
6/25	10AR20	2N30	8 30	6N24	7AR15	2N31
7/ 5	10AR27	2N31	8 37	6N27	7AR21	2N30
7/15	10AR29	2N32	8 38	6N28	7AR27	2N30
7/25	10AR25	2N32	8 35	6N28	7AR32	2N29
8/ 4	10AR17	2N33	8 27	6N25	7AR38	2N28
8/14	10AR 4	2N33	8 14	6N20	7AR44	2N28
8/24	9AR46	2N34	7 58	6N14	7AR49	2N27
9/ 3	9AR25	2N34	7 38	6N 5	7AR55	2N27
9/13	9AR 1	2N34	7 16	5N56	8AR 1	2N26
9/23	8AR35	2N33	6 52	5N45	8AR 7	2N25
10/ 3	8AR 8	2N33	6 28	5N34	8AR12	2N25
10/13	7AR41	2N32	6 3	5N22	8AR18	2N24
10/23	7AR15	2N31	5 40	5N11	8AR24	2N23
11/ 2	6AR52	2N29	5 19	5N 1	8AR29	2N23
11/12	6AR32	2N28	5 1	4N51	8AR35	2N22
11/22	6AR16	2N26	4 47	4N44	8AR41	2N21
12/ 2	6AR 5	2N24	4 38	4N38	8AR46	2N21
12/12	5AR59	2N22	4 33	4N33	8AR52	2N20
12/22	5AR59	2N20	4 34	4N31	8AR58	2N19

Stations	Date	Long.	Lat.
RETROGRADE	7/13.66	10AR29	2N32
DIRECT	12/17.69	5AR58	2N21

Date	Long.	Lat.	R.A.	Dec.	HLong.	HLat.
1/ 1	6AR 4	2N19	4 39	4N32	9AR 3	2N19
1/11	6AR14	2N17	4 50	4N34	9AR 9	2N18
1/21	6AR30	2N15	5 5	4N39	9AR15	2N18
1/31	6AR51	2N13	5 24	4N45	9AR20	2N17
2/10	7AR15	2N12	5 47	4N54	9AR26	2N16
2/20	7AR43	2N10	6 14	5N 3	9AR32	2N16
3/ 2	8AR14	2N 9	6 43	5N15	9AR37	2N15
3/12	8AR47	2N 8	7 14	5N27	9AR43	2N14
3/22	9AR22	2N 7	7 46	5N39	9AR49	2N14
4/ 1	9AR57	2N 6	8 19	5N53	9AR55	2N13
4/11	10AR32	2N 6	8 51	6N 6	10AR 0	2N12
4/21	11AR 7	2N 5	9 23	6N19	10AR 6	2N12
5/ 1	11AR39	2N 5	9 54	6N32	10AR12	2N11
5/11	12AR10	2N 5	10 22	6N44	10AR17	2N10
5/21	12AR38	2N 5	10 48	6N55	10AR23	2N10
5/31	13AR 2	2N 5	11 11	7N 5	10AR29	2N 9
6/10	13AR23	2N 6	11 30	7N13	10AR34	2N 8
6/20	13AR39	2N 6	11 44	7N20	10AR40	2N 8
6/30	13AR51	2N 7	11 55	7N24	10AR46	2N 7
7/10	13AR57	2N 7	12 1	7N27	10AR51	2N 6
7/20	13AR59	2N 7	12 2	7N28	10AR57	2N 6
7/30	13AR55	2N 8	11 58	7N27	11AR 3	2N 5
8/ 9	13AR46	2N 8	11 50	7N24	11AR 9	2N 4
8/19	13AR32	2N 9	11 37	7N19	11AR14	2N 4
8/29	13AR14	2N 9	11 20	7N12	11AR20	2N 3
9/ 8	12AR52	2N 9	11 0	7N 4	11AR26	2N 2
9/18	12AR28	2N 8	10 37	6N54	11AR31	2N 2
9/28	12AR 2	2N 8	10 13	6N43	11AR37	2N 1
10/ 8	11AR34	2N 7	9 48	6N32	11AR43	2N 1
10/18	11AR 8	2N 6	9 24	6N21	11AR48	2N 0
10/28	10AR42	2N 5	9 1	6N 9	11AR54	1N59
11/ 7	10AR19	2N 4	8 40	5N59	12AR 0	1N59
11/17	9AR59	2N 3	8 22	5N50	12AR 6	1N58
11/27	9AR44	2N 1	8 9	5N43	12AR11	1N57
12/ 7	9AR34	1N59	8 0	5N37	12AR17	1N57
12/17	9AR28	1N58	7 56	5N33	12AR23	1N56
12/27	9AR29	1N56	7 57	5N32	12AR28	1N55

Stations	Date	Long.	Lat.
RETROGRADE	7/17.53	13AR59	2N 7
DIRECT	12/21.44	9AR28	1N57

1922

Date	Long.	Lat.	R.A.	Dec.	HLong.	HLat.
1/ 6	9AR35	1N54	8 3	5N33	12AR34	1N55
1/16	9AR46	1N52	8 14	5N36	12AR40	1N54
1/26	10AR 2	1N51	8 30	5N41	12AR45	1N53
2/ 5	10AR23	1N49	8 50	5N47	12AR51	1N53
2/15	10AR48	1N48	9 13	5N56	12AR57	1N52
2/25	11AR17	1N47	9 40	6N 6	13AR 3	1N51
3/ 7	11AR48	1N46	10 10	6N17	13AR 8	1N51
3/17	12AR21	1N45	10 41	6N29	13AR14	1N50
3/27	12AR56	1N44	11 13	6N42	13AR20	1N49
4/ 6	13AR32	1N43	11 46	6N55	13AR25	1N49
4/16	14AR 7	1N43	12 19	7N 9	13AR31	1N48
4/26	14AR41	1N42	12 51	7N21	13AR37	1N47
5/ 6	15AR14	1N42	13 22	7N34	13AR43	1N47
5/16	15AR44	1N42	13 50	7N46	13AR48	1N46
5/26	16AR12	1N42	14 16	7N56	13AR54	1N45
6/ 5	16AR36	1N42	14 38	8N 5	14AR 0	1N45
6/15	16AR56	1N42	14 57	8N13	14AR 6	1N44
6/25	17AR12	1N42	15 12	8N20	14AR11	1N43
7/ 5	17AR23	1N42	15 22	8N24	14AR17	1N43
7/15	17AR29	1N42	15 27	8N27	14AR23	1N42
7/25	17AR30	1N43	15 28	8N27	14AR28	1N41
8/ 4	17AR25	1N43	15 24	8N26	14AR34	1N41
8/14	17AR16	1N43	15 15	8N22	14AR40	1N40
8/24	17AR 1	1N43	15 2	8N17	14AR46	1N39
9/ 3	16AR43	1N43	14 44	8N 9	14AR51	1N38
9/13	16AR21	1N43	14 24	8N 1	14AR57	1N38
9/23	15AR56	1N42	14 1	7N51	15AR 3	1N37
10/ 3	15AR29	1N42	13 36	7N40	15AR 9	1N36
10/13	15AR 2	1N41	13 11	7N29	15AR14	1N36
10/23	14AR35	1N40	12 46	7N18	15AR20	1N35
11/ 2	14AR10	1N39	12 23	7N 7	15AR26	1N34
11/12	13AR47	1N38	12 3	6N57	15AR32	1N34
11/22	13AR28	1N37	11 45	6N48	15AR37	1N33
12/ 2	13AR13	1N35	11 32	6N41	15AR43	1N32
12/12	13AR 3	1N34	11 24	6N36	15AR49	1N32
12/22	12AR59	1N32	11 20	6N33	15AR55	1N31

Stations	Date	Long.	Lat.
RETROGRADE	7/21.47	17AR30	1N43
DIRECT	12/25.13	12AR58	1N32

Date	Long.	Lat.	R.A.	Dec.	HLong.	HLat.
1/ 1	13AR 0	1N31	11 22	6N32	16AR 0	1N30
1/11	13AR 6	1N29	11 28	6N33	16AR 6	1N30
1/21	13AR18	1N28	11 40	6N36	16AR12	1N29
1/31	13AR35	1N26	11 56	6N41	16AR18	1N28
2/10	13AR57	1N25	12 17	6N49	16AR23	1N28
2/20	14AR23	1N24	12 41	6N57	16AR29	1N27
3/ 2	14AR52	1N23	13 9	7N 8	16AR35	1N26
3/12	15AR23	1N22	13 39	7N19	16AR41	1N26
3/22	15AR57	1N21	14 10	7N31	16AR46	1N25
4/ 1	16AR32	1N20	14 43	7N44	16AR52	1N24
4/11	17AR 8	1N19	15 16	7N57	16AR58	1N24
4/21	17AR43	1N19	15 50	8N10	17AR 4	1N23
5/ 1	18AR17	1N18	16 22	8N23	17AR10	1N22
5/11	18AR50	1N18	16 52	8N35	17AR15	1N21
5/21	19AR20	1N18	17 21	8N46	17AR21	1N21
5/31	19AR48	1N17	17 47	8N56	17AR27	1N20
6/10	20AR12	1N17	18 9	9N 5	17AR33	1N19
6/20	20AR31	1N17	18 28	9N13	17AR39	1N19
6/30	20AR47	1N17	18 42	9N18	17AR44	1N18
7/10	20AR57	1N17	18 52	9N22	17AR50	1N17
7/20	21AR 3	1N17	18 57	9N24	17AR56	1N17
7/30	21AR 3	1N17	18 58	9N25	18AR 2	1N16
8/ 9	20AR58	1N17	18 53	9N23	18AR 7	1N15
8/19	20AR48	1N17	18 43	9N19	18AR13	1N15
8/29	20AR33	1N17	18 30	9N13	18AR19	1N14
9/ 8	20AR14	1N17	18 12	9N 6	18AR25	1N13
9/18	19AR52	1N16	17 51	8N57	18AR31	1N12
9/28	19AR26	1N16	17 27	8N47	18AR37	1N12
10/ 8	18AR59	1N15	17 2	8N36	18AR42	1N11
10/18	18AR32	1N14	16 37	8N25	18AR48	1N10
10/28	18AR 5	1N14	16 12	8N14	18AR54	1N10
11/ 7	17AR40	1N13	15 49	8N 3	19AR 0	1N 9
11/17	17AR17	1N11	15 28	7N53	19AR 6	1N 8
11/27	16AR58	1N10	15 11	7N45	19AR11	1N 8
12/ 7	16AR44	1N 9	14 59	7N38	19AR17	1N 7
12/17	16AR35	1N 8	14 50	7N34	19AR23	1N 6
12/27	16AR31	1N 6	14 47	7N31	19AR29	1N 6

Stations	Date	Long.	Lat.
RETROGRADE	7/25.44	21AR 4	1N17
DIRECT	12/28.87	16AR31	1N 6

1924

Date	Long.	Lat.	R.A.	Dec.	HLong.	HLat.
1/ 6	16AP33	1N 5	14 49	7N30	19AR35	1N 5
1/16	16AR40	1N 4	14 57	7N32	19AR41	1N 4
1/26	16AP53	1N 3	15 9	7N36	19AR46	1N 3
2/ 5	17AP10	1N 1	15 26	7N42	19AR52	1N 3
2/15	17AR33	1N 0	15 47	7N49	19AR58	1N 2
2/25	17AP59	0N59	16 12	7N58	20AR 4	1N 1
3/ 6	18AP29	0N58	16 40	8N 8	20AP10	1N 1
3/16	19AR 1	0N57	17 11	8N20	20AR16	1N 0
3/26	19AR35	0N56	17 43	8N32	20AR22	0N59
4/ 5	20AP11	0N56	18 17	8N45	20AR27	0N59
4/15	20AP46	0N55	18 50	8N58	20AR33	0N58
4/25	21AR22	0N54	19 24	9N10	20AR39	0N57
5/ 5	21AR56	0N54	19 56	9N23	20AR45	0N56
5/15	22AR29	0N53	20 27	9N35	20AR51	0N56
5/25	22AR59	0N53	20 56	9N45	20AR57	0N55
6/ 4	23AP27	0N52	21 22	9N55	21AR 3	0N54
6/14	23AP50	0N52	21 44	10N 4	21AR 9	0N54
6/24	24AP10	0N52	22 3	10N11	21AR14	0N53
7/ 4	24AR25	0N52	22 17	10N16	21AR20	0N52
7/14	24AP35	0N51	22 27	10N20	21AR26	0N51
7/24	24AP40	0N51	22 32	10N21	21AR32	0N51
8/ 3	24AP40	0N51	22 32	10N21	21AR38	0N50
8/13	24AR35	0N51	22 27	10N19	21AR44	0N49
8/23	24AR24	0N50	22 17	10N14	21AR50	0N49
9/ 2	24AP 9	0N50	22 2	10N 8	21AR56	0N48
9/12	23AR49	0N49	21 44	10N 1	22AR 2	0N47
9/22	23AP26	0N49	21 23	9N52	22AR 8	0N47
10/ 2	23AR 0	0N48	20 59	9N42	22AR14	0N46
10/12	22AP33	0N48	20 33	9N31	22AR19	0N45
10/22	22AR 5	0N47	20 7	9N20	22AR25	0N44
11/ 1	21AP38	0N46	19 42	9N 9	22AR31	0N44
11/11	21AP13	0N45	19 19	8N59	22AR37	0N43
11/21	20AR51	0N44	18 59	8N49	22AR43	0N42
12/ 1	20AP32	0N43	18 42	8N41	22AR49	0N42
12/11	20AP18	0N42	18 29	8N35	22AR55	0N41
12/21	20AR10	0N41	18 21	8N31	23AR 1	0N40
12/31	20AP 6	0N40	18 19	8N29	23AR 7	0N39

Stations	Date	Long.	Lat.
RETROGRADE	7/28.54	24AR41	0N51
DIRECT	12/31.60	20AR 6	0N40

Date	Long.	Lat.	R.A.	Dec.	HLong.	HLat.
1/10	20AR 9	0N39	18 21	8N29	23AR13	0N39
1/20	20AR17	0N38	18 29	8N31	23AR19	0N38
1/30	20AR31	0N37	18 43	8N35	23AR25	0N37
2/ 9	20AR49	0N36	19 0	8N41	23AR31	0N36
2/19	21AR12	0N35	19 22	8N49	23AR37	0N36
3/ 1	21AR39	0N34	19 48	8N58	23AR43	0N35
3/11	22AR 9	0N33	20 17	9N 8	23AR49	0N34
3/21	22AR42	0N32	20 48	9N20	23AR55	0N34
3/31	23AR17	0N31	21 21	9N32	24AR 1	0N33
4/10	23AR53	0N31	21 55	9N45	24AR 7	0N32
4/20	24AR29	0N30	22 29	9N57	24AR13	0N31
4/30	25AR 5	0N29	23 3	10N10	24AR19	0N31
5/10	25AR39	0N29	23 36	10N22	24AR25	0N30
5/20	26AR12	0N28	24 7	10N33	24AR31	0N29
5/30	26AR42	0N27	24 36	10N44	24AR37	0N29
6/ 9	27AR10	0N27	25 3	10N53	24AR43	0N28
6/19	27AR33	0N26	25 25	11N 1	24AR49	0N27
6/29	27AR53	0N26	25 44	11N 8	24AR55	0N26
7/ 9	28AR 8	0N25	25 58	11N13	25AR 1	0N26
7/19	28AR18	0N25	26 8	11N16	25AR 7	0N25
7/29	28AR22	0N24	26 13	11N17	25AR13	0N24
8/ 8	28AR22	0N24	26 12	11N16	25AR19	0N23
8/18	28AR16	0N23	26 7	11N13	25AR25	0N23
8/28	28AR 5	0N23	25 56	11N 9	25AR31	0N22
9/ 7	27AR49	0N22	25 41	11N 3	25AR37	0N21
9/17	27AR29	0N22	25 22	10N55	25AR43	0N21
9/27	27AR 5	0N21	25 0	10N46	25AR49	0N20
10/ 7	26AR39	0N20	24 36	10N36	25AR55	0N19
10/17	26AR11	0N19	24 10	10N25	26AR 1	0N18
10/27	25AR43	0N19	23 44	10N14	26AR 7	0N18
11/ 6	25AR16	0N18	23 18	10N 3	26AR13	0N17
11/16	24AR51	0N17	22 55	9N53	26AR19	0N16
11/26	24AR29	0N16	22 34	9N44	26AR25	0N15
12/ 6	24AR10	0N15	22 17	9N37	26AR31	0N15
12/16	23AR57	0N14	22 5	9N31	26AR38	0N14
12/26	23AR49	0N13	21 58	9N27	26AR44	0N13

Stations	Date	Long.	Lat.
RETROGRADE	8/ 1.73	28AR23	0N24

1926

Date	Long.	Lat.	R.A.	Dec.	HLong.	HLat.
1/ 5	23AR46	0N13	21 56	9N26	26AR50	0N12
1/15	23AR50	0N12	21 59	9N26	26AR56	0N12
1/25	23AR58	0N11	22 8	9N28	27AR 2	0N11
2/ 4	24AR13	0N10	22 21	9N33	27AR 8	0N10
2/14	24AR32	0N 9	22 40	9N39	27AR14	0N10
2/24	24AR56	0N 8	23 3	9N47	27AR20	0N 9
3/ 6	25AR24	0N 8	23 29	9N57	27AR26	0N 8
3/16	25AR55	0N 7	23 59	10N 7	27AR33	0N 7
3/26	26AR28	0N 6	24 31	10N19	27AR39	0N 7
4/ 5	27AR 3	0N 6	25 4	10N31	27AR45	0N 6
4/15	27AR40	0N 5	25 39	10N43	27AR51	0N 5
4/25	28AR16	0N 4	26 14	10N56	27AR57	0N 4
5/ 5	28AR52	0N 3	26 49	11N 8	28AR 3	0N 4
5/15	29AR27	0N 3	27 22	11N20	28AR 9	0N 3
5/25	0TA 1	0N 2	27 54	11N31	28AR16	0N 2
6/ 4	0TA31	0N 1	28 24	11N41	28AR22	0N 1
6/14	0TA59	0N 1	28 50	11N50	28AR28	0N 1
6/24	1TA22	0S 0	29 13	11N57	28AR34	0S 0
7/ 4	1TA42	0S 1	29 32	12N 3	28AR40	0S 1
7/14	1TA57	0S 2	29 47	12N 8	28AR46	0S 2
7/24	2TA 6	0S 2	29 56	12N10	28AR53	0S 2
8/ 3	2TA11	0S 3	30 1	12N11	28AR59	0S 3
8/13	2TA10	0S 4	30 0	12N10	29AR 5	0S 4
8/23	2TA 3	0S 5	29 54	12N 7	29AR11	0S 5
9/ 2	1TA51	0S 6	29 43	12N 2	29AR17	0S 5
9/12	1TA35	0S 6	29 28	11N56	29AR24	0S 6
9/22	1TA14	0S 7	29 8	11N48	29AR30	0S 7
10/ 2	0TA50	0S 8	28 45	11N39	29AR36	0S 8
10/12	0TA24	0S 9	28 20	11N29	29AR42	0S 8
10/22	29AR55	0S10	27 54	11N18	29AR49	0S 9
11/ 1	29AR27	0S10	27 27	11N 7	29AR55	0S10
11/11	29AR 0	0S11	27 1	10N57	0TA 1	0S11
11/21	28AR35	0S12	26 37	10N47	0TA 7	0S11
12/ 1	28AR13	0S13	26 17	10N39	0TA14	0S12
12/11	27AR55	0S13	26 0	10N32	0TA20	0S13
12/21	27AR42	0S14	25 48	10N26	0TA26	0S14
12/31	27AR34	0S15	25 41	10N23	0TA32	0S14

Stations	Date	Long.	Lat.
DIRECT	1/ 4.41	23AR46	0N13
RETROGRADE	8/ 6.06	2TA11	0S 3

Date	Long.	Lat.	R.A.	Dec.	HLong.	HLat.
1/10	27AR32	0S15	25 39	10N22	0TA39	0S15
1/20	27AR36	0S16	25 43	10N23	0TA45	0S16
1/30	27AR46	0S17	25 53	10N25	0TA51	0S17
2/ 9	28AR 1	0S17	26 7	10N30	0TA57	0S17
2/19	28AR21	0S18	26 26	10N37	1TA 4	0S18
3/ 1	28AR46	0S18	26 50	10N45	1TA10	0S19
3/11	29AR14	0S19	27 18	10N55	1TA16	0S20
3/21	29AR46	0S20	27 48	11N 5	1TA23	0S21
3/31	0TA20	0S20	28 21	11N17	1TA29	0S21
4/10	0TA56	0S21	28 55	11N29	1TA35	0S22
4/20	1TA33	0S22	29 31	11N41	1TA42	0S23
4/30	2TA10	0S22	30 7	11N53	1TA48	0S24
5/10	2TA47	0S23	30 42	12N 5	1TA54	0S24
5/20	3TA22	0S24	31 17	12N16	2TA 1	0S25
5/30	3TA56	0S25	31 49	12N27	2TA 7	0S26
6/ 9	4TA27	0S26	32 20	12N36	2TA13	0S27
6/19	4TA54	0S26	32 47	12N45	2TA20	0S27
6/29	5TA18	0S27	33 10	12N52	2TA26	0S28
7/ 9	5TA38	0S28	33 29	12N57	2TA33	0S29
7/19	5TA52	0S29	33 44	13N 1	2TA39	0S30
7/29	6TA 2	0S30	33 53	13N 3	2TA45	0S30
8/ 8	6TA 6	0S32	33 58	13N 4	2TA52	0S31
8/18	6TA 5	0S33	33 57	13N 2	2TA58	0S32
8/28	5TA58	0S34	33 51	12N59	3TA 5	0S33
9/ 7	5TA46	0S35	33 39	12N54	3TA11	0S34
9/17	5TA29	0S36	33 23	12N47	3TA17	0S34
9/27	5TA 8	0S37	33 3	12N39	3TA24	0S35
10/ 7	4TA43	0S38	32 40	12N30	3TA30	0S36
10/17	4TA16	0S39	32 14	12N20	3TA37	0S37
10/27	3TA47	0S40	31 46	12N10	3TA43	0S37
11/ 6	3TA19	0S40	31 19	11N59	3TA50	0S38
11/16	2TA51	0S41	30 53	11N49	3TA56	0S39
11/26	2TA26	0S42	30 29	11N40	4TA 3	0S40
12/ 6	2TA 4	0S42	30 8	11N32	4TA 9	0S41
12/16	1TA46	0S43	29 51	11N25	4TA16	0S41
12/26	1TA33	0S43	29 39	11N20	4TA22	0S42

Stations	Date	Long.	Lat.
DIRECT	1/ 8.25	27AR32	0S15
RETROGRADE	8/10.56	6TA 6	0S32

1928

Date	Long.	Lat.	R.A.	Dec.	HLong.	HLat.
1/ 5	1TA26	0S44	29 32	11N18	4TA29	0S43
1/15	1TA25	0S44	29 31	11N17	4TA35	0S44
1/25	1TA29	0S44	29 36	11N18	4TA42	0S44
2/ 4	1TA40	0S45	29 46	11N21	4TA48	0S45
2/14	1TA56	0S45	30 1	11N27	4TA55	0S46
2/24	2TA17	0S45	30 21	11N33	5TA 1	0S47
3/ 5	2TA42	0S46	30 46	11N42	5TA 8	0S48
3/15	3TA12	0S46	31 14	11N51	5TA14	0S48
3/25	3TA44	0S47	31 46	12N 2	5TA21	0S49
4/ 4	4TA19	0S47	32 20	12N13	5TA27	0S50
4/14	4TA56	0S48	32 55	12N25	5TA34	0S51
4/24	5TA34	0S49	33 32	12N37	5TA40	0S52
5/ 4	6TA12	0S49	34 9	12N49	5TA47	0S52
5/14	6TA49	0S50	34 45	13N 0	5TA54	0S53
5/24	7TA25	0S51	35 21	13N11	6TA 0	0S54
6/ 3	7TA59	0S52	35 54	13N21	6TA 7	0S55
6/13	8TA30	0S53	36 25	13N30	6TA13	0S55
6/23	8TA58	0S54	36 53	13N38	6TA20	0S56
7/ 3	9TA23	0S56	37 17	13N45	6TA27	0S57
7/13	9TA42	0S57	37 37	13N50	6TA33	0S58
7/23	9TA57	0S58	37 52	13N53	6TA40	·0S59
8/ 2	10TA 7	0S59	38 1	13N55	6TA47	0S59
8/12	10TA11	1S 1	38 6	13N55	6TA53	1S 0
8/22	10TA 9	1S 2	38 5	13N53	7TA 0	1S 1
9/ 1	10TA 2	1S 4	37 58	13N50	7TA 7	1S 2
9/11	9TA50	1S 5	37 46	13N44	7TA13	1S 3
9/21	9TA32	1S 6	37 30	13N38	7TA20	1S 3
10/ 1	9TA10	1S 8	37 9	13N29	7TA27	1S 4
10/11	8TA45	1S 9	36 45	13N20	7TA33	1S 5
10/21	8TA17	1S10	36 18	13N10	7TA40	1S 6
10/31	7TA48	1S11	35 50	13N 0	7TA47	1S 7
11/10	7TA19	1S11	35 22	12N50	7TA53	1S 7
11/20	6TA51	1S12	34 55	12N40	8TA 0	1S 8
11/30	6TA26	1S13	34 30	12N32	8TA 7	1S 9
12/10	6TA 3	1S13	34 9	12N24	8TA14	1S10
12/20	5TA46	1S13	33 52	12N18	8TA20	1S11
12/30	5TA33	1S13	33 40	12N14	8TA27	1S11

Stations	Date	Long.	Lat.
DIRECT	1/12.20	1TA25	0S44
RETROGRADE	8/14.24	10TA11	1S 1

Date	Long.	Lat.	R.A.	Dec.	HLong.	HLat.
1/ 9	5TA27	1S14	33 34	12N11	8TA34	1S12
1/19	5TA26	1S14	33 33	12N11	8TA41	1S13
1/29	5TA31	1S14	33 38	12N13	8TA47	1S14
2/ 8	5TA42	1S14	33 49	12N16	8TA54	1S15
2/18	5TA59	1S14	34 5	12N22	9TA 1	1S15
2/28	6TA21	1S14	34 27	12N29	9TA 8	1S16
3/10	6TA47	1S14	34 52	12N37	9TA15	1S17
3/20	7TA18	1S14	35 22	12N47	9TA21	1S18
3/30	7TA51	1S15	35 54	12N57	9TA28	1S19
4/ 9	8TA27	1S15	36 29	13N 8	9TA35	1S19
4/19	9TA 5	1S16	37 6	13N20	9TA42	1S20
4/29	9TA43	1S17	37 44	13N31	9TA49	1S21
5/ 9	10TA22	1S17	38 22	13N43	9TA56	1S22
5/19	11TA 0	1S18	39 0	13N54	10TA 2	1S23
5/29	11TA37	1S19	39 36	14N 4	10TA 9	1S23
6/ 8	12TA12	1S20	40 11	14N14	10TA16	1S24
6/18	12TA44	1S22	40 42	14N22	10TA23	1S25
6/28	13TA13	1S23	41 11	14N29	10TA30	1S26
7/ 8	13TA37	1S24	41 36	14N35	10TA37	1S27
7/18	13TA57	1S26	41 56	14N40	10TA44	1S28
7/28	14TA13	1S28	42 12	14N43	10TA51	1S28
8/ 7	14TA22	1S29	42 22	14N44	10TA58	1S29
8/17	14TA26	1S31	42 26	14N44	11TA 5	1S30
8/27	14TA25	1S33	42 25	14N42	11TA12	1S31
9/ 6	14TA17	1S34	42 19	14N38	11TA19	1S32
9/16	14TA 4	1S36	42 6	14N32	11TA26	1S32
9/26	13TA47	1S38	41 49	14N26	11TA33	1S33
10/ 6	13TA24	1S39	41 28	14N17	11TA40	1S34
10/16	12TA58	1S40	41 2	14N 8	11TA47	1S35
10/26	12TA30	1S42	40 35	13N59	11TA54	1S36
11/ 5	12TA 0	1S43	40 6	13N49	12TA 1	1S37
11/15	11TA30	1S43	39 37	13N39	12TA 8	1S37
11/25	11TA 2	1S44	39 10	13N30	12TA15	1S38
12/ 5	10TA36	1S44	38 44	13N21	12TA22	1S39
12/15	10TA14	1S44	38 23	13N14	12TA29	1S40
12/25	9TA56	1S45	38 6	13N 9	12TA36	1S41

Stations	Date	Long.	Lat.
DIRECT	1/15.24	5TA26	1S14
RETROGRADE	8/19.13	14TA27	1S31

1930

Date	Long.	Lat.	R.A.	Dec.	HLong.	HLat.
1/ 4	9TA44	1S44	37 54	13N 5	12TA43	1S42
1/14	9TA38	1S44	37 47	13N 3	12TA50	1S42
1/24	9TA37	1S44	37 47	13N 3	12TA57	1S43
2/ 3	9TA43	1S44	37 53	13N 5	13TA 4	1S44
2/13	9TA55	1S44	38 4	13N 9	13TA11	1S45
2/23	10TA13	1S43	38 21	13N15	13TA18	1S46
3/ 5	10TA36	1S43	38 43	13N22	13TA25	1S47
3/15	11TA 3	1S43	39 10	13N31	13TA33	1S47
3/25	11TA34	1S43	39 41	13N40	13TA40	1S48
4/ 4	12TA 9	1S44	40 15	13N50	13TA47	1S49
4/14	12TA46	1S44	40 51	14N 1	13TA54	1S50
4/24	13TA24	1S45	41 29	14N12	14TA 1	1S51
5/ 4	14TA 4	1S45	42 9	14N23	14TA 8	1S52
5/14	14TA44	1S46	42 48	14N34	14TA16	1S52
5/24	15TA23	1S47	43 27	14N45	14TA23	1S53
6/ 3	16TA 1	1S48	44 5	14N55	14TA30	1S54
6/13	16TA36	1S49	44 40	15N 3	14TA37	1S55
6/23	17TA 9	1S51	45 14	15N11	14TA45	1S56
7/ 3	17TA39	1S53	45 43	15N18	14TA52	1S57
7/13	18TA 4	1S54	46 9	15N23	14TA59	1S57
7/23	18TA25	1S56	46 30	15N27	15TA 6	1S58
8/ 2	18TA40	1S58	46 47	15N30	15TA14	1S59
8/12	18TA50	2S 0	46 57	15N30	15TA21	2S 0
8/22	18TA55	2S 2	47 2	15N30	15TA28	2S 1
9/ 1	18TA53	2S 4	47 1	15N27	15TA35	2S 2
9/11	18TA46	2S 6	46 54	15N23	15TA43	2S 2
9/21	18TA33	2S 8	46 42	15N18	15TA50	2S 3
10/ 1	18TA14	2S10	46 24	15N11	15TA57	2S 4
10/11	17TA51	2S12	46 2	15N 3	16TA 5	2S 5
10/21	17TA25	2S13	45 36	14N54	16TA12	2S 6
10/31	16TA56	2S15	45 7	14N45	16TA20	2S 7
11/10	16TA25	2S16	44 37	14N35	16TA27	2S 8
11/20	15TA55	2S16	44 7	14N26	16TA34	2S 8
11/30	15TA26	2S17	43 39	14N17	16TA42	2S 9
12/10	15TA 0	2S17	43 13	14N 9	16TA49	2S10
12/20	14TA37	2S17	42 51	14N 3	16TA57	2S11
12/30	14TA19	2S17	42 33	13N58	17TA 4	2S12

Stations	Date	Long.	Lat.
DIRECT	1/19.44	9TA37	1S44
RETROGRADE	8/24.28	18TA55	2S 3

Date	Long.	Lat.	R.A.	Dec.	HLong.	HLat.
1/ 9	14TA 7	2S16	42 21	13N55	17TA11	2S13
1/19	14TA 1	2S16	42 15	13N53	17TA19	2S13
1/29	14TA 1	2S15	42 15	13N54	17TA26	2S14
2/ 8	14TA 8	2S15	42 21	13N56	17TA34	2S15
2/18	14TA20	2S14	42 33	14N 0	17TA41	2S16
2/28	14TA39	2S14	42 51	14N 6	17TA49	2S17
3/10	15TA 2	2S13	43 15	14N13	17TA56	2S18
3/20	15TA31	2S13	43 42	14N22	18TA 4	2S19
3/30	16TA 3	2S13	44 14	14N31	18TA11	2S19
4/ 9	16TA38	2S13	44 50	14N41	18TA19	2S20
4/19	17TA17	2S13	45 28	14N52	18TA27	2S21
4/29	17TA56	2S14	46 7	15N 2	18TA34	2S22
5/ 9	18TA37	2S15	46 48	15N13	18TA42	2S23
5/19	19TA18	2S15	47 29	15N23	18TA49	2S24
5/29	19TA58	2S17	48 10	15N33	18TA57	2S25
6/ 8	20TA37	2S18	48 49	15N42	19TA 5	2S25
6/18	21TA14	2S19	49 26	15N50	19TA12	2S26
6/28	21TA48	2S21	50 1	15N57	19TA20	2S27
7/ 8	22TA19	2S23	50 32	16N 3	19TA27	2S28
7/18	22TA45	2S25	50 59	16N 8	19TA35	2S29
7/28	23TA 7	2S27	51 21	16N11	19TA43	2S30
8/ 7	23TA23	2S29	51 39	16N13	19TA51	2S31
8/17	23TA34	2S32	51 50	16N13	19TA58	2S32
8/27	23TA38	2S34	51 55	16N12	20TA 6	2S32
9/ 6	23TA37	2S37	51 55	16N 9	20TA14	2S33
9/16	23TA30	2S39	51 48	16N 5	20TA21	2S34
9/26	23TA16	2S41	51 35	15N59	20TA29	2S35
10/ 6	22TA58	2S44	51 17	15N53	20TA37	2S36
10/16	22TA34	2S46	50 54	15N45	20TA45	2S37
10/26	22TA 7	2S47	50 27	15N36	20TA53	2S38
11/ 5	21TA37	2S49	49 57	15N28	21TA 0	2S39
11/15	21TA 6	2S50	49 26	15N18	21TA 8	2S39
11/25	20TA35	2S51	48 55	15N10	21TA16	2S40
12/ 5	20TA 5	2S51	48 26	15N 2	21TA24	2S41
12/15	19TA38	2S51	47 59	14N54	21TA32	2S42
12/25	19TA15	2S51	47 36	14N48	21TA40	2S43

Stations	Date	Long.	Lat.
DIRECT	1/23.77	14TA 0	2S16
RETROGRADE	8/29.75	23TA39	2S35

1932

Date	Long.	Lat.	R.A.	Dec.	HLong.	HLat.
1/ 4	18TA57	2S50	47 18	14N44	21TA47	2S44
1/14	18TA45	2S49	47 6	14N41	21TA55	2S45
1/24	18TA39	2S49	46 59	14N41	22TA 3	2S46
2/ 3	18TA39	2S48	47 0	14N42	22TA11	2S46
2/13	18TA46	2S47	47 6	14N44	22TA19	2S47
2/23	19TA 0	2S46	47 19	14N49	22TA27	2S48
3/ 4	19TA19	2S45	47 38	14N55	22TA35	2S49
3/14	19TA43	2S44	48 2	15N 2	22TA43	2S50
3/24	20TA13	2S44	48 31	15N10	22TA51	2S51
4/ 3	20TA46	2S44	49 5	15N19	22TA59	2S52
4/13	21TA23	2S44	49 42	15N29	23TA 7	2S53
4/23	22TA 2	2S44	50 21	15N39	23TA15	2S53
5/ 3	22TA44	2S44	51 3	15N49	23TA23	2S54
5/13	23TA26	2S45	51 45	15N59	23TA31	2S55
5/23	24TA 8	2S46	52 28	16N 8	23TA39	2S56
6/ 2	24TA50	2S47	53 11	16N17	23TA47	2S57
6/12	25TA30	2S48	53 52	16N25	23TA56	2S58
6/22	26TA 9	2S50	54 31	16N33	24TA 4	2S59
7/ 2	26TA44	2S52	55 7	16N39	24TA12	3S 0
7/12	27TA16	2S54	55 40	16N44	24TA20	3S 1
7/22	27TA43	2S56	56 9	16N48	24TA28	3S 1
8/ 1	28TA 6	2S59	56 32	16N50	24TA36	3S 2
8/11	28TA23	3S 1	56 51	16N52	24TA44	3S 3
8/21	28TA35	3S 4	57 3	16N51	24TA53	3S 4
8/31	28TA40	3S 7	57 9	16N50	25TA 1	3S 5
9/10	28TA40	3S10	57 9	16N47	25TA 9	3S 6
9/20	28TA32	3S13	57 2	16N42	25TA17	3S 7
9/30	28TA19	3S16	56 49	16N37	25TA26	3S 8
10/10	28TA 0	3S18	56 31	16N30	25TA34	3S 9
10/20	27TA36	3S20	56 7	16N23	25TA42	3S 9
10/30	27TA 8	3S22	55 39	16N14	25TA51	3S10
11/ 9	26TA38	3S24	55 9	16N 6	25TA59	3S11
11/19	26TA 6	3S25	54 37	15N58	26TA 7	3S12
11/29	25TA34	3S26	54 5	15N49	26TA16	3S13
12/ 9	25TA 3	3S26	53 34	15N42	26TA24	3S14
12/19	24TA36	3S26	53 6	15N36	26TA32	3S15
12/29	24TA12	3S25	52 42	15N30	26TA41	3S16

Stations	Date	Long.	Lat.
DIRECT	1/28.34	18TA38	2S48
RETROGRADE	9/ 3.55	28TA41	3S 8

Date	Long.	Lat.	R.A.	Dec.	HLong.	HLat.
1/ 8	23TA53	3S25	52 23	15N27	26TA49	3S17
1/18	23TA41	3S24	52 10	15N25	26TA58	3S17
1/28	23TA35	3S22	52 4	15N24	27TA 6	3S18
2/ 7	23TA35	3S21	52 4	15N26	27TA15	3S19
2/17	23TA43	3S20	52 11	15N29	27TA23	3S20
2/27	23TA56	3S18	52 25	15N34	27TA32	3S21
3/ 9	24TA16	3S17	52 44	15N40	27TA40	3S22
3/19	24TA42	3S16	53 10	15N47	27TA49	3S23
3/29	25TA12	3S15	53 40	15N55	27TA57	3S24
4/ 8	25TA47	3S15	54 15	16N 3	28TA 6	3S25
4/18	26TA25	3S15	54 54	16N12	28TA14	3S26
4/28	27TA 6	3S14	55 35	16N22	28TA23	3S26
5/ 8	27TA49	3S15	56 19	16N31	28TA32	3S27
5/18	28TA33	3S15	57 3	16N40	28TA40	3S28
5/28	29TA17	3S16	57 48	16N48	28TA49	3S29
6/ 7	0GE 0	3S17	58 33	16N56	28TA58	3S30
6/17	0GE42	3S19	59 16	17N 4	29TA 6	3S31
6/27	1GE22	3S21	59 57	17N10	29TA15	3S32
7/ 7	1GE59	3S23	60 36	17N15	29TA24	3S33
7/17	2GE33	3S25	61 11	17N19	29TA32	3S34
7/27	3GE 2	3S28	61 41	17N22	29TA41	3S35
8/ 6	3GE26	3S31	62 7	17N24	29TA50	3S36
8/16	3GE45	3S34	62 27	17N24	29TA59	3S36
8/26	3GE58	3S37	62 41	17N23	0GE 8	3S37
9/ 5	4GE 4	3S41	62 48	17N21	0GE16	3S38
9/15	4GE 4	3S44	62 48	17N18	0GE25	3S39
9/25	3GE58	3S47	62 42	17N13	0GE34	3S40
10/ 5	3GE44	3S51	62 29	17N 8	0GE43	3S41
10/15	3GE26	3S54	62 10	17N 1	0GE52	3S42
10/25	3GE 1	3S56	61 46	16N54	1GE 1	3S43
11/ 4	2GE33	3S58	61 18	16N47	1GE10	3S44
11/14	2GE 2	4S 0	60 46	16N39	1GE19	3S45
11/24	1GE29	4S 1	60 13	16N31	1GE28	3S46
12/ 4	0GE56	4S 2	59 39	16N24	1GE37	3S46
12/14	0GE24	4S 2	59 7	16N17	1GE46	3S47
12/24	29TA55	4S 2	58 38	16N12	1GE55	3S48

Stations	Date	Long.	Lat.
DIRECT	2/ 1.10	23TA34	3S22
RETROGRADE	9/ 9.84	4GE 5	3S42

1934

Date	Long.	Lat.	R.A.	Dec.	HLong.	HLat.
1/ 3	29TA31	4S 1	58 12	16N 8	2GE 4	3S49
1/13	29TA11	4S 0	57 53	16N 5	2GE13	3S50
1/23	28TA58	3S59	57 39	16N 3	2GE22	3S51
2/ 2	28TA52	3S57	57 32	16N 4	2GE31	3S52
2/12	28TA53	3S55	57 32	16N 5	2GE40	3S53
2/22	29TA 0	3S53	57 40	16N 9	2GE50	3S54
3/ 4	29TA14	3S52	57 54	16N13	2GE59	3S55
3/14	29TA35	3S50	58 14	16N19	3GE 8	3S56
3/24	0GE 1	3S49	58 41	16N26	3GE17	3S57
4/ 3	0GE33	3S47	59 13	16N34	3GE26	3S57
4/13	1GE 9	3S47	59 49	16N42	3GE36	3S58
4/23	1GE49	3S46	60 30	16N50	3GE45	3S59
5/ 3	2GE31	3S46	61 13	16N59	3GE54	4S 0
5/13	3GE15	3S46	61 59	17N 7	4GE 3	4S 1
5/23	4GE 1	3S46	62 46	17N15	4GE13	4S 2
6/ 2	4GE47	3S47	63 33	17N22	4GE22	4S 3
6/12	5GE33	3S49	64 20	17N29	4GE32	4S 4
6/22	6GE17	3S50	65 6	17N35	4GE41	4S 5
7/ 2	6GE59	3S52	65 50	17N40	4GE50	4S 6
7/12	7GE38	3S55	66 31	17N44	5GE 0	4S 7
7/22	8GE14	3S57	67 8	17N47	5GE `9	4S 8
8/ 1	8GE45	4S 0	67 41	17N49	5GE19	4S 8
8/11	9GE12	4S 4	68 9	17N49	5GE28	4S 9
8/21	9GE32	4S 7	68 31	17N49	5GE38	4S10
8/31	9GE47	4S11	68 46	17N47	5GE47	4S11
9/10	9GE55	4S15	68 55	17N45	5GE57	4S12
9/20	9GE56	4S19	68 57	17N41	6GE 7	4S13
9/30	9GE50	4S23	68 52	17N36	6GE16	4S14
10/10	9GE37	4S26	68 39	17N31	6GE26	4S15
10/20	9GE19	4S30	68 20	17N25	6GE35	4S16
10/30	8GE54	4S33	67 56	17N18	6GE45	4S17
11/ 9	8GE26	4S35	67 26	17N11	6GE55	4S18
11/19	7GE53	4S37	66 54	17N 4	7GE 5	4S19
11/29	7GE19	4S39	66 19	16N58	7GE14	4S19
12/ 9	6GE45	4S39	65 44	16N51	7GE24	4S20
12/19	6GE12	4S39	65 10	16N46	7GE34	4S21
12/29	5GE42	4S39	64 39	16N41	7GE44	4S22

Stations	Date	Long.	Lat.
DIRECT	2/ 6.21	28TA51	3S56
RETROGRADE	9/16.59	9GE56	4S17

Date	Long.	Lat.	R.A.	Dec.	HLong.	HLat.
1/ 8	5GE17	4S38	64 13	16N38	7GE54	4S23
1/18	4GE56	4S36	63 52	16N36	8GE 3	4S24
1/28	4GE42	4S34	63 37	16N35	8GE13	4S25
2/ 7	4GE35	4S32	63 29	16N36	8GE23	4S26
2/17	4GE36	4S30	63 29	16N39	8GE33	4S27
2/27	4GE43	4S28	63 37	16N42	8GE43	4S28
3/ 9	4GE58	4S25	63 51	16N47	8GE53	4S29
3/19	5GE19	4S23	64 12	16N53	9GE 3	4S30
3/29	5GE46	4S21	64 40	16N59	9GE13	4S31
4/ 8	6GE19	4S20	65 13	17N 6	9GE23	4S31
4/18	6GE56	4S19	65 52	17N14	9GE33	4S32
4/28	7GE37	4S18	66 34	17N21	9GE43	4S33
5/ 8	8GE22	4S17	67 19	17N28	9GE53	4S34
5/18	9GE 8	4S17	68 7	17N35	10GE 4	4S35
5/28	9GE56	4S18	68 57	17N42	10GE14	4S36
6/ 7	10GE44	4S18	69 47	17N48	10GE24	4S37
6/17	11GE32	4S20	70 37	17N53	10GE34	4S38
6/27	12GE19	4S21	71 26	17N57	10GE44	4S39
7/ 7	13GE 3	4S24	72 12	18N 1	10GE55	4S40
7/17	13GE45	4S26	72 56	18N 3	11GE 5	4S41
7/27	14GE24	4S29	73 37	18N 5	11GE15	4S42
8/ 6	14GE58	4S32	74 13	18N 5	11GE26	4S42
8/16	15GE27	4S36	74 43	18N 5	11GE36	4S43
8/26	15GE50	4S40	75 8	18N 3	11GE47	4S44
9/ 5	16GE 6	4S44	75 26	18N 1	11GE57	4S45
9/15	16GE16	4S49	75 37	17N57	12GE 7	4S46
9/25	16GE19	4S53	75 40	17N53	12GE18	4S47
10/ 5	16GE15	4S58	75 36	17N48	12GE28	4S48
10/15	16GE 4	5S 2	75 25	17N43	12GE39	4S49
10/25	15GE46	5S 6	75 6	17N37	12GE50	4S50
11/ 4	15GE21	5S 9	74 41	17N31	13GE 0	4S51
11/14	14GE52	5S12	74 12	17N25	13GE11	4S52
11/24	14GE19	5S14	73 38	17N19	13GE21	4S53
12/ 4	13GE44	5S16	73 2	17N14	13GE32	4S53
12/14	13GE 9	5S17	72 25	17N 9	13GE43	4S54
12/24	12GE34	5S17	71 49	17N 4	13GE54	4S55

Stations	Date	Long.	Lat.
DIRECT	2/11.61	4GE35	4S31
RETROGRADE	9/24.01	16GE19	4S53

1936

Date	Long.	Lat.	R.A.		Dec.	HLong.	HLat.
1/ 3	12GE 3	5S16	71	17	17N 1	14GE 4	4S56
1/13	11GE35	5S15	70	48	16N59	14GE15	4S57
1/23	11GE14	5S13	70	26	16N58	14GE26	4S58
2/ 2	10GE59	5S10	70	10	16N58	14GE37	4S59
2/12	10GE51	5S 8	70	1	17N 0	14GE48	5S 0
2/22	10GE50	5S 5	70	0	17N 3	14GE59	5S 1
3/ 3	10GE58	5S 2	70	7	17N 7	15GE 9	5S 2
3/13	11GE12	4S59	70	22	17N11	15GE20	5S 3
3/23	11GE34	4S57	70	44	17N17	15GE31	5S 3
4/ 2	12GE 2	4S54	71	13	17N23	15GE42	5S 4
4/12	12GE35	4S52	71	47	17N29	15GE54	5S 5
4/22	13GE14	4S50	72	27	17N36	16GE 5	5S 6
5/ 2	13GE57	4S49	73	11	17N42	16GE16	5S 7
5/12	14GE43	4S48	73	59	17N48	16GE27	5S 8
5/22	15GE32	4S48	74	50	17N53	16GE38	5S 9
6/ 1	16GE22	4S48	75	42	17N58	16GE49	5S10
6/11	17GE13	4S49	76	35	18N 2	17GE 0	5S11
6/21	18GE 3	4S50	77	28	18N 6	17GE12	5S12
7/ 1	18GE53	4S52	78	20	18N 8	17GE23	5S13
7/11	19GE41	4S54	79	11	18N10	17GE34	5S13
7/21	20GE26	4S57	79	58	18N10	17GE46	5S14
7/31	21GE 8	5S 0	80	42	18N10	17GE57	5S15
8/10	21GE45	5S 4	81	21	18N 8	18GE 8	5S16
8/20	22GE17	5S 8	81	55	18N 6	18GE20	5S17
8/30	22GE44	5S12	82	23	18N 3	18GE31	5S18
9/ 9	23GE 4	5S17	82	44	18N 0	18GE43	5S19
9/19	23GE17	5S22	82	58	17N55	18GE54	5S20
9/29	23GE22	5S27	83	4	17N51	19GE 6	5S21
10/ 9	23GE20	5S32	83	2	17N45	19GE18	5S21
10/19	23GE10	5S37	82	52	17N40	19GE29	5S22
10/29	22GE53	5S41	82	34	17N35	19GE41	5S23
11/ 8	22GE30	5S45	82	10	17N29	19GE53	5S24
11/18	22GE 1	5S49	81	40	17N24	20GE 4	5S25
11/28	21GE27	5S51	81	6	17N20	20GE16	5S26
12/ 8	20GE51	5S53	80	28	17N16	20GE28	5S27
12/18	20GE14	5S54	79	50	17N12	20GE40	5S28
12/28	19GE38	5S54	79	12	17N 9	20GE52	5S28

Stations	Date	Long.	Lat.
DIRECT	2/17.51	10GE50	5S 6
RETROGRADE	10/ 1.18	23GE22	5S28

Date	Long.	Lat.	R.A.	Dec.	HLong.	HLat.
1/ 7	19GE 4	5S53	78 37	17N 8	21GE 4	5S29
1/17	18GE35	5S52	78 7	17N 7	21GE16	5S30
1/27	18GE12	5S49	77 42	17N 7	21GE28	5S31
2/ 6	17GE55	5S46	77 24	17N 9	21GE40	5S32
2/16	17GE45	5S43	77 14	17N11	21GE52	5S33
2/26	17GE44	5S40	77 12	17N15	22GE 4	5S34
3/ 8	17GE50	5S36	77 19	17N19	22GE16	5S35
3/18	18GE 4	5S32	77 33	17N24	22GE28	5S35
3/28	18GE26	5S29	77 55	17N29	22GE40	5S36
4/ 7	18GE55	5S26	78 25	17N34	22GE52	5S37
4/17	19GE29	5S23	79 1	17N39	23GE 5	5S38
4/27	20GE 9	5S21	79 42	17N45	23GE17	5S39
5/ 7	20GE54	5S19	80 28	17N49	23GE29	5S40
5/17	21GE42	5S18	81 19	17N54	23GE42	5S41
5/27	22GE33	5S18	82 12	17N57	23GE54	5S41
6/ 6	23GE26	5S17	83 7	18N 0	24GE 7	5S42
6/16	24GE20	5S18	84 3	18N 2	24GE19	5S43
6/26	25GE14	5S19	85 0	18N 3	24GE32	5S44
7/ 6	26GE 7	5S20	85 56	18N 3	24GE44	5S45
7/16	26GE58	5S23	86 50	18N 2	24GE57	5S46
7/26	27GE48	5S25	87 41	18N 0	25GE 9	5S47
8/ 5	28GE33	5S29	88 29	17N58	25GE22	5S47
8/15	29GE15	5S33	89 13	17N54	25GE35	5S48
8/25	29GE51	5S37	89 51	17N50	25GE47	5S49
9/ 4	0CN22	5S42	90 23	17N45	26GE 0	5S50
9/14	0CN46	5S47	90 48	17N40	26GE13	5S51
9/24	1CN 2	5S52	91 5	17N34	26GE26	5S52
10/ 4	1CN12	5S58	91 15	17N29	26GE39	5S52
10/14	1CN13	6S 4	91 16	17N23	26GE52	5S53
10/24	1CN 5	6S 9	91 8	17N17	27GE 5	5S54
11/ 3	0CN51	6S14	90 53	17N12	27GE18	5S55
11/13	0CN28	6S19	90 30	17N 8	27GE31	5S56
11/23	0CN 0	6S23	90 0	17N 4	27GE44	5S56
12/ 3	29GE27	6S26	89 25	17N 0	27GE57	5S57
12/13	28GE50	6S29	88 47	16N58	28GE10	5S58
12/23	28GE11	6S30	88 7	16N56	28GE24	5S59

Stations	Date	Long.	Lat.
DIRECT	2/22.90	17GE43	5S41
RETROGRADE	10/10.24	1CN13	6S 2

1938

Date	Long.	Lat.	R.A.		Dec.	HLong.	HLat.
1/ 2	27GE33	6S30	87	27	16N56	28GE37	6S 0
1/12	26GE57	6S29	86	50	16N56	28GE50	6S 0
1/22	26GE25	6S27	86	17	16N57	29GE 3	6S 1
2/ 1	25GE59	6S24	85	50	16N59	29GE17	6S 2
2/11	25GE40	6S21	85	30	17N 2	29GE30	6S 3
2/21	25GE28	6S17	85	17	17N 6	29GE44	6S 4
3/ 3	25GE25	6S13	85	14	17N10	29GE57	6S 4
3/13	25GE30	6S 8	85	19	17N14	0CN11	6S 5
3/23	25GE43	6S 4	85	33	17N19	0CN24	6S 6
4/ 2	26GE 5	6S 0	85	55	17N24	0CN38	6S 7
4/12	26GE33	5S56	86	24	17N28	0CN52	6S 7
4/22	27GE 8	5S53	87	1	17N32	1CN 5	6S 8
5/ 2	27GE49	5S50	87	44	17N36	1CN19	6S 9
5/12	28GE36	5S47	88	32	17N39	1CN33	6S10
5/22	29GE26	5S46	89	24	17N41	1CN47	6S10
6/ 1	0CN19	5S44	90	20	17N42	2CN 1	6S11
6/11	1CN15	5S44	91	18	17N43	2CN15	6S12
6/21	2CN12	5S44	92	18	17N42	2CN29	6S13
7/ 1	3CN10	5S45	93	18	17N40	2CN43	6S13
7/11	4CN 7	5S46	94	18	17N37	2CN57	6S14
7/21	5CN 3	5S48	95	17	17N33	3CN11	6S15
7/31	5CN57	5S51	96	13	17N29	3CN25	6S16
8/10	6CN48	5S54	97	5	17N23	3CN40	6S16
8/20	7CN35	5S58	97	54	17N17	3CN54	6S17
8/30	8CN16	6S 2	98	37	17N10	4CN 8	6S18
9/ 9	8CN52	6S 7	99	14	17N 2	4CN22	6S19
9/19	9CN21	6S13	99	44	16N55	4CN37	6S19
9/29	9CN43	6S19	100	6	16N48	4CN51	6S20
10/ 9	9CN57	6S25	100	20	16N41	5CN 6	6S21
10/19	10CN 3	6S31	100	25	16N34	5CN20	6S21
10/29	10CN 0	6S37	100	21	16N28	5CN35	6S22
11/ 8	9CN48	6S43	100	9	16N23	5CN50	6S23
11/18	9CN28	6S49	99	48	16N19	6CN 4	6S23
11/28	9CN 2	6S53	99	20	16N16	6CN19	6S24
12/ 8	8CN29	6S57	98	46	16N14	6CN34	6S25
12/18	7CN52	7S 0	98	8	16N14	6CN49	6S25
12/28	7CN12	7S 1	97	26	16N14	7CN 4	6S26

Stations	Date	Long.	Lat.
DIRECT	3/ 2.00	25GE25	6S13
RETROGRADE	10/20.41	10CN 3	6S32

Date	Long.	Lat.	R.A.	Dec.	HLong.	HLat.
1/ 7	6CN32	7S 2	96 45	16N16	7CN19	6S27
1/17	5CN53	7S 1	96 5	16N18	7CN34	6S27
1/27	5CN18	6S59	95 29	16N22	7CN49	6S28
2/ 6	4CN49	6S56	94 59	16N26	8CN 4	6S29
2/16	4CN26	6S52	94 36	16N31	8CN19	6S29
2/26	4CN11	6S47	94 21	16N36	8CN34	6S30
3/ 8	4CN 5	6S42	94 14	16N41	8CN49	6S31
3/18	4CN 8	6S37	94 17	16N46	9CN 5	6S31
3/28	4CN20	6S32	94 30	16N51	9CN20	6S32
4/ 7	4CN40	6S27	94 50	16N55	9CN35	6S32
4/17	5CN 8	6S22	95 20	16N59	9CN51	6S33
4/27	5CN43	6S18	95 57	17N 2	10CN 6	6S34
5/ 7	6CN25	6S14	96 40	17N 4	10CN22	6S34
5/17	7CN12	6S11	97 30	17N 5	10CN38	6S35
5/27	8CN 4	6S 8	98 24	17N 4	10CN53	6S35
6/ 6	9CN 0	6S 6	99 22	17N 3	11CN 9	6S36
6/16	9CN59	6S 5	100 23	17N 0	11CN25	6S36
6/26	11CN 0	6S 5	101 27	16N56	11CN41	6S37
7/ 6	12CN 2	6S 5	102 31	16N51	11CN57	6S38
7/16	13CN 4	6S 6	103 35	16N44	12CN12	6S38
7/26	14CN 5	6S 7	104 38	16N37	12CN28	6S39
8/ 5	15CN 4	6S10	105 38	16N28	12CN45	6S39
8/15	16CN 1	6S13	106 36	16N19	13CN 1	6S40
8/25	16CN54	6S17	107 30	16N 9	13CN17	6S40
9/ 4	17CN42	6S21	108 19	15N59	13CN33	6S41
9/14	18CN24	6S26	109 2	15N48	13CN49	6S41
9/24	19CN 0	6S32	109 38	15N38	14CN 6	6S42
10/ 4	19CN29	6S38	110 6	15N28	14CN22	6S42
10/14	19CN49	6S44	110 26	15N19	14CN38	6S43
10/24	20CN 1	6S51	110 37	15N11	14CN55	6S43
11/ 3	20CN 4	6S58	110 39	15N 4	15CN11	6S44
11/13	19CN57	7S 4	110 31	14N58	15CN28	6S44
11/23	19CN42	7S10	110 15	14N54	15CN45	6S45
12/ 3	19CN18	7S16	109 50	14N52	16CN 1	6S45
12/13	18CN47	7S20	109 18	14N52	16CN18	6S45
12/23	18CN10	7S24	108 40	14N53	16CN35	6S46

Stations	Date	Long.	Lat.
DIRECT	3/ 9.93	4CN 5	6S41
RETROGRADE	10/31.89	20CN 4	6S56

1940

Date	Long.	Lat.	R.A.		Dec.	HLong.	HLat.
1/ 2	17CN30	7S26	107	59	14N56	16CN52	6S46
1/12	16CN48	7S27	107	16	15N 0	17CN 9	6S47
1/22	16CN 7	7S26	106	34	15N 6	17CN26	6S47
2/ 1	15CN28	7S24	105	55	15N12	17CN43	6S47
2/11	14CN55	7S21	105	21	15N19	18CN 0	6S48
2/21	14CN28	7S16	104	54	15N26	18CN17	6S48
3/ 2	14CN 9	7S11	104	35	15N33	18CN35	6S49
3/12	13CN59	7S 5	104	25	15N40	18CN52	6S49
3/22	13CN58	6S59	104	25	15N46	19CN 9	6S49
4/ 1	14CN 6	6S53	104	34	15N51	19CN27	6S50
4/11	14CN24	6S47	104	53	15N55	19CN44	6S50
4/21	14CN51	6S42	105	21	15N58	20CN 2	6S50
5/ 1	15CN25	6S36	105	57	16N 0	20CN20	6S51
5/11	16CN 7	6S31	106	40	16N 0	20CN37	6S51
5/21	16CN55	6S27	107	30	15N58	20CN55	6S51
5/31	17CN49	6S24	108	26	15N55	21CN13	6S51
6/10	18CN47	6S21	109	26	15N51	21CN31	6S52
6/20	19CN49	6S19	110	29	15N44	21CN49	6S52
6/30	20CN53	6S17	111	35	15N37	22CN 7	6S52
7/10	21CN59	6S17	112	43	15N27	22CN25	6S52
7/20	23CN 6	6S17	113	51	15N17	22CN43	6S53
7/30	24CN13	6S18	114	58	15N 5	23CN 1	6S53
8/ 9	25CN18	6S19	116	4	14N52	23CN19	6S53
8/19	26CN21	6S22	117	8	14N38	23CN38	6S53
8/29	27CN21	6S25	118	8	14N24	23CN56	6S54
9/ 8	28CN17	6S29	119	3	14N 9	24CN14	6S54
9/18	29CN 8	6S34	119	53	13N55	24CN33	6S54
9/28	29CN52	6S39	120	36	13N41	24CN51	6S54
10/ 8	0LE29	6S45	121	12	13N27	25CN10	6S54
10/18	0LE58	6S52	121	39	13N15	25CN29	6S54
10/28	1LE18	6S58	121	58	13N 4	25CN48	6S54
11/ 7	1LE28	7S 5	122	7	12N55	26CN 6	6S54
11/17	1LE29	7S12	122	6	12N48	26CN25	6S55
11/27	1LE20	7S19	121	56	12N43	26CN44	6S55
12/ 7	1LE 2	7S25	121	36	12N41	27CN 3	6S55
12/17	0LE35	7S30	121	8	12N42	27CN22	6S55
12/27	0LE 1	7S34	120	33	12N45	27CN42	6S55

Stations	Date	Long.	Lat.
DIRECT	3/17.92	13CN57	7S 2
RETROGRADE	11/12.82	1LE30	7S 9

Date	Long.	Lat.	R.A.	Dec.	HLong.	HLat.
1/ 6	29CN21	7S37	119 53	12N50	28CN 1	6S55
1/16	28CN38	7S39	119 10	12N57	28CN20	6S55
1/26	27CN55	7S38	118 27	13N 6	28CN40	6S55
2/ 5	27CN13	7S37	117 45	13N15	28CN59	6S55
2/15	26CN34	7S33	117 7	13N25	29CN18	6S55
2/25	26CN 2	7S29	116 36	13N35	29CN38	6S55
3/ 7	25CN37	7S24	116 12	13N45	29CN58	6S55
3/17	25CN22	7S17	115 57	13N54	0LE17	6S55
3/27	25CN15	7S10	115 52	14N 2	0LE37	6S55
4/ 6	25CN19	7S 3	115 57	14N 8	0LE57	6S55
4/16	25CN33	6S56	116 12	14N13	1LE17	6S54
4/26	25CN56	6S50	116 37	14N15	1LE37	6S54
5/ 6	26CN28	6S43	117 10	14N16	1LE57	6S54
5/16	27CN 8	6S37	117 52	14N14	2LE17	6S54
5/26	27CN56	6S32	118 41	14N11	2LE37	6S54
6/ 5	28CN50	6S27	119 36	14N 5	2LE58	6S54
6/15	29CN50	6S23	120 37	13N57	3LE18	6S54
6/25	0LE54	6S20	121 42	13N47	3LE38	6S53
7/ 5	2LE 1	6S17	122 50	13N35	3LE59	6S53
7/15	3LE11	6S15	124 0	13N21	4LE19	6S53
7/25	4LE23	6S15	125 12	13N 6	4LE40	6S53
8/ 4	5LE35	6S14	126 24	12N49	5LE 1	6S52
8/14	6LE47	6S15	127 34	12N32	5LE21	6S52
8/24	7LE58	6S17	128 43	12N13	5LE42	6S52
9/ 3	9LE 5	6S19	129 50	11N53	6LE 3	6S51
9/13	10LE10	6S22	130 52	11N34	6LE24	6S51
9/23	11LE 9	6S26	131 49	11N14	6LE45	6S51
10/ 3	12LE 3	6S30	132 41	10N56	7LE 6	6S50
10/13	12LE51	6S36	133 25	10N38	7LE27	6S50
10/23	13LE30	6S42	134 2	10N21	7LE49	6S50
11/ 2	14LE 1	6S48	134 30	10N 7	8LE10	6S49
11/12	14LE22	6S55	134 48	9N54	8LE31	6S49
11/22	14LE33	7S 1	134 57	9N45	8LE53	6S48
12/ 2	14LE33	7S 8	134 55	9N38	9LE14	6S48
12/12	14LE23	7S14	134 44	9N35	9LE36	6S47
12/22	14LE 3	7S20	134 23	9N35	9LE58	6S47

Stations	Date	Long.	Lat.
DIRECT	3/28.24	25CN15	7S10
RETROGRADE	11/27.38	14LE34	7S 5

1942

Date	Long.	Lat.	R.A.		Dec.	HLong.	HLat.
1/ 1	13LE34	7S25	133	53	9N39	10LE19	6S46
1/11	12LE58	7S28	133	17	9N45	10LE41	6S46
1/21	12LE16	7S30	132	36	9N55	11LE 3	6S45
1/31	11LE31	7S31	131	53	10N 6	11LE25	6S45
2/10	10LE46	7S30	131	9	10N19	11LE47	6S44
2/20	10LE 3	7S27	130	28	10N33	12LE 9	6S44
3/ 2	9LE25	7S23	129	52	10N47	12LE31	6S43
3/12	8LE53	7S17	129	22	11N 0	12LE54	6S42
3/22	8LE30	7S11	129	1	11N12	13LE16	6S42
4/ 1	8LE16	7S 3	128	50	11N23	13LE38	6S41
4/11	8LE13	6S56	128	49	11N31	14LE 1	6S40
4/21	8LE20	6S48	128	58	11N37	14LE23	6S40
5/ 1	8LE38	6S40	129	17	11N40	14LE46	6S39
5/11	9LE 5	6S33	129	46	11N40	15LE 9	6S38
5/21	9LE42	6S25	130	24	11N38	15LE31	6S37
5/31	10LE27	6S19	131	10	11N32	15LE54	6S36
6/10	11LE20	6S13	132	3	11N24	16LE17	6S36
6/20	12LE19	6S 8	133	2	11N13	16LE40	6S35
6/30	13LE24	6S 3	134	7	11N 0	17LE 3	6S34
7/10	14LE33	5S59	135	15	10N44	17LE26	6S33
7/20	15LE46	5S56	136	27	10N26	17LE49	6S32
7/30	17LE 2	5S54	137	41	10N 7	18LE13	6S31
8/ 9	18LE19	5S52	138	56	9N45	18LE36	6S30
8/19	19LE37	5S52	140	10	9N22	18LE59	6S29
8/29	20LE54	5S52	141	24	8N58	19LE23	6S28
9/ 8	22LE10	5S52	142	37	8N34	19LE46	6S27
9/18	23LE23	5S54	143	46	8N 9	20LE10	6S26
9/28	24LE33	5S57	144	51	7N44	20LE34	6S25
10/ 8	25LE37	6S 0	145	51	7N20	20LE57	6S24
10/18	26LE36	6S 4	146	45	6N57	21LE21	6S23
10/28	27LE27	6S 8	147	32	6N36	21LE45	6S22
11/ 7	28LE10	6S13	148	11	6N16	22LE 9	6S21
11/17	28LE44	6S19	148	41	6N 0	22LE33	6S20
11/27	29LE 8	6S24	149	1	5N46	22LE57	6S19
12/ 7	29LE21	6S30	149	11	5N36	23LE21	6S17
12/17	29LE22	6S36	149	11	5N30	23LE45	6S16
12/27	29LE13	6S41	149	0	5N28	24LE10	6S15

Stations	Date	Long.	Lat.
DIRECT	4/ 9.19	8LE13	6S57
RETROGRADE	12/13.58	29LE23	6S34

Date	Long.	Lat.	R.A.	Dec.	HLong.	HLat.
1/ 6	28LE53	6S46	148 40	5N31	24LE34	6S14
1/16	28LE24	6S50	148 11	5N37	24LE58	6S12
1/26	27LE47	6S53	147 35	5N47	25LE23	6S11
2/ 5	27LE 4	6S54	146 54	6N 0	25LE47	6S10
2/15	26LE18	6S53	146 11	6N16	26LE12	6S 8
2/25	25LE31	6S51	145 28	6N33	26LE37	6S 7
3/ 7	24LE47	6S48	144 48	6N51	27LE 1	6S 6
3/17	24LE 8	6S43	144 12	7N 8	27LE26	6S 4
3/27	23LE36	6S36	143 44	7N25	27LE51	6S 3
4/ 6	23LE13	6S29	143 25	7N39	28LE16	6S 1
4/16	23LE 0	6S22	143 15	7N50	28LE41	6S 0
4/26	22LE58	6S13	143 16	7N59	29LE 6	5S58
5/ 6	23LE 7	6S 5	143 27	8N 4	29LE31	5S57
5/16	23LE26	5S57	143 48	8N 5	29LE57	5S55
5/26	23LE56	5S49	144 19	8N 3	0VI22	5S54
6/ 5	24LE36	5S42	144 59	7N57	0VI47	5S52
6/15	25LE24	5S35	145 47	7N48	1VI13	5S50
6/25	26LE20	5S28	146 42	7N35	1VI38	5S49
7/ 5	27LE23	5S22	147 44	7N20	2VI 4	5S47
7/15	28LE32	5S17	148 51	7N 1	2VI29	5S45
7/25	29LE46	5S13	150 2	6N40	2VI55	5S44
8/ 4	1VI 4	5S 9	151 16	6N17	3VI20	5S42
8/14	2VI24	5S 6	152 32	5N51	3VI46	5S40
8/24	3VI46	5S 4	153 50	5N24	4VI12	5S38
9/ 3	5VI 9	5S 2	155 8	4N56	4VI38	5S37
9/13	6VI31	5S 1	156 25	4N27	5VI 4	5S35
9/23	7VI52	5S 1	157 40	3N58	5VI30	5S33
10/ 3	9VI10	5S 2	158 52	3N28	5VI56	5S31
10/13	10VI25	5S 3	160 1	2N59	6VI22	5S29
10/23	11VI35	5S 5	161 4	2N31	6VI48	5S27
11/ 2	12VI38	5S 7	162 2	2N 5	7VI14	5S25
11/12	13VI34	5S10	162 53	1N41	7VI41	5S23
11/22	14VI22	5S14	163 35	1N20	8VI 7	5S21
12/ 2	15VI 0	5S17	164 9	1N 2	8VI33	5S19
12/12	15VI28	5S22	164 33	0N47	9VI 0	5S17
12/22	15VI44	5S26	164 46	0N37	9VI26	5S15

Stations	Date	Long.	Lat.
DIRECT	4/22.99	22LE58	6S16
RETROGRADE	12/31.12	15VI49	5S29

1944

Date	Long.	Lat.	R.A.		Dec.	HLong.	HLat.
1/ 1	15VI49	5S30	164	49	0N32	9VI53	5S13
1/11	15VI42	5S33	164	42	0N31	10VI19	5S11
1/21	15VI24	5S36	164	24	0N35	10VI46	5S 9
1/31	14VI56	5S39	163	57	0N43	11VI13	5S 7
2/10	14VI20	5S40	163	23	0N56	11VI39	5S 4
2/20	13VI37	5S40	162	44	1N13	12VI 6	5S 2
3/ 1	12VI50	5S39	162	1	1N32	12VI33	5S 0
3/11	12VI 3	5S36	161	19	1N52	13VI 0	4S58
3/21	11VI18	5S32	160	39	2N13	13VI27	4S56
3/31	10VI37	5S26	160	3	2N33	13VI54	4S53
4/10	10VI 4	5S20	159	35	2N51	14VI21	4S51
4/20	9VI40	5S13	159	15	3N 7	14VI48	4S49
4/30	9VI26	5S 6	159	5	3N19	15VI15	4S46
5/10	9VI23	4S58	159	5	3N27	15VI42	4S44
5/20	9VI31	4S50	159	16	3N32	16VI 9	4S41
5/30	9VI50	4S42	159	36	3N32	16VI36	4S39
6/ 9	10VI20	4S34	160	7	3N28	17VI 4	4S37
6/19	11VI 0	4S27	160	47	3N20	17VI31	4S34
6/29	11VI49	4S20	161	35	3N 7	17VI58	4S32
7/ 9	12VI46	4S14	162	30	2N52	18VI26	4S29
7/19	13VI51	4S 8	163	32	2N32	18VI53	4S27
7/29	15VI 2	4S 3	164	39	2N10	19VI20	4S24
8/ 8	16VI18	3S58	165	51	1N45	19VI48	4S22
8/18	17VI38	3S54	167	7	1N18	20VI15	4S19
8/28	19VI 2	3S50	168	25	0N49	20VI43	4S16
9/ 7	20VI27	3S47	169	44	0N18	21VI11	4S14
9/17	21VI53	3S45	171	4	0S13	21VI38	4S11
9/27	23VI19	3S43	172	24	0S45	22VI 6	4S 8
10/ 7	24VI44	3S41	173	42	1S18	22VI34	4S 6
10/17	26VI 6	3S40	174	58	1S49	23VI 1	4S 3
10/27	27VI25	3S40	176	10	2S20	23VI29	4S 0
11/ 6	28VI39	3S40	177	18	2S50	23VI57	3S58
11/16	29VI47	3S41	178	20	3S17	24VI25	3S55
11/26	0LI48	3S41	179	16	3S42	24VI52	3S52
12/ 6	1LI40	3S43	180	3	4S 4	25VI20	3S49
12/16	2LI23	3S44	180	42	4S22	25VI48	3S46
12/26	2LI55	3S46	181	11	4S36	26VI16	3S44

Stations	Date	Long.	Lat.
DIRECT	5/ 7.76	9VI22	4S59

Date	Long.	Lat.	R.A.	Dec.	HLong.	HLat.
1/ 5	3LI15	3S47	181 29	4S46	26VI44	3S41
1/15	3LI24	3S49	181 36	4S51	27VI12	3S38
1/25	3LI21	3S50	181 33	4S51	27VI40	3S35
2/ 4	3LI 6	3S51	181 19	4S46	28VI 8	3S32
2/14	2LI41	3S51	180 56	4S36	28VI36	3S29
2/24	2LI 6	3S50	180 24	4S22	29VI 4	3S26
3/ 6	1LI25	3S49	179 47	4S 4	29VI32	3S23
3/16	0LI39	3S47	179 5	3S43	0LI 0	3S20
3/26	29VI51	3S43	178 23	3S22	0LI28	3S17
4/ 5	29VI 5	3S39	177 42	2S59	0LI56	3S14
4/15	28VI23	3S34	177 6	2S38	1LI24	3S11
4/25	27VI48	3S29	176 36	2S19	1LI52	3S 8
5/ 5	27VI21	3S22	176 13	2S 2	2LI20	3S 5
5/15	27VI 4	3S16	176 0	1S50	2LI48	3S 2
5/25	26VI58	3S 9	175 58	1S41	3LI16	2S59
6/ 4	27VI 3	3S 3	176 5	1S37	3LI44	2S56
6/14	27VI20	2S56	176 23	1S38	4LI12	2S53
6/24	27VI47	2S50	176 51	1S43	4LI40	2S50
7/ 4	28VI25	2S43	177 28	1S52	5LI 9	2S47
7/14	29VI13	2S37	178 14	2S 6	5LI37	2S44
7/24	0LI 9	2S32	179 7	2S23	6LI 5	2S40
8/ 3	1LI12	2S27	180 8	2S43	6LI33	2S37
8/13	2LI22	2S22	181 14	3S 7	7LI 1	2S34
8/23	3LI38	2S18	182 26	3S33	7LI29	2S31
9/ 2	4LI59	2S14	183 41	4S 1	7LI57	2S28
9/12	6LI22	2S10	184 59	4S31	8LI25	2S25
9/22	7LI48	2S 7	186 20	5S 2	8LI54	2S21
10/ 2	9LI16	2S 4	187 42	5S34	9LI22	2S18
10/12	10LI43	2S 1	189 4	6S 6	9LI50	2S15
10/22	12LI10	1S58	190 25	6S38	10LI18	2S12
11/ 1	13LI34	1S56	191 44	7S 9	10LI46	2S 9
11/11	14LI55	1S54	193 0	7S38	11LI14	2S 5
11/21	16LI12	1S53	194 11	8S 6	11LI42	2S 2
12/ 1	17LI22	1S51	195 18	8S32	12LI10	1S59
12/11	18LI26	1S50	196 18	8S55	12LI38	1S55
12/21	19LI21	1S48	197 10	9S15	13LI 6	1S52
12/31	20LI 7	1S47	197 53	9S31	13LI34	1S49

Stations	Date	Long.	Lat.
RETROGRADE	1/17.32	3LI25	3S49
DIRECT	5/25.29	26VI58	3S 9

1946

Date	Long.	Lat.	R.A.	Dec.	HLong.	HLat.
1/10	20LI42	1S46	198 27	9S43	14LI 2	1S46
1/20	21LI 6	1S45	198 50	9S51	14LI30	1S42
1/30	21LI19	1S43	199 2	9S55	14LI58	1S39
2/ 9	21LI19	1S42	199 3	9S53	15LI26	1S36
2/19	21LI 8	1S40	198 53	9S48	15LI54	1S32
3/ 1	20LI46	1S38	198 33	9S37	16LI22	1S29
3/11	20LI14	1S36	198 4	9S23	16LI50	1S26
3/21	19LI35	1S33	197 29	9S 6	17LI18	1S23
3/31	18LI50	1S30	196 48	8S46	17LI46	1S19
4/10	18LI 3	1S26	196 6	8S25	18LI14	1S16
4/20	17LI17	1S22	195 24	8S 3	18LI42	1S13
4/30	16LI34	1S18	194 45	7S43	19LI 9	1S 9
5/10	15LI56	1S13	194 12	7S24	19LI37	1S 6
5/20	15LI26	1S 9	193 46	7S 8	20LI 5	1S 3
5/30	15LI 6	1S 4	193 29	6S56	20LI33	0S59
6/ 9	14LI56	1S 0	193 22	6S48	21LI 0	0S56
6/19	14LI57	0S55	193 25	6S44	21LI28	0S53
6/29	15LI10	0S51	193 38	6S45	21LI56	0S49
7/ 9	15LI33	0S46	194 1	6S50	22LI23	0S46
7/19	16LI 7	0S42	194 34	6S59	22LI51	0S43
7/29	16LI50	0S38	195 16	7S12	23LI18	0S39
8/ 8	17LI42	0S34	196 6	7S29	23LI46	0S36
8/18	18LI43	0S31	197 4	7S48	24LI13	0S33
8/28	19LI50	0S27	198 8	8S11	24LI41	0S29
9/ 7	21LI 3	0S24	199 18	8S35	25LI 8	0S26
9/17	22LI21	0S21	200 32	9S 1	25LI35	0S23
9/27	23LI43	0S17	201 50	9S29	26LI 3	0S19
10/ 7	25LI 7	0S14	203 11	9S57	26LI30	0S16
10/17	26LI33	0S11	204 33	10S25	26LI57	0S13
10/27	27LI59	0S 8	205 56	10S54	27LI25	0S 9
11/ 6	29LI25	0S 6	207 19	11S21	27LI52	0S 6
11/16	0SC48	0S 3	208 40	11S48	28LI19	0S 3
11/26	2SC 9	0N 0	209 58	12S13	28LI46	0N 0
12/ 6	3SC25	0N 3	211 12	12S36	29LI13	0N 4
12/16	4SC35	0N 7	212 22	12S57	29LI40	0N 7
12/26	5SC39	0N10	213 24	13S15	0SC 7	0N10

Stations	Date	Long.	Lat.
RETROGRADE	2/ 4.31	21LI20	1S43
DIRECT	6/12.91	14LI55	0S58

Date	Long.	Lat.	R.A.		Dec.	HLong.	HLat.
1/ 5	6SC35	0N13	214	20	13S31	0SC34	0N14
1/15	7SC22	0N16	215	6	13S43	1SC 1	0N17
1/25	7SC58	0N20	215	43	13S51	1SC28	0N20
2/ 4	8SC24	0N24	216	9	13S56	1SC54	0N23
2/14	8SC38	0N28	216	24	13S57	2SC21	0N27
2/24	8SC41	0N32	216	28	13S54	2SC48	0N30
3/ 6	8SC32	0N36	216	21	13S47	3SC14	0N33
3/16	8SC13	0N40	216	3	13S37	3SC41	0N36
3/26	7SC43	0N44	215	36	13S24	4SC 8	0N39
4/ 5	7SC 7	0N48	215	2	13S 8	4SC34	0N43
4/15	6SC24	0N52	214	22	12S51	5SC 1	0N46
4/25	5SC38	0N55	213	39	12S32	5SC27	0N49
5/ 5	4SC53	0N59	212	56	12S14	5SC53	0N52
5/15	4SC 9	1N 2	212	15	11S56	6SC20	0N55
5/25	3SC30	1N 5	211	39	11S40	6SC46	0N59
6/ 4	2SC58	1N 8	211	9	11S27	7SC12	1N 2
6/14	2SC35	1N10	210	48	11S16	7SC38	1N 5
6/24	2SC22	1N13	210	36	11S10	8SC 4	1N 8
7/ 4	2SC19	1N15	210	34	11S 7	8SC30	1N11
7/14	2SC27	1N16	210	42	11S 8	8SC56	1N14
7/24	2SC45	1N18	211	0	11S13	9SC22	1N17
8/ 3	3SC14	1N20	211	29	11S21	9SC48	1N20
8/13	3SC53	1N21	212	6	11S32	10SC14	1N23
8/23	4SC41	1N23	212	53	11S47	10SC39	1N26
9/ 2	5SC36	1N25	213	47	12S 4	11SC 5	1N29
9/12	6SC39	1N26	214	48	12S23	11SC31	1N33
9/22	7SC48	1N28	215	55	12S44	11SC56	1N36
10/ 2	9SC 2	1N30	217	8	13S 5	12SC22	1N39
10/12	10SC19	1N32	218	24	13S28	12SC47	1N42
10/22	11SC40	1N34	219	44	13S51	13SC12	1N45
11/ 1	13SC 2	1N37	221	5	14S13	13SC38	1N47
11/11	14SC25	1N39	222	28	14S35	14SC 3	1N50
11/21	15SC47	1N42	223	50	14S56	14SC28	1N53
12/ 1	17SC 8	1N46	225	11	15S16	14SC53	1N56
12/11	18SC25	1N49	226	29	15S34	15SC18	1N59
12/21	19SC39	1N53	227	43	15S50	15SC43	2N 2
12/31	20SC47	1N57	228	53	16S 5	16SC 8	2N 5

Stations	Date	Long.	Lat.
RETROGRADE	2/21.29	8SC41	0N30
DIRECT	7/ 1.64	2SC19	1N14

1948

Date	Long.	Lat.	R.A.	Dec.	HLong.	HLat.
1/10	21SC48	2N 1	229 56	16S16	16SC33	2N 8
1/20	22SC42	2N 6	230 51	16S25	16SC58	2N11
1/30	23SC27	2N11	231 38	16S32	17SC23	2N14
2/ 9	24SC 2	2N16	232 15	16S35	17SC47	2N16
2/19	24SC27	2N21	232 41	16S36	18SC12	2N19
2/29	24SC41	2N27	232 57	16S34	18SC37	2N22
3/10	24SC44	2N33	233 1	16S29	19SC 1	2N25
3/20	24SC36	2N38	232 54	16S22	19SC25	2N28
3/30	24SC17	2N43	232 37	16S12	19SC50	2N30
4/ 9	23SC50	2N49	232 10	16S 1	20SC14	2N33
4/19	23SC15	2N53	231 36	15S47	20SC38	2N36
4/29	22SC34	2N58	230 56	15S33	21SC 2	2N39
5/ 9	21SC50	3N 1	230 13	15S19	21SC26	2N41
5/19	21SC 5	3N 4	229 29	15S 4	21SC50	2N44
5/29	20SC22	3N 6	228 47	14S51	22SC14	2N47
6/ 8	19SC43	3N 8	228 9	14S39	22SC38	2N49
6/18	19SC11	3N 9	227 37	14S30	23SC 2	2N52
6/28	18SC46	3N 9	227 12	14S23	23SC26	2N54
7/ 8	18SC31	3N 9	226 57	14S18	23SC50	2N57
7/18	18SC25	3N 9	226 51	14S17	24SC13	3N 0
7/28	18SC29	3N 8	226 55	14S19	24SC37	3N 2
8/ 7	18SC44	3N 7	227 10	14S24	25SC 0	3N 5
8/17	19SC 9	3N 7	227 34	14S31	25SC24	3N 7
8/27	19SC43	3N 6	228 8	14S41	25SC47	3N10
9/ 6	20SC27	3N 5	228 51	14S53	26SC10	3N12
9/16	21SC18	3N 5	229 42	15S 7	26SC33	3N15
9/26	22SC16	3N 5	230 40	15S21	26SC56	3N17
10/ 6	23SC20	3N 5	231 44	15S37	27SC20	3N20
10/16	24SC29	3N 6	232 54	15S54	27SC43	3N22
10/26	25SC42	3N 7	234 8	16S10	28SC 5	3N25
11/ 5	26SC58	3N 8	235 25	16S26	28SC28	3N27
11/15	28SC15	3N10	236 44	16S42	28SC51	3N29
11/25	29SC33	3N12	238 4	16S56	29SC14	3N32
12/ 5	0SA51	3N14	239 24	17S10	29SC36	3N34
12/15	2SA 6	3N17	240 42	17S22	29SC59	3N36
12/25	3SA19	3N21	241 58	17S32	0SA22	3N39

Stations	Date	Long.	Lat.
RETROGRADE	3/ 7.61	24SC44	2N31
DIRECT	7/18.55	18SC25	3N 9

1949

Date	Long.	Lat.	R.A.		Dec.	HLong.	HLat.
1/ 4	4SA28	3N25	243	9	17S41	0SA44	3N41
1/14	5SA31	3N29	244	15	17S48	1SA 6	3N43
1/24	6SA28	3N34	245	15	17S52	1SA29	3N46
2/ 3	7SA18	3N40	246	7	17S55	1SA51	3N48
2/13	7SA59	3N46	246	51	17S56	2SA13	3N50
2/23	8SA31	3N52	247	25	17S55	2SA35	3N52
3/ 5	8SA53	3N58	247	48	17S52	2SA57	3N55
3/15	9SA 4	4N 5	248	1	17S47	3SA19	3N57
3/25	9SA 5	4N11	248	4	17S41	3SA41	3N59
4/ 4	8SA56	4N17	247	55	17S33	4SA 3	4N 1
4/14	8SA37	4N23	247	37	17S25	4SA24	4N 3
4/24	8SA10	4N29	247	10	17S15	4SA46	4N 5
5/ 4	7SA36	4N34	246	35	17S 5	5SA 8	4N 7
5/14	6SA57	4N38	245	55	16S55	5SA29	4N 9
5/24	6SA14	4N41	245	12	16S45	5SA51	4N12
6/ 3	5SA31	4N43	244	28	16S35	6SA12	4N14
6/13	4SA49	4N44	243	46	16S27	6SA33	4N16
6/23	4SA12	4N44	243	7	16S20	6SA55	4N18
7/ 3	3SA40	4N44	242	35	16S15	7SA16	4N20
7/13	3SA15	4N42	242	9	16S11	7SA37	4N22
7/23	2SA59	4N41	241	52	16S10	7SA58	4N24
8/ 2	2SA52	4N38	241	45	16S11	8SA19	4N26
8/12	2SA55	4N36	241	47	16S14	8SA40	4N28
8/22	3SA 8	4N33	242	0	16S19	9SA 1	4N29
9/ 1	3SA30	4N31	242	22	16S26	9SA21	4N31
9/11	4SA 1	4N28	242	54	16S34	9SA42	4N33
9/21	4SA41	4N26	243	34	16S43	10SA 3	4N35
10/ 1	5SA28	4N24	244	22	16S53	10SA23	4N37
10/11	6SA22	4N22	245	17	17S 4	10SA44	4N39
10/21	7SA22	4N21	246	19	17S15	11SA 4	4N41
10/31	8SA27	4N21	247	25	17S26	11SA25	4N42
11/10	9SA35	4N21	248	36	17S36	11SA45	4N44
11/20	10SA46	4N21	249	50	17S45	12SA 5	4N46
11/30	11SA59	4N22	251	5	17S54	12SA25	4N48
12/10	13SA11	4N24	252	21	18S 1	12SA45	4N50
12/20	14SA23	4N26	253	36	18S 8	13SA 5	4N51
12/30	15SA34	4N29	254	50	18S12	13SA25	4N53

Stations	Date	Long.	Lat.
RETROGRADE	3/21.09	9SA 6	4N 8
DIRECT	8/ 4.00	2SA52	4N38

1950

Date	Long.	Lat.	R.A.		Dec.	HLong.	HLat.
1/ 9	16SA41	4N32	256	0	18S16	13SA45	4N55
1/19	17SA43	4N37	257	6	18S17	14SA 5	4N56
1/29	18SA41	4N41	258	7	18S18	14SA25	4N58
2/ 8	19SA32	4N46	259	1	18S16	14SA44	5N 0
2/18	20SA16	4N52	259	47	18S14	15SA 4	5N 1
2/28	20SA52	4N58	260	25	18S10	15SA24	5N 3
3/10	21SA19	5N 5	260	54	18S 6	15SA43	5N 5
3/20	21SA36	5N11	261	12	18S 0	16SA 2	5N 6
3/30	21SA44	5N18	261	21	17S54	16SA22	5N 8
4/ 9	21SA42	5N25	261	19	17S47	16SA41	5N 9
4/19	21SA30	5N31	261	7	17S40	17SA 0	5N11
4/29	21SA10	5N37	260	47	17S33	17SA19	5N12
5/ 9	20SA42	5N42	260	18	17S26	17SA39	5N14
5/19	20SA 8	5N47	259	43	17S19	17SA58	5N15
5/29	19SA29	5N50	259	3	17S12	18SA17	5N17
6/ 8	18SA48	5N53	258	20	17S 7	18SA35	5N18
6/18	18SA 7	5N54	257	37	17S 2	18SA54	5N20
6/28	17SA27	5N54	256	56	16S58	19SA13	5N21
7/ 8	16SA51	5N53	256	19	16S56	19SA32	5N23
7/18	16SA21	5N51	255	48	16S55	19SA50	5N24
7/28	15SA58	5N49	255	24	16S55	20SA 9	5N26
8/ 7	15SA43	5N46	255	8	16S57	20SA27	5N27
8/17	15SA37	5N42	255	1	17S 0	20SA46	5N28
8/27	15SA40	5N38	255	4	17S 4	21SA 4	5N30
9/ 6	15SA52	5N34	255	16	17S 9	21SA23	5N31
9/16	16SA13	5N30	255	38	17S15	21SA41	5N32
9/26	16SA43	5N27	256	8	17S22	21SA59	5N34
10/ 6	17SA21	5N23	256	47	17S29	22SA17	5N35
10/16	18SA 6	5N20	257	33	17S36	22SA35	5N36
10/26	18SA57	5N18	258	27	17S42	22SA53	5N37
11/ 5	19SA54	5N16	259	25	17S48	23SA11	5N39
11/15	20SA54	5N15	260	29	17S54	23SA29	5N40
11/25	21SA59	5N14	261	36	17S59	23SA47	5N41
12/ 5	23SA 5	5N14	262	45	18S 2	24SA 5	5N42
12/15	24SA13	5N15	263	56	18S 5	24SA22	5N44
12/25	25SA20	5N16	265	7	18S 6	24SA40	5N45

Stations	Date	Long.	Lat.
RETROGRADE	4/ 1.84	21SA44	5N20
DIRECT	8/18.73	15SA37	5N41

Date	Long.	Lat.	R.A.		Dec.		HLong.	HLat.
1/ 4	26SA27	5N18	266	17	18S	6	24SA58	5N46
1/14	27SA31	5N21	267	24	18S	4	25SA15	5N47
1/24	28SA32	5N24	268	28	18S	2	25SA33	5N48
2/ 3	29SA29	5N29	269	27	17S58		25SA50	5N49
2/13	0CP20	5N33	270	21	17S53		26SA 7	5N51
2/23	1CP 5	5N39	271	7	17S48		26SA25	5N52
3/ 5	1CP42	5N44	271	47	17S42		26SA42	5N53
3/15	2CP12	5N51	272	18	17S35		26SA59	5N54
3/25	2CP33	5N57	272	39	17S28		27SA16	5N55
4/ 4	2CP45	6N 4	272	52	17S21		27SA33	5N56
4/14	2CP48	6N10	272	54	17S15		27SA50	5N57
4/24	2CP41	6N17	272	48	17S 8		28SA 7	5N58
5/ 4	2CP26	6N23	272	32	17S 3		28SA24	5N59
5/14	2CP 4	6N28	272	9	16S57		28SA41	6N 0
5/24	1CP34	6N33	271	38	16S53		28SA58	6N 1
6/ 3	1CP 0	6N37	271	2	16S50		29SA15	6N 2
6/13	0CP22	6N39	270	23	16S47		29SA31	6N 3
6/23	29SA42	6N41	269	41	16S46		29SA48	6N 4
7/ 3	29SA 3	6N41	269	0	16S45		0CP 4	6N 5
7/13	28SA25	6N40	268	22	16S46		0CP21	6N 6
7/23	27SA52	6N38	267	48	16S47		0CP37	6N 7
8/ 2	27SA25	6N36	267	19	16S50		0CP54	6N 8
8/12	27SA 5	6N32	266	58	16S53		1CP10	6N 9
8/22	26SA52	6N28	266	45	16S57		1CP26	6N10
9/ 1	26SA48	6N23	266	40	17S 1		1CP42	6N11
9/11	26SA52	6N19	266	45	17S 6		1CP59	6N12
9/21	27SA 6	6N14	266	58	17S11		2CP15	6N12
10/ 1	27SA27	6N 9	267	21	17S16		2CP31	6N13
10/11	27SA57	6N 5	267	52	17S21		2CP47	6N14
10/21	28SA34	6N 1	268	30	17S25		3CP 3	6N15
10/31	29SA18	5N58	269	16	17S29		3CP19	6N16
11/10	0CP 7	5N55	270	7	17S32		3CP34	6N17
11/20	1CP 1	5N53	271	4	17S34		3CP50	6N17
11/30	1CP59	5N51	272	4	17S35		4CP 6	6N18
12/10	3CP 0	5N50	273	8	17S35		4CP22	6N19
12/20	4CP 2	5N50	274	13	17S33		4CP37	6N20
12/30	5CP 5	5N50	275	19	17S31		4CP53	6N21

Stations	Date	Long.	Lat.
RETROGRADE	4/12.11	2CP48	6N 9
DIRECT	8/31.78	26SA48	6N23

1952

Date	Long.	Lat.	R.A.		Dec.	HLong.	HLat.
1/ 9	6CP 8	5N52	276	24	17S27	5CP 8	6N21
1/19	7CP 9	5N54	277	27	17S22	5CP24	6N22
1/29	8CP 7	5N57	278	28	17S16	5CP39	6N23
2/ 8	9CP 2	6N 0	279	24	17S 9	5CP55	6N23
2/18	9CP52	6N 4	280	16	17S 1	6CP10	6N24
2/28	10CP37	6N 9	281	2	16S53	6CP25	6N25
3/ 9	11CP14	6N14	281	41	16S45	6CP41	6N26
3/19	11CP45	6N20	282	12	16S37	6CP56	6N26
3/29	12CP 8	6N26	282	35	16S29	7CP11	6N27
4/ 8	12CP23	6N32	282	50	16S21	7CP26	6N28
4/18	12CP29	6N39	282	55	16S14	7CP41	6N28
4/28	12CP27	6N45	282	52	16S 8	7CP56	6N29
5/ 8	12CP16	6N51	282	41	16S 4	8CP11	6N30
5/18	11CP57	6N56	282	21	16S 0	8CP26	6N30
5/28	11CP32	7N 1	281	55	15S57	8CP41	6N31
6/ 7	11CP 1	7N 5	281	23	15S56	8CP55	6N31
6/17	10CP26	7N 8	280	46	15S56	9CP10	6N32
6/27	9CP48	7N 9	280	7	15S57	9CP25	6N33
7/ 7	9CP10	7N10	279	28	15S59	9CP40	6N33
7/17	8CP33	7N 9	278	50	16S 2	9CP54	6N34
7/27	7CP59	7N 7	278	15	16S 6	10CP 9	6N34
8/ 6	7CP29	7N 5	277	44	16S10	10CP23	6N35
8/16	7CP 5	7N 1	277	20	16S15	10CP38	6N35
8/26	6CP48	6N57	277	3	16S20	10CP52	6N36
9/ 5	6CP39	6N52	276	53	16S25	11CP 6	6N36
9/15	6CP38	6N47	276	52	16S30	11CP21	6N37
9/25	6CP45	6N42	277	0	16S35	11CP35	6N37
10/ 5	7CP 1	6N37	277	16	16S39	11CP49	6N38
10/15	7CP24	6N32	277	41	16S43	12CP 3	6N38
10/25	7CP55	6N27	278	13	16S46	12CP18	6N39
11/ 4	8CP32	6N23	278	52	16S48	12CP32	6N39
11/14	9CP15	6N20	279	37	16S49	12CP46	6N40
11/24	10CP 4	6N17	280	27	16S48	13CP 0	6N40
12/ 4	10CP56	6N15	281	22	16S46	13CP14	6N41
12/14	11CP52	6N13	282	19	16S43	13CP28	6N41
12/24	12CP49	6N12	283	19	16S39	13CP42	6N42

Stations	Date	Long.	Lat.
RETROGRADE	4/20.13	12CP29	6N40
DIRECT	9/11.31	6CP38	6N49

Date	Long.	Lat.	R.A.	Dec.	HLong.	HLat.
1/ 3	13CP48	6N12	284 20	16S34	13CP55	6N42
1/13	14CP47	6N13	285 20	16S27	14CP 9	6N43
1/23	15CP45	6N14	286 19	16S19	14CP23	6N43
2/ 2	16CP40	6N16	287 16	16S11	14CP37	6N43
2/12	17CP33	6N19	288 10	16S 1	14CP50	6N44
2/22	18CP21	6N23	288 59	15S52	15CP 4	6N44
3/ 4	19CP 4	6N27	289 43	15S42	15CP18	6N45
3/14	19CP42	6N32	290 21	15S32	15CP31	6N45
3/24	20CP13	6N37	290 51	15S23	15CP45	6N45
4/ 3	20CP37	6N43	291 15	15S14	15CP58	6N46
4/13	20CP53	6N48	291 30	15S 5	16CP11	6N46
4/23	21CP 1	6N54	291 38	14S58	16CP25	6N46
5/ 3	21CP 1	7N 0	291 37	14S53	16CP38	6N47
5/13	20CP54	7N 6	291 28	14S48	16CP51	6N47
5/23	20CP38	7N11	291 12	14S45	17CP 5	6N47
6/ 2	20CP16	7N16	290 49	14S44	17CP18	6N48
6/12	19CP48	7N20	290 20	14S44	17CP31	6N48
6/22	19CP16	7N22	289 47	14S45	17CP44	6N48
7/ 2	18CP41	7N24	289 11	14S48	17CP57	6N49
7/12	18CP 4	7N25	288 33	14S52	18CP10	6N49
7/22	17CP28	7N25	287 56	14S57	18CP23	6N49
8/ 1	16CP53	7N23	287 22	15S 3	18CP36	6N49
8/11	16CP23	7N20	286 50	15S 9	18CP49	6N50
8/21	15CP57	7N17	286 25	15S16	19CP 2	6N50
8/31	15CP37	7N13	286 5	15S22	19CP15	6N50
9/10	15CP25	7N 8	285 53	15S28	19CP28	6N51
9/20	15CP20	7N 3	285 48	15S34	19CP41	6N51
9/30	15CP22	6N57	285 51	15S39	19CP53	6N51
10/10	15CP33	6N52	286 3	15S43	20CP 6	6N51
10/20	15CP51	6N47	286 22	15S46	20CP19	6N51
10/30	16CP17	6N42	286 49	15S48	20CP31	6N52
11/ 9	16CP49	6N38	287 23	15S49	20CP44	6N52
11/19	17CP28	6N34	288 3	15S48	20CP57	6N52
11/29	18CP11	6N30	288 48	15S46	21CP 9	6N52
12/ 9	18CP59	6N28	289 37	15S42	21CP22	6N53
12/19	19CP50	6N26	290 29	15S37	21CP34	6N53
12/29	20CP43	6N24	291 24	15S31	21CP46	6N53

Stations	Date	Long.	Lat.
RETROGRADE	4/28.13	21CP 2	6N57
DIRECT	9/21.45	15CP19	7N 2

1954

Date	Long.	Lat.	R.A.		Dec.	HLong.	HLat.
1/ 8	21CP38	6N24	292	20	15S23	21CP59	6N53
1/18	22CP33	6N24	293	16	15S14	22CP11	6N53
1/28	23CP28	6N25	294	12	15S 5	22CP23	6N53
2/ 7	24CP21	6N27	295	5	14S54	22CP36	6N54
2/17	25CP11	6N29	295	55	14S43	22CP48	6N54
2/27	25CP57	6N32	296	42	14S32	23CP 0	6N54
3/ 9	26CP39	6N36	297	23	14S21	23CP12	6N54
3/19	27CP16	6N40	298	0	14S10	23CP24	6N54
3/29	27CP47	6N45	298	30	14S 0	23CP37	6N54
4/ 8	28CP11	6N50	298	53	13S50	23CP49	6N54
4/18	28CP28	6N55	299	9	13S41	24CP 1	6N55
4/28	28CP37	7N 1	299	17	13S34	24CP13	6N55
5/ 8	28CP39	7N 6	299	18	13S29	24CP25	6N55
5/18	28CP33	7N12	299	11	13S24	24CP37	6N55
5/28	28CP20	7N16	298	57	13S22	24CP48	6N55
6/ 7	28CP 1	7N21	298	36	13S22	25CP 0	6N55
6/17	27CP35	7N25	298	10	13S23	25CP12	6N55
6/27	27CP 5	7N27	297	40	13S25	25CP24	6N55
7/ 7	26CP32	7N29	297	6	13S30	25CP36	6N55
7/17	25CP57	7N30	296	31	13S35	25CP47	6N55
7/27	25CP22	7N30	295	55	13S42	25CP59	6N55
8/ 6	24CP48	7N28	295	21	13S49	26CP11	6N56
8/16	24CP17	7N26	294	51	13S57	26CP22	6N56
8/26	23CP50	7N23	294	24	14S 4	26CP34	6N56
9/ 5	23CP29	7N18	294	3	14S12	26CP46	6N56
9/15	23CP14	7N14	293	49	14S19	26CP57	6N56
9/25	23CP 6	7N 9	293	42	14S25	27CP 9	6N56
10/ 5	23CP 6	7N 4	293	43	14S30	27CP20	6N56
10/15	23CP13	6N58	293	51	14S34	27CP32	6N56
10/25	23CP27	6N53	294	6	14S37	27CP43	6N56
11/ 4	23CP49	6N48	294	29	14S39	27CP54	6N56
11/14	24CP17	6N43	294	59	14S38	28CP 6	6N56
11/24	24CP52	6N39	295	34	14S37	28CP17	6N56
12/ 4	25CP31	6N36	296	15	14S33	28CP28	6N56
12/14	26CP15	6N33	296	59	14S28	28CP40	6N56
12/24	27CP 2	6N31	297	48	14S22	28CP51	6N56

Stations	Date	Long.	Lat.
RETROGRADE	5/ 5.34	28CP39	7N 5
DIRECT	9/30.52	23CP 5	7N 6

Date	Long.	Lat.	R.A.		Dec.	HLong.	HLat.
1/ 3	27CP52	6N29	298	38	14S14	29CP 2	6N56
1/13	28CP44	6N28	299	30	14S 5	29CP13	6N56
1/23	29CP36	6N28	300	22	13S55	29CP24	6N56
2/ 2	0AQ27	6N28	301	14	13S44	29CP35	6N56
2/12	1AQ18	6N30	302	4	13S32	29CP47	6N56
2/22	2AQ 6	6N32	302	51	13S20	29CP58	6N56
3/ 4	2AQ50	6N34	303	35	13S 8	0AQ 9	6N56
3/14	3AQ31	6N38	304	15	12S55	0AQ20	6N56
3/24	4AQ 7	6N41	304	49	12S44	0AQ31	6N56
4/ 3	4AQ37	6N46	305	18	12S33	0AQ42	6N56
4/13	5AQ 0	6N50	305	40	12S23	0AQ52	6N56
4/23	5AQ17	6N55	305	56	12S14	1AQ 3	6N56
5/ 3	5AQ28	7N 0	306	5	12S 7	1AQ14	6N56
5/13	5AQ30	7N 5	306	6	12S 1	1AQ25	6N56
5/23	5AQ26	7N10	306	1	11S57	1AQ36	6N56
6/ 2	5AQ15	7N15	305	48	11S55	1AQ47	6N55
6/12	4AQ57	7N19	305	30	11S56	1AQ57	6N55
6/22	4AQ33	7N22	305	6	11S58	2AQ 8	6N55
7/ 2	4AQ 5	7N25	304	38	12S 1	2AQ19	6N55
7/12	3AQ34	7N27	304	6	12S 7	2AQ29	6N55
7/22	3AQ 0	7N28	303	33	12S13	2AQ40	6N55
8/ 1	2AQ26	7N27	302	59	12S21	2AQ51	6N55
8/11	1AQ53	7N26	302	26	12S29	3AQ 1	6N55
9/21	1AQ22	7N24	301	56	12S38	3AQ12	6N55
8/31	0AQ55	7N21	301	30	12S47	3AQ22	6N55
9/10	0AQ33	7N17	301	9	12S55	3AQ33	6N55
9/20	0AQ17	7N13	300	54	13S 3	3AQ43	6N54
9/30	0AQ 7	7N 8	300	45	13S 9	3AQ54	6N54
10/10	0AQ 4	7N 3	300	43	13S15	4AQ 4	6N54
10/20	0AQ 9	6N57	300	49	13S19	4AQ15	6N54
10/30	0AQ21	6N52	301	2	13S22	4AQ25	6N54
11/ 9	0AQ39	6N47	301	22	13S23	4AQ35	6N54
11/19	1AQ 5	6N43	301	48	13S22	4AQ46	6N54
11/29	1AQ36	6N39	302	20	13S20	4AQ56	6N54
12/ 9	2AQ12	6N35	302	57	13S15	5AQ 6	6N54
12/19	2AQ53	6N32	303	38	13S 9	5AQ17	6N53
12/29	3AQ37	6N29	304	22	13S 2	5AQ27	6N53

Stations	Date	Long.	Lat.
RETROGRADE	5/11.90	5AQ30	7N 5
DIRECT	10/ 8.65	0AQ 4	7N 3

1956

Date	Long.	Lat.	R.A.	Dec.	HLong.	HLat.
1/ 8	4AQ24	6N28	305 9	12S53	5AQ37	6N53
1/18	5AQ12	6N26	305 58	12S43	5AQ47	6N53
1/28	6AQ 2	6N26	306 47	12S32	5AQ57	6N53
2/ 7	6AQ51	6N26	307 35	12S20	6AQ 7	6N53
2/17	7AQ39	6N27	308 22	12S 7	6AQ17	6N52
2/27	8AQ24	6N29	309 7	11S54	6AQ28	6N52
3/ 8	9AQ 7	6N31	309 48	11S41	6AQ38	6N52
3/18	9AQ46	6N34	310 26	11S28	6AQ48	6N52
3/28	10AQ21	6N37	310 58	11S16	6AQ58	6N52
4/ 7	10AQ50	6N41	311 26	11S 5	7AQ 8	6N52
4/17	11AQ13	6N45	311 47	10S55	7AQ18	6N51
4/27	11AQ30	6N50	312 3	10S46	7AQ28	6N51
5/ 7	11AQ40	6N55	312 11	10S38	7AQ37	6N51
5/17	11AQ44	6N59	312 13	10S33	7AQ47	6N51
5/27	11AQ40	7N 4	312 9	10S30	7AQ57	6N51
6/ 6	11AQ30	7N 8	311 58	10S28	8AQ 7	6N51
6/16	11AQ14	7N12	311 41	10S29	8AQ17	6N50
6/26	10AQ52	7N15	311 19	10S32	8AQ27	6N50
7/ 6	10AQ25	7N18	310 52	10S36	8AQ36	6N50
7/16	9AQ55	7N19	310 22	10S42	8AQ46	6N50
7/26	9AQ23	7N20	309 51	10S50	8AQ56	6N50
8/ 5	8AQ50	7N20	309 19	10S58	9AQ 6	6N49
8/15	8AQ18	7N19	308 47	11S 7	9AQ15	6N49
8/25	7AQ47	7N17	308 18	11S17	9AQ25	6N49
9/ 4	7AQ20	7N14	307 52	11S26	9AQ35	6N49
9/14	6AQ58	7N10	307 31	11S35	9AQ44	6N48
9/24	6AQ41	7N 6	307 15	11S44	9AQ54	6N48
10/ 4	6AQ30	7N 1	307 6	11S51	10AQ 3	6N48
10/14	6AQ26	6N56	307 3	11S57	10AQ13	6N48
10/24	6AQ28	6N51	307 7	12S 1	10AQ23	6N48
11/ 3	6AQ38	6N46	307 18	12S 3	10AQ32	6N47
11/13	6AQ54	6N42	307 35	12S 4	10AQ42	6N47
11/23	7AQ17	6N37	307 58	12S 3	10AQ51	6N47
12/ 3	7AQ46	6N33	308 28	12S 0	11AQ 1	6N47
12/13	8AQ19	6N29	309 2	11S55	11AQ10	6N46
12/23	8AQ58	6N26	309 40	11S48	11AQ19	6N46

Stations	Date	Long.	Lat.
RETROGRADE	5/16.90	11AQ44	6N59
DIRECT	10/14.99	6AQ25	6N56

Date	Long.	Lat.	R.A.	Dec.	HLong.	HLat.
1/ 2	9AQ39	6N24	310 21	11S40	11AQ29	6N46
1/12	10AQ24	6N22	311 5	11S30	11AQ38	6N46
1/22	11AQ10	6N20	311 51	11S19	11AQ47	6N45
2/ 1	11AQ57	6N20	312 37	11S 8	11AQ57	6N45
2/11	12AQ43	6N20	313 22	10S55	12AQ 6	6N45
2/21	13AQ29	6N21	314 7	10S41	12AQ15	6N45
3/ 3	14AQ13	6N22	314 49	10S28	12AQ25	6N44
3/13	14AQ54	6N24	315 28	10S14	12AQ34	6N44
3/23	15AQ32	6N27	316 4	10S 1	12AQ43	6N44
4/ 2	16AQ 5	6N30	316 35	9S49	12AQ52	6N44
4/12	16AQ33	6N33	317 1	9S37	13AQ 2	6N43
4/22	16AQ56	6N37	317 22	9S27	13AQ11	6N43
5/ 2	17AQ13	6N41	317 37	9S18	13AQ20	6N43
5/12	17AQ23	6N45	317 45	9S11	13AQ29	6N43
5/22	17AQ26	6N49	317 47	9S 6	13AQ38	6N42
6/ 1	17AQ23	6N54	317 43	9S 3	13AQ47	6N42
6/11	17AQ14	6N58	317 33	9S 2	13AQ56	6N42
6/21	16AQ59	7N 1	317 17	9S 3	14AQ 5	6N41
7/ 1	16AQ38	7N 4	316 56	9S 6	14AQ14	6N41
7/11	16AQ12	7N 6	316 31	9S11	14AQ23	6N41
7/21	15AQ44	7N 8	316 3	9S18	14AQ32	6N41
7/31	15AQ13	7N 9	315 33	9S26	14AQ41	6N40
8/10	14AQ41	7N 9	315 2	9S36	14AQ50	6N40
8/20	14AQ 9	7N 8	314 32	9S45	14AQ59	6N40
8/30	13AQ39	7N 6	314 3	9S56	15AQ 8	6N39
9/ 9	13AQ12	7N 3	313 38	10S 6	15AQ17	6N39
9/19	12AQ50	6N59	313 17	10S15	15AQ26	6N39
9/29	12AQ32	6N55	313 2	10S24	15AQ35	6N38
10/ 9	12AQ21	6N51	312 52	10S31	15AQ44	6N38
10/19	12AQ15	6N46	312 48	10S37	15AQ53	6N38
10/29	12AQ17	6N42	312 51	10S41	16AQ 1	6N37
11/ 8	12AQ25	6N37	313 0	10S44	16AQ10	6N37
11/18	12AQ40	6N32	313 16	10S44	16AQ19	6N37
11/28	13AQ 1	6N28	313 37	10S43	16AQ28	6N37
12/ 8	13AQ28	6N24	314 4	10S39	16AQ37	6N36
12/18	13AQ59	6N20	314 36	10S34	16AQ45	6N36
12/28	14AQ35	6N17	315 12	10S27	16AQ54	6N36

Stations	Date	Long.	Lat.
RETROGRADE	5/22.49	17AQ26	6N50
DIRECT	10/21.73	12AQ15	6N45

1958

Date	Long.	Lat.	R.A.	Dec.	HLong.	HLat.
1/ 7	15AQ15	6N14	315 51	10S18	17AQ 3	6N35
1/17	15AQ57	6N13	316 32	10S 7	17AQ11	6N35
1/27	16AQ41	6N11	317 15	9S56	17AQ20	6N35
2/ 6	17AQ26	6N11	317 59	9S43	17AQ29	6N34
2/16	18AQ11	6N10	318 42	9S30	17AQ37	6N34
2/26	18AQ55	6N11	319 24	9S16	17AQ46	6N34
3/ 8	19AQ37	6N12	320 4	9S 3	17AQ55	6N33
3/18	20AQ16	6N14	320 41	8S49	18AQ 3	6N33
3/28	20AQ53	6N16	321 15	8S35	18AQ12	6N33
4/ 7	21AQ25	6N19	321 45	8S23	18AQ20	6N32
4/17	21AQ52	6N22	322 10	8S11	18AQ29	6N32
4/27	22AQ14	6N25	322 29	8S 1	18AQ37	6N32
5/ 7	22AQ30	6N29	322 44	7S53	18AQ46	6N31
5/17	22AQ40	6N33	322 52	7S46	18AQ54	6N31
5/27	22AQ43	6N37	322 54	7S41	19AQ 3	6N30
6/ 6	22AQ41	6N41	322 50	7S38	19AQ11	6N30
6/16	22AQ32	6N44	322 41	7S38	19AQ20	6N30
6/26	22AQ17	6N48	322 26	7S39	19AQ28	6N29
7/ 6	21AQ57	6N50	322 6	7S43	19AQ36	6N29
7/16	21AQ33	6N52	321 42	7S48	19AQ45	6N29
7/26	21AQ 5	6N54	321 15	7S56	19AQ53	6N28
8/ 5	20AQ35	6N55	320 46	8S 4	20AQ 2	6N28
8/15	20AQ 4	6N54	320 16	8S14	20AQ10	6N28
8/25	19AQ33	6N53	319 47	8S25	20AQ18	6N27
9/ 4	19AQ 3	6N52	319 20	8S35	20AQ27	6N27
9/14	18AQ37	6N49	318 55	8S46	20AQ35	6N27
9/24	18AQ15	6N46	318 35	8S55	20AQ43	6N26
10/ 4	17AQ57	6N42	318 19	9S 4	20AQ51	6N26
10/14	17AQ45	6N38	318 9	9S12	21AQ 0	6N25
10/24	17AQ39	6N33	318 5	9S18	21AQ 8	6N25
11/ 3	17AQ40	6N29	318 7	9S22	21AQ16	6N25
11/13	17AQ47	6N24	318 15	9S24	21AQ24	6N24
11/23	18AQ 1	6N20	318 29	9S24	21AQ33	6N24
12/ 3	18AQ20	6N15	318 50	9S23	21AQ41	6N24
12/13	18AQ46	6N12	319 15	9S19	21AQ49	6N23
12/23	19AQ16	6N 8	319 45	9S13	21AQ57	6N23

Stations	Date	Long.	Lat.
RETROGRADE	5/27.70	22AQ43	6N37
DIRECT	10/27.92	17AQ39	6N31

Date	Long.	Lat.	R.A.	Dec.	HLong.	HLat.
1/ 2	19AQ50	6N 5	320 19	9S 5	22AQ 5	6N22
1/12	20AQ28	6N 3	320 56	8S56	22AQ13	6N22
1/22	21AQ 8	6N 1	321 35	8S45	22AQ21	6N22
2/ 1	21AQ51	5N59	322 16	8S33	22AQ30	6N21
2/11	22AQ34	5N59	322 57	8S20	22AQ38	6N21
2/21	23AQ17	5N58	323 38	8S 7	22AQ46	6N20
3/ 3	23AQ59	5N59	324 18	7S53	22AQ54	6N20
3/13	24AQ40	6N 0	324 56	7S39	23AQ 2	6N20
3/23	25AQ18	6N 1	325 32	7S25	23AQ10	6N19
4/ 2	25AQ53	6N 3	326 4	7S11	23AQ18	6N19
4/12	26AQ24	6N 6	326 33	6S59	23AQ26	6N18
4/22	26AQ50	6N 9	326 57	6S47	23AQ34	6N18
5/ 2	27AQ11	6N12	327 15	6S37	23AQ42	6N18
5/12	27AQ26	6N15	327 29	6S29	23AQ50	6N17
5/22	27AQ36	6N19	327 37	6S23	23AQ58	6N17
6/ 1	27AQ39	6N22	327 39	6S18	24AQ 6	6N16
6/11	27AQ37	6N26	327 35	6S16	24AQ13	6N16
6/21	27AQ28	6N29	327 26	6S15	24AQ21	6N16
7/ 1	27AQ14	6N32	327 11	6S17	24AQ29	6N15
7/11	26AQ54	6N34	326 52	6S22	24AQ37	6N15
7/21	26AQ31	6N36	326 29	6S28	24AQ45	6N14
7/31	26AQ 4	6N38	326 3	6S35	24AQ53	6N14
8/10	25AQ34	6N38	325 36	6S44	25AQ 1	6N14
8/20	25AQ 4	6N38	325 7	6S55	25AQ 9	6N13
8/30	24AQ34	6N37	324 39	7S 5	25AQ16	6N13
9/ 9	24AQ 5	6N35	324 12	7S16	25AQ24	6N12
9/19	23AQ39	6N33	323 48	7S27	25AQ32	6N12
9/29	23AQ17	6N30	323 28	7S37	25AQ40	6N11
10/ 9	23AQ 0	6N26	323 13	7S46	25AQ47	6N11
10/19	22AQ48	6N22	323 3	7S54	25AQ55	6N11
10/29	22AQ42	6N18	322 58	8S 0	26AQ 3	6N10
11/ 8	22AQ42	6N14	323 0	8S 4	26AQ11	6N10
11/18	22AQ48	6N 9	323 8	8S 6	26AQ18	6N 9
11/28	23AQ 1	6N 5	323 21	8S 6	26AQ26	6N 9
12/ 8	23AQ20	6N 1	323 40	8S 3	26AQ34	6N 8
12/18	23AQ44	5N57	324 4	7S59	26AQ41	6N 8
12/28	24AQ13	5N54	324 33	7S53	26AQ49	6N 8

Stations	Date	Long.	Lat.
RETROGRADE	6/ 1.64	27AQ39	6N22
DIRECT	11/ 2.67	22AQ41	6N16

1960

Date	Long.	Lat.	R.A.	Dec.	HLong.	HLat.
1/ 7	24AQ46	5N51	325 5	7S45	26AQ57	6N 7
1/17	25AQ22	5N49	325 40	7S35	27AQ 4	6N 7
1/27	26AQ 1	5N47	326 18	7S24	27AQ12	6N 6
2/ 6	26AQ42	5N45	326 57	7S12	27AQ20	6N 6
2/16	27AQ23	5N45	327 36	6S59	27AQ27	6N 5
2/26	28AQ 5	5N44	328 16	6S45	27AQ35	6N 5
3/ 7	28AQ46	5N45	328 54	6S31	27AQ42	6N 5
3/17	29AQ25	5N46	329 31	6S17	27AQ50	6N 4
3/27	0PI 2	5N47	330 5	6S 3	27AQ58	6N 4
4/ 6	0PI35	5N49	330 36	5S49	28AQ 5	6N 3
4/16	1PI 5	5N51	331 3	5S37	28AQ13	6N 3
4/26	1PI31	5N54	331 25	5S26	28AQ20	6N 2
5/ 6	1PI51	5N56	331 43	5S16	28AQ28	6N 2
5/16	2PI 6	5N59	331 56	5S 8	28AQ35	6N 1
5/26	2PI15	6N 3	332 4	5S 2	28AQ43	6N 1
6/ 5	2PI18	6N 6	332 5	4S58	28AQ50	6N 1
6/15	2PI15	6N 9	332 2	4S56	28AQ58	6N 0
6/25	2PI 7	6N12	331 53	4S56	29AQ 5	6N 0
7/ 5	1PI53	6N15	331 39	4S58	29AQ13	5N59
7/15	1PI34	6N17	331 20	5S 3	29AQ20	5N59
7/25	1PI10	6N19	330 58	5S 9	29AQ27	5N58
8/ 4	0PI44	6N20	330 33	5S17	29AQ35	5N58
8/14	0PI15	6N20	330 6	5S27	29AQ42	5N57
8/24	29AQ46	6N20	329 38	5S37	29AQ50	5N57
9/ 3	29AQ16	6N19	329 11	5S48	29AQ57	5N56
9/13	28AQ48	6N17	328 45	5S59	0PI 4	5N56
9/23	28AQ23	6N15	328 22	6S10	0PI12	5N56
10/ 3	28AQ 1	6N12	328 2	6S20	0PI19	5N55
10/13	27AQ44	6N 9	327 47	6S29	0PI26	5N55
10/23	27AQ32	6N 5	327 37	6S37	0PI34	5N54
11/ 2	27AQ26	6N 1	327 33	6S43	0PI41	5N54
11/12	27AQ25	5N57	327 34	6S47	0PI48	5N53
11/22	27AQ32	5N53	327 41	6S49	0PI56	5N53
12/ 2	27AQ44	5N49	327 54	6S48	1PI 3	5N52
12/12	28AQ 2	5N45	328 12	6S46	1PI10	5N52
12/22	28AQ25	5N41	328 35	6S41	1PI17	5N51

Stations	Date	Long.	Lat.
RETROGRADE	6/ 5.32	2PI18	6N 6
DIRECT	11/ 7.07	27AQ25	5N59

Date	Long.	Lat.	R.A.	Dec.	HLong.	HLat.
1/ 1	28AQ53	5N38	329 3	6S35	1PI25	5N51
1/11	29AQ25	5N35	329 34	6S26	1PI32	5N50
1/21	0PI 0	5N33	330 8	6S16	1PI39	5N50
1/31	0PI38	5N31	330 44	6S 5	1PI46	5N50
2/10	1PI18	5N30	331 22	5S52	1PI54	5N49
2/20	1PI58	5N29	332 0	5S39	2PI 1	5N49
3/ 2	2PI38	5N29	332 37	5S25	2PI 8	5N48
3/12	3PI18	5N29	333 14	5S11	2PI15	5N48
3/22	3PI56	5N30	333 50	4S56	2PI22	5N47
4/ 1	4PI31	5N31	334 22	4S43	2PI30	5N47
4/11	5PI 4	5N33	334 52	4S29	2PI37	5N46
4/21	5PI33	5N35	335 18	4S17	2PI44	5N46
5/ 1	5PI57	5N37	335 40	4S 6	2PI51	5N45
5/11	6PI16	5N40	335 57	3S57	2PI58	5N45
5/21	6PI30	5N42	336 9	3S49	3PI 5	5N44
5/31	6PI39	5N45	336 16	3S43	3PI12	5N44
6/10	6PI42	5N48	336 17	3S39	3PI19	5N43
6/20	6PI39	5N51	336 13	3S38	3PI27	5N43
6/30	6PI30	5N54	336 4	3S38	3PI34	5N42
7/10	6PI16	5N56	335 51	3S41	3PI41	5N42
7/20	5PI58	5N58	335 33	3S46	3PI48	5N41
7/30	5PI35	6N 0	335 11	3S53	3PI55	5N41
8/ 9	5PI 9	6N 1	334 46	4S 2	4PI 2	5N40
8/19	4PI41	6N 1	334 20	4S11	4PI 9	5N40
8/29	4PI12	6N 1	333 53	4S22	4PI16	5N39
9/ 8	3PI43	6N 0	333 27	4S33	4PI23	5N39
9/18	3PI15	5N58	333 1	4S45	4PI30	5N38
9/28	2PI50	5N56	332 39	4S56	4PI37	5N38
10/ 8	2PI29	5N53	332 20	5S 6	4PI44	5N37
10/18	2PI12	5N50	332 5	5S15	4PI51	5N37
10/28	2PI 0	5N46	331 56	5S22	4PI58	5N37
11/ 7	1PI54	5N43	331 51	5S28	5PI 5	5N36
11/17	1PI54	5N39	331 53	5S31	5PI12	5N36
11/27	2PI 0	5N35	332 0	5S33	5PI19	5N35
12/ 7	2PI12	5N31	332 12	5S32	5PI26	5N35
12/17	2PI29	5N27	332 30	5S30	5PI33	5N34
12/27	2PI52	5N24	332 52	5S25	5PI40	5N34

Stations		Date	Long.	Lat.
RETROGRADE		6/ 9.82	6PI42	5N48
DIRECT		11/12.11	1PI53	5N41

1962

Date	Long.	Lat.	R.A.	Dec.	HLong.	HLat.
1/ 6	3PI19	5N21	333 19	5S18	5PI46	5N33
1/16	3PI50	5N19	333 49	5S 9	5PI53	5N33
1/26	4PI25	5N16	334 22	4S59	6PI 0	5N32
2/ 5	5PI 2	5N15	334 57	4S47	6PI 7	5N32
2/15	5PI40	5N13	335 33	4S34	6PI14	5N31
2/25	6PI19	5N13	336 10	4S21	6PI21	5N31
3/ 7	6PI59	5N12	336 46	4S 7	6PI28	5N30
3/17	7PI37	5N13	337 22	3S52	6PI35	5N30
3/27	8PI14	5N13	337 56	3S38	6PI41	5N29
4/ 6	8PI49	5N14	338 27	3S25	6PI48	5N29
4/16	9PI20	5N16	338 56	3S12	6PI55	5N28
4/26	9PI48	5N17	339 21	3S 0	7PI 2	5N28
5/ 6	10PI11	5N20	339 42	2S49	7PI 9	5N27
5/16	10PI30	5N22	339 58	2S40	7PI16	5N27
5/26	10PI43	5N24	340 10	2S32	7PI22	5N26
6/ 5	10PI51	5N27	340 16	2S27	7PI29	5N26
6/15	10PI54	5N30	340 17	2S24	7PI36	5N25
6/25	10PI50	5N32	340 13	2S23	7PI43	5N24
7/ 5	10PI41	5N35	340 4	2S24	7PI50	5N24
7/15	10PI27	5N37	339 50	2S27	7PI56	5N23
7/25	10PI 9	5N39	339 32	2S32	8PI 3	5N23
8/ 4	9PI46	5N40	339 11	2S39	8PI10	5N22
8/14	9PI21	5N41	338 47	2S48	8PI17	5N22
8/24	8PI53	5N41	338 21	2S58	8PI23	5N21
9/ 3	8PI24	5N41	337 55	3S 9	8PI30	5N21
9/13	7PI56	5N40	337 29	3S20	8PI37	5N20
9/23	7PI29	5N38	337 5	3S32	8PI43	5N20
10/ 3	7PI 4	5N36	336 43	3S43	8PI50	5N19
10/13	6PI44	5N33	336 24	3S53	8PI57	5N19
10/23	6PI27	5N30	336 10	4S 2	9PI 3	5N18
11/ 2	6PI16	5N27	336 1	4S 9	9PI10	5N18
11/12	6PI10	5N23	335 57	4S14	9PI17	5N17
11/22	6PI10	5N19	335 58	4S18	9PI23	5N17
12/ 2	6PI16	5N16	336 5	4S19	9PI30	5N16
12/12	6PI28	5N12	336 17	4S18	9PI37	5N16
12/22	6PI45	5N 9	336 35	4S15	9PI43	5N15

Stations	Date	Long.	Lat.
RETROGRADE	6/14.14	10PI54	5N30
DIRECT	11/16.95	6PI 9	5N21

Date	Long.	Lat.	R.A.	Dec.	HLong.	HLat.
1/ 1	7PI 7	5N 6	336 56	4S10	9PI50	5N15
1/11	7PI34	5N 3	337 22	4S 3	9PI57	5N14
1/21	8PI 4	5N 1	337 52	3S54	10PI 3	5N14
1/31	8PI38	4N59	338 24	3S43	10PI10	5N13
2/10	9PI14	4N57	338 58	3S31	10PI16	5N13
2/20	9PI52	4N56	339 33	3S18	10PI23	5N12
3/ 2	10PI30	4N55	340 9	3S 5	10PI30	5N12
3/12	11PI 9	4N55	340 44	2S50	10PI36	5N11
3/22	11PI46	4N55	341 19	2S36	10PI43	5N11
4/ 1	12PI22	4N55	341 52	2S22	10PI49	5N10
4/11	12PI55	4N56	342 22	2S 9	10PI56	5N 9
4/21	13PI26	4N58	342 50	1S56	11PI 3	5N 9
5/ 1	13PI53	4N59	343 14	1S44	11PI 9	5N 8
5/11	14PI15	5N 1	343 34	1S34	11PI16	5N 8
5/21	14PI33	5N 3	343 49	1S25	11PI22	5N 7
5/31	14PI46	5N 6	344 0	1S18	11PI29	5N 7
6/10	14PI53	5N 8	344 6	1S13	11PI35	5N 6
6/20	14PI55	5N10	344 7	1S10	11PI42	5N 6
6/30	14PI51	5N13	344 3	1S 9	11PI48	5N 5
7/10	14PI42	5N15	343 53	1S11	11PI55	5N 5
7/20	14PI28	5N17	343 40	1S15	12PI 1	5N 4
7/30	14PI 9	5N18	343 22	1S20	12PI 8	5N 4
8/ 9	13PI47	5N19	343 1	1S28	12PI14	5N 3
8/19	13PI22	5N20	342 37	1S37	12PI21	5N 3
8/29	12PI54	5N20	342 12	1S47	12PI27	5N 2
9/ 8	12PI26	5N20	341 46	1S58	12PI34	5N 2
9/18	11PI58	5N19	341 21	2S10	12PI40	5N 1
9/28	11PI32	5N17	340 57	2S21	12PI46	5N 0
10/ 8	11PI 8	5N15	340 36	2S32	12PI53	5N 0
10/18	10PI47	5N12	340 18	2S42	12PI59	4N59
10/28	10PI31	5N 9	340 4	2S51	13PI 6	4N59
11/ 7	10PI20	5N 6	339 55	2S58	13PI12	4N58
11/17	10PI15	5N 3	339 51	3S 3	13PI19	4N58
11/27	10PI15	5N 0	339 53	3S 6	13PI25	4N57
12/ 7	10PI21	4N56	340 0	3S 7	13PI31	4N57
12/17	10PI33	4N53	340 12	3S 6	13PI38	4N56
12/27	10PI50	4N50	340 29	3S 2	13PI44	4N56

Stations	Date	Long.	Lat.
RETROGRADE	6/18.33	14PI55	5N10
DIRECT	11/21.50	10PI14	5N 1

1964

Date	Long.	Lat.	R.A.	Dec.	HLong.	HLat.
1/ 6	11PI12	4N47	340 50	2S57	13PI51	4N55
1/16	11PI39	4N44	341 16	2S49	13PI57	4N55
1/26	12PI 9	4N42	341 45	2S40	14PI 3	4N54
2/ 5	12PI42	4N40	342 16	2S29	14PI10	4N53
2/15	13PI17	4N38	342 49	2S17	14PI16	4N53
2/25	13PI54	4N37	343 24	2S 4	14PI22	4N52
3/ 6	14PI32	4N37	343 59	1S50	14PI29	4N52
3/16	15PI 9	4N36	344 33	1S36	14PI35	4N51
3/26	15PI46	4N36	345 7	1S22	14PI42	4N51
4/ 5	16PI21	4N37	345 39	1S 8	14PI48	4N50
4/15	16PI54	4N38	346 9	0S55	14PI54	4N50
4/25	17PI23	4N39	346 35	0S42	15PI 1	4N49
5/ 5	17PI49	4N40	346 58	0S31	15PI 7	4N49
5/15	18PI11	4N42	347 18	0S21	15PI13	4N48
5/25	18PI28	4N44	347 33	0S12	15PI19	4N47
6/ 4	18PI40	4N46	347 43	0S 6	15PI26	4N47
6/14	18PI47	4N48	347 48	0S 1	15PI32	4N46
6/24	18PI48	4N50	347 49	0N 1	15PI38	4N46
7/ 4	18PI44	4N52	347 44	0N 1	15PI45	4N45
7/14	18PI34	4N54	347 35	0S 0	15PI51	4N45
7/24	18PI20	4N56	347 21	0S 5	15PI57	4N44
8/ 3	18PI 1	4N57	347 3	0S11	16PI 3	4N44
8/13	17PI39	4N58	346 42	0S18	16PI10	4N43
8/23	17PI14	4N59	346 19	0S28	16PI16	4N43
9/ 2	16PI46	4N59	345 54	0S38	16PI22	4N42
9/12	16PI19	4N58	345 28	0S49	16PI28	4N41
9/22	15PI51	4N57	345 4	1S 1	16PI35	4N41
10/ 2	15PI25	4N55	344 40	1S12	16PI41	4N40
10/12	15PI 1	4N53	344 19	1S23	16PI47	4N40
10/22	14PI42	4N51	344 2	1S33	16PI53	4N39
11/ 1	14PI26	4N48	343 49	1S42	17PI 0	4N39
11/11	14PI16	4N45	343 40	1S48	17PI 6	4N38
11/21	14PI10	4N42	343 37	1S53	17PI12	4N38
12/ 1	14PI11	4N39	343 39	1S56	17PI18	4N37
12/11	14PI17	4N36	343 46	1S57	17PI24	4N36
12/21	14PI29	4N33	343 58	1S55	17PI31	4N36
12/31	14PI47	4N30	344 15	1S51	17PI37	4N35

Stations	Date	Long.	Lat.
RETROGRADE	6/21.38	18PI48	4N50
DIRECT	11/24.92	14PI10	4N41

Date	Long.	Lat.	R.A.	Dec.	HLong.	HLat.
1/10	15PI 9	4N27	344 36	1S45	17PI43	4N35
1/20	15PI35	4N24	345 1	1S37	17PI49	4N34
1/30	16PI 5	4N22	345 30	1S28	17PI55	4N34
2/ 9	16PI38	4N21	346 1	1S17	18PI 2	4N33
2/19	17PI13	4N19	346 33	1S 4	18PI 8	4N33
3/ 1	17PI49	4N18	347 7	0S51	18PI14	4N32
3/11	18PI26	4N17	347 41	0S38	18PI20	4N31
3/21	19PI 3	4N17	348 15	0S24	18PI26	4N31
3/31	19PI38	4N17	348 48	0S10	18PI32	4N30
4/10	20PI13	4N18	349 19	0N 4	18PI38	4N30
4/20	20PI44	4N18	349 48	0N17	18PI45	4N29
4/30	21PI13	4N19	350 14	0N29	18PI51	4N29
5/10	21PI38	4N21	350 36	0N40	18PI57	4N28
5/20	21PI59	4N22	350 55	0N50	19PI 3	4N27
5/30	22PI15	4N24	351 9	0N58	19PI 9	4N27
6/ 9	22PI27	4N26	351 19	1N 4	19PI15	4N26
6/19	22PI33	4N27	351 24	1N 8	19PI21	4N26
6/29	22PI34	4N29	351 24	1N10	19PI27	4N25
7/ 9	22PI29	4N31	351 19	1N10	19PI33	4N25
7/19	22PI19	4N33	351 9	1N 8	19PI40	4N24
7/29	22PI 5	4N34	350 55	1N 3	19PI46	4N24
8/ 8	21PI46	4N35	350 37	0N57	19PI52	4N23
8/18	21PI23	4N36	350 17	0N49	19PI58	4N22
8/28	20PI58	4N37	349 53	0N39	20PI 4	4N22
9/ 7	20PI31	4N36	349 29	0N29	20PI10	4N21
9/17	20PI 3	4N36	349 4	0N17	20PI16	4N21
9/27	19PI36	4N35	348 39	0N 6	20PI22	4N20
10/ 7	19PI11	4N33	348 16	0S 6	20PI28	4N20
10/17	18PI48	4N31	347 56	0S16	20PI34	4N19
10/27	18PI28	4N29	347 39	0S26	20PI40	4N18
11/ 6	18PI13	4N26	347 26	0S34	20PI46	4N18
11/16	18PI 3	4N24	347 18	0S41	20PI52	4N17
11/26	17PI59	4N21	347 15	0S45	20PI58	4N17
12/ 6	18PI 0	4N18	347 17	0S48	21PI 4	4N16
12/16	18PI 6	4N15	347 24	0S48	21PI11	4N16
12/26	18PI19	4N12	347 37	0S46	21PI17	4N15

Stations	Date	Long.	Lat.
RETROGRADE	6/25.38	22PI34	4N29
DIRECT	11/29.13	17PI58	4N20

1966

Date	Long.	Lat.	R.A.	Dec.	HLong.	HLat.
1/ 5	18PI36	4N 9	347 54	0S41	21PI23	4N14
1/15	18PI58	4N 6	348 15	0S35	21PI29	4N14
1/25	19PI24	4N 4	348 40	0S27	21PI35	4N13
2/ 4	19PI54	4N 2	349 8	0S17	21PI41	4N13
2/14	20PI27	4N 1	349 39	0S 6	21PI47	4N12
2/24	21PI 1	3N59	350 11	0N 6	21PI53	4N12
3/ 6	21PI37	3N58	350 44	0N19	21PI59	4N11
3/16	22PI13	3N58	351 18	0N33	22PI 5	4N10
3/26	22PI50	3N57	351 51	0N47	22PI11	4N10
4/ 5	23PI25	3N57	352 23	1N 1	22PI17	4N 9
4/15	23PI58	3N58	352 54	1N15	22PI23	4N 9
4/25	24PI29	3N58	353 22	1N27	22PI29	4N 8
5/ 5	24PI57	3N59	353 47	1N39	22PI35	4N 7
5/15	25PI22	4N 0	354 9	1N50	22PI40	4N 7
5/25	25PI42	4N 2	354 27	1N59	22PI46	4N 6
6/ 4	25PI57	4N 3	354 41	2N 7	22PI52	4N 6
6/14	26PI 8	4N 5	354 50	2N12	22PI58	4N 5
6/24	26PI13	4N 6	354 54	2N16	23PI 4	4N 5
7/ 4	26PI14	4N 8	354 54	2N18	23PI10	4N 4
7/14	26PI 8	4N10	354 48	2N17	23PI16	4N 3
7/24	25PI58	4N11	354 38	2N14	23PI22	4N 3
8/ 3	25PI43	4N12	354 24	2N 9	23PI28	4N 2
8/13	25PI24	4N13	354 6	2N 3	23PI34	4N 2
8/23	25PI 2	4N14	353 45	1N54	23PI40	4N 1
9/ 2	24PI36	4N14	353 22	1N45	23PI46	4N 1
9/12	24PI 9	4N14	352 58	1N34	23PI52	4N 0
9/22	23PI42	4N13	352 33	1N22	23PI58	3N59
10/ 2	23PI15	4N12	352 9	1N11	24PI 4	3N59
10/12	22PI50	4N10	351 46	0N59	24PI10	3N58
10/22	22PI27	4N 9	351 26	0N49	24PI16	3N58
11/ 1	22PI 9	4N 6	351 10	0N39	24PI21	3N57
11/11	21PI54	4N 4	350 58	0N31	24PI27	3N56
11/21	21PI45	4N 1	350 50	0N25	24PI33	3N56
12/ 1	21PI41	3N59	350 47	0N21	24PI39	3N55
12/11	21PI42	3N56	350 50	0N19	24PI45	3N55
12/21	21PI49	3N53	350 57	0N19	24PI51	3N54
12/31	22PI 2	3N50	351 10	0N22	24PI57	3N53

Stations	Date	Long.	Lat.
RETROGRADE	6/29.25	26PI14	4N 7
DIRECT	12/ 3.25	21PI40	3N58

Date	Long.	Lat.	R.A.	Dec.	HLong.	HLat.
1/10	22PI19	3N48	351 27	0N26	25PI 3	3N53
1/20	22PI42	3N45	351 49	0N33	25PI 9	3N52
1/30	23PI 8	3N43	352 13	0N42	25PI15	3N52
2/ 9	23PT38	3N41	352 41	0N52	25PI20	3N51
2/19	24PI10	3N40	353 12	1N 3	25PI26	3N51
3/ 1	24PI44	3N39	353 44	1N15	25PI32	3N50
3/11	25PI20	3N38	354 17	1N29	25PI38	3N49
3/21	25PI56	3N37	354 50	1N42	25PI44	3N49
3/31	26PI32	3N37	355 23	1N56	25PI50	3N48
4/10	27PI 6	3N37	355 54	2N10	25PI56	3N48
4/20	27PI39	3N37	356 24	2N23	26PI 1	3N47
4/30	28PI 9	3N38	356 52	2N36	26PI 7	3N46
5/10	28PI37	3N38	357 17	2N47	26PI13	3N46
5/20	29PI 0	3N39	357 38	2N58	26PI19	3N45
5/30	29PI20	3N41	357 55	3N 6	26PI25	3N45
6/ 9	29PI35	3N42	358 8	3N13	26PI31	3N44
6/19	29PI45	3N43	358 17	3N19	26PI37	3N43
6/29	29PI49	3N45	358 21	3N22	26PI42	3N43
7/ 9	29PI49	3N46	358 20	3N23	26PI48	3N42
7/19	29PI43	3N47	358 14	3N22	26PI54	3N42
7/29	29PI33	3N49	358 4	3N19	27PI 0	3N41
8/ 8	29PI17	3N50	357 49	3N14	27PI 6	3N40
8/18	28PI58	3N50	357 31	3N 7	27PI12	3N40
8/28	28PI35	3N51	357 10	2N58	27PI17	3N39
9/ 7	28PI10	3N51	356 47	2N48	27PI23	3N39
9/17	27PI43	3N50	356 23	2N37	27PI29	3N38
9/27	27PI16	3N50	355 58	2N25	27PI35	3N37
10/ 7	26PI49	3N49	355 34	2N14	27PI41	3N37
10/17	26PI24	3N47	355 12	2N 3	27PI47	3N36
10/27	26PI 2	3N45	354 52	1N52	27PI52	3N36
11/ 6	25PI44	3N43	354 36	1N43	27PI58	3N35
11/16	25PI30	3N41	354 25	1N36	28PI 4	3N34
11/26	25PI21	3N39	354 17	1N30	28PI10	3N34
12/ 6	25PI18	3N36	354 15	1N26	28PI16	3N33
12/16	25PI20	3N33	354 18	1N24	28PI21	3N33
12/26	25PI27	3N31	354 26	1N25	28PI27	3N32

Stations	Date	Long.	Lat.
RETROGRADE	7/ 3.13	29PI50	3N45
DIRECT	12/ 7.22	25PI18	3N36

1968

Date	Long.	Lat.	R.A.	Dec.	HLong.	HLat.
1/ 5	25PI40	3N28	354 39	1N28	28PI33	3N31
1/15	25PI58	3N26	354 57	1N33	28PI39	3N31
1/25	26PI21	3N24	355 18	1N40	28PI45	3N30
2/ 4	26PI47	3N22	355 43	1N49	28PI50	3N30
2/14	27PI17	3N20	356 11	1N59	28PI56	3N29
2/24	27PI50	3N19	356 41	2N11	29PI 2	3N28
3/ 5	28PI24	3N18	357 13	2N23	29PI 8	3N28
3/15	28PI59	3N17	357 46	2N36	29PI13	3N27
3/25	29PI35	3N16	358 19	2N50	29PI19	3N27
4/ 4	0AR10	3N16	358 51	3N 4	29PI25	3N26
4/14	0AR44	3N16	359 22	3N17	29PI31	3N25
4/24	1AR16	3N16	359 52	3N30	29PI37	3N25
5/ 4	1AR46	3N16	0 19	3N42	29PI42	3N24
5/14	2AR13	3N17	0 43	3N54	29PI48	3N24
5/24	2AR36	3N18	1 4	4N 3	29PI54	3N23
6/ 3	2AR55	3N19	1 21	4N12	0 0	3N22
6/13	3AR 9	3N20	1 34	4N19	0AR 5	3N22
6/23	3AR18	3N21	1 42	4N23	0AR11	3N21
7/ 3	3AR22	3N22	1 45	4N26	0AR17	3N21
7/13	3AR21	3N23	1 43	4N27	0AR23	3N20
7/23	3AR15	3N25	1 37	4N25	0AR28	3N19
8/ 2	3AR 4	3N26	1 27	4N22	0AR34	3N19
8/12	2AR48	3N26	1 12	4N16	0AR40	3N18
8/22	2AR28	3N27	0 54	4N 9	0AR46	3N17
9/ 1	2AR 5	3N27	0 32	4N 0	0AR51	3N17
9/11	1AR40	3N27	0 9	3N50	0AR57	3N16
9/21	1AR13	3N27	359 45	3N39	1AR 3	3N16
10/ 1	0AR46	3N26	359 20	3N27	1AR 9	3N15
10/11	0AR19	3N25	358 56	3N16	1AR14	3N14
10/21	29PI55	3N23	358 34	3N 5	1AR20	3N14
10/31	29PI33	3N22	358 15	2N54	1AR26	3N13
11/10	29PI16	3N20	358 0	2N46	1AR31	3N13
11/20	29PI 2	3N18	357 48	2N38	1AR37	3N12
11/30	28PI54	3N15	357 42	2N33	1AR43	3N11
12/10	28PI51	3N13	357 40	2N30	1AR49	3N11
12/20	28PI54	3N11	357 44	2N28	1AR54	3N10
12/30	29PI 2	3N 8	357 52	2N30	2AR 0	3N10

Stations	Date	Long.	Lat.
RETROGRADE	7/ 5.95	3AR22	3N23
DIRECT	12/10.13	28PI51	3N13

Date	Long.	Lat.	R.A.	Dec.	HLong.	HLat.
1/ 9	29PI16	3N 6	358 5	2N33	2AR 6	3N 9
1/19	29PI34	3N 4	358 23	2N38	2AR12	3N 8
1/29	29PI57	3N 2	358 45	2N46	2AR17	3N 8
2/ 8	0AP24	3N 0	359 10	2N55	2AR23	3N 7
2/18	0AP53	2N58	359 38	3N 5	2AR29	3N 6
2/28	1AR26	2N57	0 8	3N17	2AR34	3N 6
3/10	2AP 0	2N56	0 40	3N29	2AR40	3N 5
3/20	2AR35	2N55	1 13	3N43	2AR46	3N 5
3/30	3AP11	2N55	1 45	3N56	2AR52	3N 4
4/ 9	3AR45	2N54	2 17	4N10	2AR57	3N 3
4/19	4AR19	2N54	2 49	4N23	3AR 3	3N 3
4/29	4AP51	2N54	3 18	4N36	3AR 9	3N 2
5/ 9	5AR20	2N55	3 44	4N48	3AR14	3N 1
5/19	5AP46	2N55	4 8	4N58	3AR20	3N 1
5/29	6AP 9	2N56	4 29	5N 8	3AR26	3N 0
6/ 8	6AP27	2N57	4 45	5N16	3AR32	3N 0
6/18	6AP40	2N58	4 57	5N22	3AR37	2N59
6/28	6AP49	2N58	5 5	5N26	3AR43	2N58
7/ 8	6AR53	2N59	5 8	5N29	3AR49	2N58
7/18	6AR51	3N 0	5 6	5N29	3AR54	2N57
7/28	6AR44	3N 1	4 59	5N27	4AR 0	2N56
8/ 7	6AP32	3N 2	4 48	5N23	4AR 6	2N56
8/17	6AP16	3N 3	4 33	5N17	4AR11	2N55
8/27	5AP56	3N 3	4 14	5N 9	4AR17	2N55
9/ 6	5AP33	3N 3	3 53	5N 0	4AR23	2N54
9/16	5AR 7	3N 3	3 29	4N50	4AR29	2N53
9/26	4AP40	3N 2	3 5	4N39	4AR34	2N53
10/ 6	4AR13	3N 2	2 40	4N27	4AR40	2N52
10/16	3AR47	3N 1	2 17	4N16	4AR46	2N51
10/26	3AR23	2N59	1 55	4N 5	4AR51	2N51
11/ 5	3AP 2	2N58	1 36	3N55	4AR57	2N50
11/15	2AP45	2N56	1 21	3N47	5AR 3	2N50
11/25	2AR32	2N54	1 10	3N40	5AR 8	2N49
12/ 5	2AR24	2N52	1 4	3N35	5AR14	2N48
12/15	2AR22	2N49	1 3	3N32	5AR20	2N48
12/25	2AP26	2N47	1 7	3N31	5AR25	2N47

Stations	Date	Long.	Lat.
RETROGRADE	7/ 9.78	6AR53	3N 0
DIRECT	12/13.93	2AR22	2N50

1970

Date	Long.	Lat.	R.A.	Dec.	HLong.	HLat.
1/ 4	2AP34	2N45	1 16	3N33	5AR31	2N46
1/14	2AP49	2N43	1 30	3N37	5AR37	2N46
1/24	3AP 7	2N41	1 48	3N42	5AR42	2N45
2/ 3	3AP31	2N39	2 10	3N50	5AR48	2N45
2/13	3AP58	2N38	2 35	3N59	5AR54	2N44
2/23	4AR28	2N36	3 4	4N10	6AR 0	2N43
3/ 5	5AP 0	2N35	3 34	4N22	6AR 5	2N43
3/15	5AR34	2N34	4 6	4N34	6AR11	2N42
3/25	6AR10	2N33	4 38	4N47	6AR17	2N41
4/ 4	6AP45	2N33	5 11	5N 1	6AR22	2N41
4/14	7AR19	2N32	5 43	5N14	6AR28	2N40
4/24	7AR53	2N32	6 14	5N27	6AR34	2N39
5/ 4	8AP24	2N32	6 43	5N40	6AR39	2N39
5/14	8AP53	2N32	7 9	5N51	6AR45	2N38
5/24	9AR19	2N33	7 33	6N 2	6AR51	2N38
6/ 3	9AP40	2N33	7 53	6N11	6AR56	2N37
6/13	9AR58	2N34	8 9	6N18	7AR 2	2N36
6/23	10AP11	2N35	8 20	6N24	7AR 8	2N36
7/ 3	10AP19	2N35	8 28	6N28	7AR13	2N35
7/13	10AP22	2N36	8 30	6N30	7AR19	2N34
7/23	10AR20	2N37	8 28	6N30	7AR25	2N34
8/ 2	10AR12	2N37	8 21	6N27	7AR30	2N33
8/12	10AR 0	2N38	8 9	6N23	7AR36	2N32
8/22	9AR43	2N38	7 54	6N17	7AR42	2N32
9/ 1	9AR23	2N38	7 35	6N 9	7AR47	2N31
9/11	8AR59	2N38	7 13	5N59	7AR53	2N31
9/21	8AP34	2N38	6 49	5N49	7AR59	2N30
10/ 1	8AR 7	2N38	6 25	5N38	8AR 4	2N29
10/11	7AR40	2N37	6 0	5N26	8AR10	2N29
10/21	7AR14	2N36	5 37	5N15	8AR16	2N28
10/31	6AR50	2N34	5 15	5N 5	8AR21	2N27
11/10	6AR29	2N33	4 57	4N55	8AR27	2N27
11/20	6AP13	2N31	4 42	4N47	8AR33	2N26
11/30	6AR 0	2N29	4 32	4N40	8AR38	2N25
12/10	5AR54	2N27	4 26	4N36	8AR44	2N25
12/20	5AR52	2N25	4 25	4N33	8AR50	2N24
12/30	5AR56	2N23	4 30	4N33	8AR55	2N23

Stations	Date	Long.	Lat.
RETROGRADE	7/13.61	10AR22	2N36
DIRECT	12/17.71	5AR52	2N26

Date	Long.	Lat.	R.A.	Dec.	HLong.	HLat.
1/ 9	6AR 6	2N21	4 39	4N35	9AR 1	2N23
1/19	6AR20	2N20	4 54	4N39	9AR 7	2N22
1/29	6AR40	2N18	5 12	4N45	9AR13	2N22
2/ 8	7AR 3	2N16	5 35	4N53	9AR18	2N21
2/18	7AR31	2N15	6 0	5N 3	9AR24	2N20
2/28	8AR 1	2N13	6 29	5N14	9AR30	2N20
3/10	8AR34	2N12	7 0	5N25	9AR35	2N19
3/20	9AR 8	2N11	7 32	5N38	9AR41	2N18
3/30	9AR43	2N11	8 4	5N51	9AR47	2N18
4/ 9	10AR18	2N10	8 37	6N 5	9AR52	2N17
4/19	10AR53	2N10	9 9	6N18	9AR58	2N16
4/29	11AR26	2N10	9 40	6N31	10AR 4	2N16
5/ 9	11AR57	2N 9	10 8	6N43	10AR 9	2N15
5/19	12AR25	2N10	10 35	6N54	10AR15	2N14
5/29	12AR51	2N10	10 58	7N 4	10AR21	2N14
6/ 8	13AR12	2N10	11 18	7N13	10AR26	2N13
6/18	13AR29	2N10	11 33	7N20	10AR32	2N12
6/28	13AR42	2N11	11 45	7N25	10AR38	2N12
7/ 8	13AR49	2N11	11 51	7N28	10AR43	2N11
7/18	13AR51	2N12	11 53	7N30	10AR49	2N10
7/28	13AR48	2N12	11 51	7N29	10AR55	2N10
8/ 7	13AR40	2N13	11 43	7N26	11AR 0	2N 9
8/17	13AR28	2N13	11 31	7N22	11AR 6	2N 8
8/27	13AR11	2N13	11 15	7N15	11AR12	2N 8
9/ 6	12AR50	2N13	10 56	7N 7	11AR17	2N 7
9/16	12AR26	2N13	10 34	6N57	11AR23	2N 7
9/26	12AR 0	2N13	10 10	6N47	11AR29	2N 6
10/ 6	11AR33	2N12	9 45	6N36	11AR34	2N 5
10/16	11AR 6	2N11	9 20	6N24	11AR40	2N 5
10/26	10AR40	2N10	8 57	6N13	11AR46	2N 4
11/ 5	10AR17	2N 9	8 36	6N 3	11AR52	2N 3
11/15	9AR56	2N 8	8 17	5N54	11AR57	2N 3
11/25	9AR40	2N 6	8 3	5N46	12AR 3	2N 2
12/ 5	9AR29	2N 4	7 53	5N40	12AR 9	2N 1
12/15	9AR22	2N 3	7 48	5N36	12AR14	2N 1
12/25	9AR21	2N 1	7 48	5N34	12AR20	2N 0

Stations	Date	Long.	Lat.
RETROGRADE	7/17.49	13AR51	2N12
DIRECT	12/21.43	9AR21	2N 1

1972

Date	Long.	Lat.	R.A.	Dec.	HLong.	HLat.
1/ 4	9AR26	1N59	7 53	5N34	12AR26	1N59
1/14	9AR36	1N57	8 3	5N36	12AR31	1N59
1/24	9AR52	1N56	8 18	5N41	12AR37	1N58
2/ 3	10AR12	1N54	8 37	5N47	12AR43	1N57
2/13	10AR36	1N53	9 0	5N55	12AR48	1N57
2/23	11AR 4	1N51	9 26	6N 5	12AR54	1N56
3/ 4	11AR35	1N50	9 55	6N16	13AR 0	1N55
3/14	12AR 7	1N49	10 26	6N28	13AR 5	1N55
3/24	12AR42	1N48	10 58	6N41	13AR11	1N54
4/ 3	13AR17	1N48	11 31	6N54	13AR17	1N53
4/13	13AR52	1N47	12 4	7N 7	13AR23	1N53
4/23	14AR27	1N47	12 36	7N20	13AR28	1N52
5/ 3	15AR 0	1N46	13 7	7N32	13AR34	1N51
5/13	15AR30	1N46	13 36	7N44	13AR40	1N51
5/23	15AR59	1N46	14 2	7N55	13AR45	1N50
6/ 2	16AR23	1N46	14 25	8N 5	13AR51	1N49
6/12	16AR44	1N46	14 44	8N13	13AR57	1N49
6/22	17AR 1	1N47	15 0	8N20	14AR 2	1N48
7/ 2	17AR13	1N47	15 11	8N24	14AR 8	1N47
7/12	17AR20	1N47	15 17	8N27	14AR14	1N47
7/22	17AR22	1N47	15 19	8N28	14AR20	1N46
8/ 1	17AR18	1N48	15 15	8N27	14AR25	1N45
8/11	17AR10	1N48	15 7	8N24	14AR31	1N45
8/21	16AR56	1N48	14 55	8N19	14AR37	1N44
8/31	16AR39	1N48	14 38	8N12	14AR42	1N43
9/10	16AR17	1N48	14 19	8N 4	14AR48	1N43
9/20	15AR53	1N47	13 56	7N54	14AR54	1N42
9/30	15AR27	1N47	13 32	7N44	15AR 0	1N41
10/10	15AR 0	1N46	13 7	7N32	15AR 5	1N41
10/20	14AR33	1N45	12 42	7N21	15AR11	1N40
10/30	14AR 7	1N44	12 19	7N10	15AR17	1N39
11/ 9	13AR44	1N43	11 58	7N 0	15AR23	1N39
11/19	13AR24	1N42	11 40	6N51	15AR28	1N38
11/29	13AR 8	1N40	11 26	6N44	15AR34	1N37
12/ 9	12AR57	1N39	11 16	6N38	15AR40	1N37
12/19	12AR52	1N37	11 12	6N35	15AR45	1N36
12/29	12AR52	1N36	11 12	6N33	15AR51	1N35

Stations	Date	Long.	Lat.
RETROGRADE	7/20.39	17AR22	1N47
DIRECT	12/24.16	12AR51	1N37

Date	Long.	Lat.	R.A.	Dec.	HLong.	HLat.
1/ 8	12AR57	1N34	11 18	6N34	15AR57	1N35
1/18	13AR 8	1N33	11 29	6N37	16AR 3	1N34
1/28	13AR24	1N31	11 44	6N42	16AR 8	1N33
2/ 7	13AR45	1N30	12 4	6N48	16AR14	1N33
2/17	14AR10	1N29	12 27	6N57	16AR20	1N32
2/27	14AR38	1N27	12 54	7N 7	16AR26	1N31
3/ 9	15AR 9	1N26	13 23	7N18	16AR31	1N30
3/19	15AR42	1N25	13 55	7N30	16AR37	1N30
3/29	16AR17	1N25	14 27	7N42	16AR43	1N29
4/ 8	16AR52	1N24	15 0	7N55	16AR49	1N28
4/18	17AR27	1N23	15 33	8N 8	16AR54	1N28
4/28	18AR 2	1N23	16 6	8N21	17AR 0	1N27
5/ 8	18AR35	1N23	16 37	8N33	17AR 6	1N26
5/18	19AR 6	1N22	17 5	8N45	17AR12	1N26
5/28	19AR33	1N22	17 32	8N55	17AR17	1N25
6/ 7	19AR58	1N22	17 55	9N 4	17AR23	1N24
6/17	20AR19	1N22	18 14	9N12	17AR29	1N24
6/27	20AR35	1N22	18 29	9N18	17AR35	1N23
7/ 7	20AR46	1N22	18 40	9N23	17AR40	1N22
7/17	20AR53	1N22	18 46	9N25	17AR46	1N22
7/27	20AR54	1N22	18 47	9N26	17AR52	1N21
8/ 6	20AR50	1N22	18 43	9N24	17AR58	1N20
8/16	20AR41	1N22	18 35	9N21	18AR 3	1N20
8/26	20AR27	1N22	18 22	9N15	18AR 9	1N19
9/ 5	20AR 9	1N22	18 5	9N 8	18AR15	1N18
9/15	19AR47	1N21	17 45	9N 0	18AR21	1N18
9/25	19AR22	1N21	17 22	8N50	18AR27	1N17
10/ 5	18AR56	1N20	16 57	8N39	18AR32	1N16
10/15	18AR28	1N20	16 32	8N28	18AR38	1N15
10/25	18AR 1	1N19	16 7	8N17	18AR44	1N15
11/ 4	17AR36	1N18	15 43	8N 6	18AR50	1N14
11/14	17AR13	1N17	15 22	7N57	18AR55	1N13
11/24	16AR53	1N16	15 5	7N48	19AR 1	1N13
12/ 4	16AR38	1N14	14 51	7N41	19AR 7	1N12
12/14	16AR28	1N13	14 42	7N36	19AR13	1N11
12/24	16AR23	1N12	14 38	7N33	19AR19	1N11

Stations	Date	Long.	Lat.
RETROGRADE	7/24.38	20AR54	1N22
DIRECT	12/27.85	16AR23	1N11

1974

Date	Long.	Lat.	R.A.	Dec.	HLong.	HLat.
1/ 3	16AR24	1N10	14 39	7N32	19AR24	1N10
1/13	16AR30	1N 9	14 45	7N33	19AR30	1N 9
1/23	16AR41	1N 8	14 57	7N36	19AR36	1N 9
2/ 2	16AR58	1N 6	15 13	7N41	19AR42	1N 8
2/12	17AR20	1N 5	15 33	7N49	19AR48	1N 7
2/22	17AR45	1N 4	15 57	7N57	19AR54	1N 6
3/ 4	18AR14	1N 3	16 25	8N 7	19AR59	1N 6
3/14	18AR46	1N 2	16 55	8N18	20AR 5	1N 5
3/24	19AR19	1N 1	17 26	8N30	20AR11	1N 4
4/ 3	19AR54	1N 0	17 59	8N43	20AR17	1N 4
4/13	20AR30	1N 0	18 33	8N56	20AR23	1N 3
4/23	21AR 5	0N59	19 6	9N 9	20AR28	1N 2
5/ 3	21AR40	0N59	19 39	9N21	20AR34	1N 2
5/13	22AR13	0N58	20 10	9N33	20AR40	1N 1
5/23	22AR43	0N58	20 39	9N44	20AR46	1N 0
6/ 2	23AR11	0N57	21 5	9N54	20AR52	1N 0
6/12	23AR35	0N57	21 28	10N 3	20AR58	0N59
6/22	23AR56	0N57	21 48	10N10	21AR 4	0N58
7/ 2	24AR12	0N57	22 3	10N16	21AR 9	0N57
7/12	24AR23	0N57	22 13	10N20	21AR15	0N57
7/22	24AR29	0N56	22 19	10N22	21AR21	0N56
8/ 1	24AR29	0N56	22 20	10N22	21AR27	0N55
8/11	24AR25	0N56	22 16	10N20	21AR33	0N55
8/21	24AR15	0N56	22 7	10N16	21AR39	0N54
8/31	24AR 1	0N55	21 53	10N10	21AR44	0N53
9/10	23AR42	0N55	21 36	10N 3	21AR50	0N52
9/20	23AR20	0N54	21 15	9N54	21AR56	0N52
9/30	22AR55	0N54	20 51	9N45	22AR 2	0N51
10/10	22AR28	0N53	20 26	9N34	22AR 8	0N50
10/20	22AR 0	0N52	20 1	9N23	22AR14	0N50
10/30	21AR33	0N52	19 36	9N12	22AR20	0N49
11/ 9	21AR 8	0N51	19 12	9N 2	22AR26	0N48
11/19	20AR45	0N50	18 51	8N52	22AR32	0N48
11/29	20AR26	0N49	18 33	8N44	22AR37	0N47
12/ 9	20AR11	0N48	18 20	8N37	22AR43	0N46
12/19	20AR 1	0N46	18 11	8N33	22AR49	0N45
12/29	19AR57	0N45	18 8	8N30	22AR55	0N45

Stations	Date	Long.	Lat.
RETROGRADE	7/28.40	24AR30	0N56
DIRECT	12/31.60	19AR57	0N45

1975

Date	Long.	Lat.	R.A.		Dec.	HLong.	HLat.
1/ 8	19AP58	0N44	18	10	8N30	23AR 1	0N44
1/18	20AR 5	0N43	18	17	8N31	23AR 7	0N43
1/28	20AP18	0N42	18	29	8N35	23AR13	0N43
2/ 7	20AR35	0N41	18	45	8N40	23AR19	0N42
2/17	20AP57	0N40	19	6	8N48	23AR25	0N41
2/27	21AR23	0N39	19	31	8N57	23AR31	0N40
3/ 9	21AP53	0N38	19	59	9N 7	23AR36	0N40
3/19	22AP25	0N37	20	30	9N18	23AR42	0N39
3/29	22AP59	0N36	21	2	9N30	23AR48	0N38
4/ 8	23AR35	0N36	21	36	9N43	23AR54	0N38
4/18	24AP11	0N35	22	10	9N55	24AR 0	0N37
4/28	24AP46	0N34	22	44	10N 8	24AR 6	0N36
5/ 8	25AP21	0N34	23	17	10N20	24AR12	0N35
5/18	25AR54	0N33	23	48	10N31	24AR18	0N35
5/28	26AP25	0N33	24	18	10N42	24AR24	0N34
6/ 7	26AP52	0N32	24	44	10N52	24AR30	0N33
6/17	27AR17	0N32	25	7	11N 0	24AR36	0N33
6/27	27AP37	0N31	25	27	11N 7	24AR42	0N32
7/ 7	27AP52	0N31	25	42	11N12	24AR48	0N31
7/17	28AP 3	0N30	25	52	11N15	24AR54	0N30
7/27	28AP 9	0N30	25	58	11N17	25AR 0	0N30
8/ 6	28AP 9	0N29	25	58	11N17	25AR 6	0N29
8/16	28AP 4	0N29	25	54	11N14	25AR12	0N28
8/26	27AR54	0N28	25	44	11N10	25AR18	0N28
9/ 5	27AP39	0N28	25	30	11N 4	25AR24	0N27
9/15	27AP20	0N27	25	12	10N57	25AR30	0N26
9/25	26AR57	0N27	24	50	10N48	25AR36	0N25
10/ 5	26AP31	0N26	24	26	10N38	25AR42	0N25
10/15	26AP 4	0N25	24	1	10N28	25AR48	0N24
10/25	25AP36	0N25	23	35	10N17	25AR54	0N23
11/ 4	25AR 9	0N24	23	9	10N 6	26AR 0	0N23
11/14	24AR43	0N23	22	46	9N56	26AR 6	0N22
11/24	24AR21	0N22	22	25	9N47	26AR12	0N21
12/ 4	24AP 2	0N21	22	7	9N39	26AR18	0N20
12/14	23AP48	0N20	21	54	9N33	26AR24	0N20
12/24	23AP39	0N19	21	46	9N29	26AR30	0N19

Stations	Date	Long.	Lat.
RETROGRADE	8/ 1.58	28AR10	0N30

1976

Date	Long.	Lat.	R.A.		Dec.	HLong.	HLat.
1/ 3	23AR35	0N18	21	43	9N27	26AR36	0N18
1/13	23AR37	0N17	21	45	9N26	26AR42	0N17
1/23	23AR45	0N17	21	53	9N29	26AR48	0N17
2/ 2	23AR58	0N16	22	5	9N33	26AR54	0N16
2/12	24AR16	0N15	22	23	9N38	27AR 0	0N15
2/22	24AR39	0N14	22	45	9N46	27AR 6	0N15
3/ 3	25AR 6	0N13	23	10	9N55	27AR12	0N14
3/13	25AR36	0N12	23	39	10N 5	27AR18	0N13
3/23	26AR 9	0N12	24	10	10N17	27AR24	0N12
4/ 2	26AR43	0N11	24	44	10N29	27AR30	0N12
4/12	27AR19	0N10	25	18	10N41	27AR36	0N11
4/22	27AR56	0N10	25	53	10N53	27AR42	0N10
5/ 2	28AR32	0N 9	26	27	11N 5	27AR48	0N 9
5/12	29AR 7	0N 8	27	1	11N17	27AR54	0N 9
5/22	29AR40	0N 8	27	33	11N28	28AR 0	0N 8
6/ 1	0TA11	0N 7	28	2	11N39	28AR 7	0N 7
6/11	0TA39	0N 6	28	29	11N48	28AR13	0N 6
6/21	1TA 3	0N 6	28	53	11N56	28AR19	0N 6
7/ 1	1TA23	0N 5	29	12	12N 2	28AR25	0N 5
7/11	1TA38	0N 4	29	27	12N 7	28AR31	0N 4
7/21	1TA49	0N 4	29	38	12N10	28AR37	0N 4
7/31	1TA54	0N 3	29	43	12N11	28AR43	0N 3
8/10	1TA54	0N 2	29	43	12N10	28AR49	0N 2
8/20	1TA49	0N 1	29	38	12N 8	28AR55	0N 1
8/30	1TA38	0N 1	29	28	12N 3	29AR 2	0N 1
9/ 9	1TA22	0S 0	29	14	11N57	29AR 8	0S 0
9/19	1TA 3	0S 1	28	55	11N49	29AR14	0S 1
9/29	0TA39	0S 2	28	33	11N40	29AR20	0S 2
10/ 9	0TA13	0S 3	28	8	11N31	29AR26	0S 2
10/19	29AR45	0S 3	27	42	11N20	29AR32	0S 3
10/29	29AR17	0S 4	27	15	11N 9	29AR38	0S 4
11/ 8	28AR50	0S 5	26	50	10N59	29AR45	0S 5
11/18	28AR24	0S 6	26	25	10N49	29AR51	0S 5
11/28	28AR 2	0S 6	26	4	10N41	29AR57	0S 6
12/ 8	27AR43	0S 7	25	47	10N33	0TA 3	0S 7
12/18	27AR29	0S 8	25	34	10N28	0TA 9	0S 8
12/28	27AR21	0S 9	25	26	10N24	0TA15	0S 8

Stations	Date	Long.	Lat.
DIRECT	1/ 4.36	23AR35	0N18
RETROGRADE	8/ 4.81	1TA55	0N 2

Date	Long.	Lat.	R.A.	Dec.	HLong.	HLat.
1/ 7	27AR18	0S 9	25 23	10N22	0TA22	0S 9
1/17	27AR20	0S10	25 26	10N22	0TA28	0S10
1/27	27AR29	0S11	25 35	10N25	0TA34	0S11
2/ 6	27AR43	0S11	25 48	10N29	0TA40	0S11
2/16	28AR 2	0S12	26 6	10N35	0TA46	0S12
2/26	28AR25	0S12	26 29	10N43	0TA53	0S13
3/ 8	28AR53	0S13	26 55	10N53	0TA59	0S14
3/18	29AR24	0S14	27 25	11N 3	1TA 5	0S14
3/28	29AR57	0S14	27 57	11N14	1TA11	0S15
4/ 7	0TA33	0S15	28 31	11N26	1TA17	0S16
4/17	1TA 9	0S16	29 7	11N38	1TA24	0S17
4/27	1TA46	0S16	29 42	11N50	1TA30	0S17
5/ 7	2TA23	0S17	30 17	12N 2	1TA36	0S18
5/17	2TA58	0S18	30 52	12N13	1TA42	0S19
5/27	3TA32	0S19	31 24	12N24	1TA49	0S20
6/ 6	4TA 3	0S20	31 54	12N34	1TA55	0S20
6/16	4TA31	0S20	32 22	12N42	2TA 1	0S21
6/26	4TA55	0S21	32 46	12N50	2TA 7	0S22
7/ 6	5TA15	0S22	33 5	12N56	2TA14	0S23
7/16	5TA31	0S23	33 21	13N 0	2TA20	0S23
7/26	5TA41	0S24	33 31	13N 2	2TA26	0S24
8/ 5	5TA46	0S25	33 36	13N 3	2TA33	0S25
8/15	5TA46	0S26	33 36	13N 2	2TA39	0S26
8/25	5TA40	0S27	33 31	12N59	2TA45	0S26
9/ 4	5TA29	0S28	33 20	12N54	2TA51	0S27
9/14	5TA13	0S29	33 5	12N48	2TA58	0S28
9/24	4TA52	0S30	32 46	12N40	3TA 4	0S29
10/ 4	4TA28	0S31	32 23	12N31	3TA10	0S30
10/14	4TA 2	0S32	31 58	12N22	3TA17	0S30
10/24	3TA33	0S33	31 31	12N11	3TA23	0S31
11/ 3	3TA 5	0S34	31 4	12N 1	3TA29	0S32
11/13	2TA37	0S34	30 37	11N51	3TA36	0S33
11/23	2TA12	0S35	30 13	11N41	3TA42	0S33
12/ 3	1TA49	0S36	29 52	11N33	3TA48	0S34
12/13	1TA31	0S36	29 34	11N26	3TA55	0S35
12/23	1TA17	0S37	29 21	11N21	4TA 1	0S36

Stations	Date	Long.	Lat.
DIRECT	1/ 7.20	27AR18	0S 9
RETROGRADE	8/ 9.23	5TA47	0S26

1978

Date	Long.	Lat.	R.A.		Dec.	HLong.	HLat.
1/ 2	1TA 9	0S37	29	14	11N18	4TA 8	0S36
1/12	1TA 6	0S38	29	11	11N16	4TA14	0S37
1/22	1TA10	0S38	29	15	11N17	4TA20	0S38
2/ 1	1TA19	0S38	29	24	11N20	4TA27	0S39
2/11	1TA34	0S39	29	38	11N25	4TA33	0S39
2/21	1TA54	0S39	29	57	11N31	4TA40	0S40
3/ 3	2TA18	0S40	30	21	11N39	4TA46	0S41
3/13	2TA47	0S40	30	48	11N49	4TA52	0S42
3/23	3TA18	0S41	31	19	11N59	4TA59	0S43
4/ 2	3TA53	0S41	31	52	12N10	5TA 5	0S43
4/12	4TA29	0S42	32	27	12N22	5TA12	0S44
4/22	5TA 6	0S42	33	3	12N33	5TA18	0S45
5/ 2	5TA43	0S43	33	40	12N45	5TA25	0S46
5/12	6TA20	0S44	34	16	12N57	5TA31	0S46
5/22	6TA56	0S45	34	51	13N 8	5TA37	0S47
6/ 1	7TA30	0S46	35	24	13N18	5TA44	0S48
6/11	8TA 2	0S47	35	55	13N27	5TA50	0S49
6/21	8TA30	0S48	36	23	13N35	5TA57	0S50
7/ 1	8TA55	0S49	36	48	13N42	6TA 3	0S50
7/11	9TA15	0S50	37	8	13N47	6TA10	0S51
7/21	9TA31	0S51	37	23	13N51	6TA16	0S52
7/31	9TA41	0S53	37	34	13N53	6TA23	0S53
8/10	9TA46	0S54	37	39	13N53	6TA29	0S53
8/20	9TA45	0S55	37	39	13N52	6TA36	0S54
8/30	9TA39	0S57	37	33	13N49	6TA42	0S55
9/ 9	9TA27	0S58	37	22	13N44	6TA49	0S56
9/19	9TA11	0S59	37	7	13N37	6TA55	0S57
9/29	8TA50	1S 0	36	47	13N30	7TA 2	0S57
10/ 9	8TA25	1S 1	36	23	13N21	7TA 9	0S58
10/19	7TA58	1S 2	35	57	13N11	7TA15	0S59
10/29	7TA29	1S 3	35	29	13N 1	7TA22	1S 0
11/ 8	7TA 0	1S 4	35	1	12N51	7TA28	1S 1
11/18	6TA32	1S 5	34	34	12N41	7TA35	1S 1
11/28	6TA 7	1S 5	34	10	12N32	7TA41	1S 2
12/ 8	5TA44	1S 6	33	48	12N24	7TA48	1S 3
12/18	5TA26	1S 6	33	30	12N18	7TA55	1S 4
12/28	5TA12	1S 6	33	18	12N13	8TA 1	1S 4

Stations	Date	Long.	Lat.
DIRECT	1/11.11	1TA 6	0S38
RETROGRADE	8/13.76	9TA46	0S54

Date	Long.	Lat.	R.A.	Dec.	HLong.	HLat.
1/ 7	5TA 5	1S 7	33 10	12N10	8TA 8	1S 5
1/17	5TA 3	1S 7	33 8	12N 9	8TA14	1S 6
1/27	5TA 7	1S 7	33 12	12N11	8TA21	1S 7
2/ 6	5TA17	1S 7	33 22	12N14	8TA28	1S 8
2/16	5TA32	1S 7	33 37	12N19	8TA34	1S 8
2/26	5TA53	1S 7	33 57	12N26	8TA41	1S 9
3/ 8	6TA18	1S 8	34 22	12N34	8TA48	1S10
3/18	6TA48	1S 8	34 50	12N43	8TA54	1S11
3/28	7TA20	1S 8	35 22	12N53	9TA 1	1S12
4/ 7	7TA56	1S 9	35 56	13N 4	9TA 8	1S12
4/17	8TA32	1S 9	36 33	13N15	9TA14	1S13
4/27	9TA10	1S10	37 10	13N27	9TA21	1S14
5/ 7	9TA49	1S11	37 47	13N38	9TA28	1S15
5/17	10TA27	1S12	38 25	13N49	9TA34	1S16
5/27	11TA 3	1S13	39 1	14N 0	9TA41	1S16
6/ 6	11TA38	1S14	39 35	14N 9	9TA48	1S17
6/16	12TA10	1S15	40 7	14N18	9TA55	1S18
6/26	12TA39	1S16	40 36	14N26	10TA 1	1S19
7/ 6	13TA 4	1S17	41 1	14N32	10TA 8	1S20
7/16	13TA24	1S19	41 22	14N37	10TA15	1S20
7/26	13TA40	1S20	41 38	14N40	10TA22	1S21
8/ 5	13TA51	1S22	41 48	14N41	10TA28	1S22
8/15	13TA55	1S24	41 54	14N41	10TA35	1S23
8/25	13TA55	1S25	41 53	14N40	10TA42	1S24
9/ 4	13TA48	1S27	41 47	14N36	10TA49	1S24
9/14	13TA36	1S28	41 36	14N31	10TA55	1S25
9/24	13TA19	1S30	41 20	14N24	11TA 2	1S26
10/ 4	12TA57	1S31	40 59	14N17	11TA 9	1S27
10/14	12TA32	1S33	40 35	14N 8	11TA16	1S28
10/24	12TA 4	1S34	40 8	13N58	11TA23	1S28
11/ 3	11TA35	1S35	39 39	13N48	11TA30	1S29
11/13	11TA 6	1S36	39 10	13N39	11TA36	1S30
11/23	10TA37	1S36	38 43	13N29	11TA43	1S31
12/ 3	10TA11	1S37	38 17	13N21	11TA50	1S32
12/13	9TA48	1S37	37 55	13N13	11TA57	1S32
12/23	9TA30	1S37	37 38	13N 8	12TA 4	1S33

Stations	Date	Long.	Lat.
DIRECT	1/15.11	5TA 3	1S 7
RETROGRADE	8/18.54	13TA56	1S24

1980

Date	Long.	Lat.	R.A.	Dec.	HLong.	HLat.
1/ 2	9TA17	1S37	37 25	13N 3	12TA11	1S34
1/12	9TA10	1S37	37 18	13N 1	12TA18	1S35
1/22	9TA 8	1S37	37 16	13N 1	12TA25	1S36
2/ 1	9TA13	1S37	37 21	13N 2	12TA31	1S37
2/11	9TA24	1S36	37 31	13N 6	12TA38	1S37
2/21	9TA40	1S36	37 47	13N11	12TA45	1S38
3/ 2	10TA 2	1S36	38 8	13N18	12TA52	1S39
3/12	10TA28	1S36	38 34	13N26	12TA59	1S40
3/22	10TA58	1S36	39 3	13N36	13TA 6	1S41
4/ 1	11TA32	1S37	39 36	13N46	13TA13	1S41
4/11	12TA 8	1S37	40 12	13N56	13TA20	1S42
4/21	12TA46	1S37	40 49	14N 7	13TA27	1S43
5/ 1	13TA25	1S38	41 28	14N18	13TA34	1S44
5/11	14TA 4	1S39	42 7	14N29	13TA41	1S45
5/21	14TA43	1S40	42 45	14N40	13TA48	1S46
5/31	15TA20	1S41	43 23	14N50	13TA55	1S46
6/10	15TA56	1S42	43 58	14N59	14TA 2	1S47
6/20	16TA28	1S44	44 31	15N 7	14TA 9	1S48
6/30	16TA58	1S45	45 1	15N14	14TA16	1S49
7/10	17TA24	1S47	45 27	15N19	14TA23	1S50
7/20	17TA45	1S48	45 48	15N23	14TA30	1S51
7/30	18TA 1	1S50	46 5	15N26	14TA37	1S51
8/ 9	18TA11	1S52	46 16	15N27	14TA45	1S52
8/19	18TA16	1S54	46 22	15N27	14TA52	1S53
8/29	18TA16	1S56	46 21	15N24	14TA59	1S54
9/ 8	18TA 9	1S58	46 15	15N21	15TA 6	1S55
9/18	17TA57	2S 0	46 4	15N16	15TA13	1S55
9/28	17TA39	2S 2	45 47	15N 9	15TA20	1S56
10/ 8	17TA17	2S 3	45 25	15N 1	15TA27	1S57
10/18	16TA51	2S 5	45 0	14N53	15TA34	1S58
10/28	16TA23	2S 6	44 32	14N43	15TA42	1S59
11/ 7	15TA53	2S 7	44 3	14N34	15TA49	2S 0
11/17	15TA23	2S 8	43 33	14N24	15TA56	2S 0
11/27	14TA54	2S 8	43 5	14N16	16TA 3	2S 1
12/ 7	14TA27	2S 9	42 39	14N 8	16TA10	2S 2
12/17	14TA 4	2S 9	42 16	14N 1	16TA18	2S 3
12/27	13TA46	2S 9	41 58	13N55	16TA25	2S 4

Stations	Date	Long.	Lat.
DIRECT	1/19.23	9TA 8	1S37
RETROGRADE	8/22.53	18TA17	1S55

Date	Long.	Lat.	R.A.	Dec.	HLong.	HLat.
1/ 6	13TA33	2S 8	41 45	13N52	16TA32	2S 5
1/16	13TA26	2S 8	41 38	13N50	16TA39	2S 6
1/26	13TA25	2S 8	41 37	13N50	16TA46	2S 6
2/ 5	13TA30	2S 7	41 42	13N52	16TA54	2S 7
2/15	13TA41	2S 7	41 53	13N56	17TA 1	2S 8
2/25	13TA59	2S 6	42 10	14N 2	17TA 8	2S 9
3/ 7	14TA21	2S 6	42 32	14N 9	17TA16	2S10
3/17	14TA48	2S 6	42 59	14N17	17TA23	2S11
3/27	15TA20	2S 6	43 29	14N26	17TA30	2S11
4/ 6	15TA54	2S 6	44 4	14N36	17TA38	2S12
4/16	16TA31	2S 6	44 41	14N46	17TA45	2S13
4/26	17TA11	2S 6	45 20	14N57	17TA52	2S14
5/ 6	17TA51	2S 7	46 0	15N 7	18TA 0	2S15
5/16	18TA31	2S 8	46 40	15N17	18TA 7	2S16
5/26	19TA11	2S 9	47 20	15N27	18TA14	2S16
6/ 5	19TA49	2S10	47 59	15N36	18TA22	2S17
6/15	20TA26	2S11	48 36	15N45	18TA29	2S18
6/25	21TA 0	2S13	49 10	15N52	18TA37	2S19
7/ 5	21TA30	2S15	49 41	15N58	18TA44	2S20
7/15	21TA57	2S17	50 8	16N 3	18TA51	2S21
7/25	22TA18	2S19	50 31	16N 7	18TA59	2S22
8/ 4	22TA35	2S21	50 48	16N 9	19TA 6	2S22
8/14	22TA46	2S23	51 0	16N 9	19TA14	2S23
8/24	22TA52	2S26	51 6	16N 8	19TA21	2S24
9/ 3	22TA51	2S28	51 6	16N 6	19TA29	2S25
9/13	22TA44	2S30	51 0	16N 2	19TA36	2S26
9/23	22TA32	2S33	50 48	15N57	19TA44	2S27
10/ 3	22TA14	2S35	50 30	15N50	19TA51	2S28
10/13	21TA51	2S37	50 8	15N43	19TA59	2S28
10/23	21TA25	2S38	49 42	15N34	20TA 6	2S29
11/ 2	20TA55	2S40	49 13	15N25	20TA14	2S30
11/12	20TA25	2S41	48 43	15N16	20TA22	2S31
11/22	19TA54	2S41	48 12	15N 7	20TA29	2S32
12/ 2	19TA24	2S42	47 43	14N59	20TA37	2S33
12/12	18TA57	2S42	47 16	14N52	20TA44	2S34
12/22	18TA34	2S42	46 52	14N45	20TA52	2S34

Stations	Date	Long.	Lat.
DIRECT	1/22.48	13TA24	2S 8
RETROGRADE	8/27.82	22TA52	2S27

1982

Date	Long.	Lat.	R.A.	Dec.	HLong.	HLat.
1/ 1	18TA15	2S41	46 34	14N41	21TA 0	2S35
1/11	18TA 2	2S41	46 21	14N38	21TA 7	2S36
1/21	17TA55	2S40	46 14	14N37	21TA15	2S37
1/31	17TA55	2S39	46 13	14N37	21TA23	2S38
2/10	18TA 0	2S38	46 18	14N40	21TA30	2S39
2/20	18TA13	2S38	46 30	14N44	21TA38	2S40
3/ 2	18TA31	2S37	46 48	14N49	21TA46	2S40
3/12	18TA54	2S36	47 11	14N56	21TA53	2S41
3/22	19TA22	2S36	47 39	15N 4	22TA 1	2S42
4/ 1	19TA55	2S36	48 11	15N13	22TA 9	2S43
4/11	20TA30	2S36	48 47	15N23	22TA17	2S44
4/21	21TA 9	2S36	49 25	15N33	22TA24	2S45
5/ 1	21TA49	2S36	50 6	15N43	22TA32	2S46
5/11	22TA30	2S37	50 48	15N52	22TA40	2S46
5/21	23TA12	2S37	51 30	16N 2	22TA48	2S47
5/31	23TA53	2S39	52 11	16N11	22TA56	2S48
6/10	24TA33	2S40	52 52	16N19	23TA 3	2S49
6/20	25TA11	2S41	53 31	16N27	23TA11	2S50
6/30	25TA46	2S43	54 7	16N33	23TA19	2S51
7/10	26TA18	2S45	54 39	16N39	23TA27	2S52
7/20	26TA45	2S48	55 8	16N43	23TA35	2S53
7/30	27TA 8	2S50	55 31	16N46	23TA43	2S53
8/ 9	27TA26	2S52	55 50	16N47	23TA51	2S54
8/19	27TA38	2S55	56 3	16N47	23TA59	2S55
8/29	27TA43	2S58	56 9	16N46	24TA 7	2S56
9/ 8	27TA43	3S 1	56 9	16N43	24TA15	2S57
9/18	27TA36	3S 3	56 3	16N39	24TA23	2S58
9/28	27TA24	3S 6	55 51	16N34	24TA31	2S59
10/ 8	27TA 6	3S 8	55 33	16N27	24TA39	3S 0
10/18	26TA43	3S11	55 11	16N20	24TA47	3S 0
10/28	26TA16	3S13	54 44	16N12	24TA55	3S 1
11/ 7	25TA46	3S14	54 14	16N 3	25TA 3	3S 2
11/17	25TA14	3S15	53 42	15N55	25TA11	3S 3
11/27	24TA42	3S16	53 10	15N47	25TA19	3S 4
12/ 7	24TA12	3S16	52 40	15N39	25TA27	3S 5
12/17	23TA44	3S16	52 12	15N32	25TA35	3S 6
12/27	23TA20	3S16	51 48	15N27	25TA43	3S 7

Stations	Date	Long.	Lat.
DIRECT	1/26.91	17TA54	2S40
RETROGRADE	9/ 2.45	27TA44	2S59

Date	Long.	Lat.	R.A.	Dec.	HLong.	HLat.
1/ 6	23TA 1	3S15	51 29	15N23	25TA51	3S 7
1/16	22TA48	3S14	51 15	15N20	25TA59	3S 8
1/26	22TA41	3S13	51 8	15N20	26TA 8	3S 9
2/ 5	22TA41	3S12	51 7	15N21	26TA16	3S10
2/15	22TA47	3S11	51 13	15N24	26TA24	3S11
2/25	23TA 0	3S10	51 26	15N28	26TA32	3S12
3/ 7	23TA19	3S 8	51 44	15N34	26TA40	3S13
3/17	23TA43	3S 8	52 8	15N40	26TA49	3S14
3/27	24TA12	3S 7	52 38	15N48	26TA57	3S15
4/ 6	24TA46	3S 6	53 11	15N57	27TA 5	3S15
4/16	25TA23	3S 6	53 49	16N 6	27TA13	3S16
4/26	26TA 3	3S 6	54 29	16N15	27TA22	3S17
5/ 6	26TA44	3S 6	55 11	16N24	27TA30	3S18
5/16	27TA27	3S 7	55 55	16N34	27TA38	3S19
5/26	28TA10	3S 8	56 39	16N42	27TA47	3S20
6/ 5	28TA53	3S 9	57 23	16N50	27TA55	3S21
6/15	29TA34	3S10	58 5	16N58	28TA 3	3S22
6/25	0GE14	3S12	58 46	17N 4	28TA12	3S23
7/ 5	0GE51	3S14	59 24	17N10	28TA20	3S23
7/15	1GE24	3S16	59 58	17N14	28TA29	3S24
7/25	1GE53	3S19	60 28	17N17	28TA37	3S25
8/ 4	2GE17	3S22	60 54	17N19	28TA46	3S26
8/14	2GE36	3S25	61 14	17N20	28TA54	3S27
8/24	2GE49	3S28	61 28	17N20	29TA 3	3S28
9/ 3	2GE55	3S31	61 35	17N18	29TA11	3S29
9/13	2GE56	3S34	61 36	17N15	29TA20	3S30
9/23	2GE50	3S37	61 30	17N10	29TA28	3S31
10/ 3	2GE37	3S40	61 18	17N 5	29TA37	3S31
10/13	2GE19	3S43	61 0	16N59	29TA45	3S32
10/23	1GE55	3S46	60 37	16N52	29TA54	3S33
11/ 2	1GE28	3S48	60 9	16N44	0GE 2	3S34
11/12	0GE57	3S50	59 38	16N36	0GE11	3S35
11/22	0GE25	3S51	59 5	16N28	0GE20	3S36
12/ 2	29TA52	3S52	58 32	16N21	0GE28	3S37
12/12	29TA21	3S52	58 0	16N14	0GE37	3S38
12/22	28TA52	3S52	57 31	16N 8	0GE46	3S39

Stations	Date	Long.	Lat.
DIRECT	1/31.57	22TA40	3S12
RETROGRADE	9/ 8.48	2GE56	3S33

1984

Date	Long.	Lat.	R.A.	Dec.	HLong.	HLat.
1/ 1	28TA27	3S51	57 6	16N 4	0GE54	3S40
1/11	28TA 8	3S50	56 46	16N 0	1GE 3	3S40
1/21	27TA54	3S49	56 32	15N59	1GE12	3S41
1/31	27TA47	3S47	56 24	15N59	1GE21	3S42
2/10	27TA47	3S45	56 24	16N 0	1GE29	3S43
2/20	27TA53	3S44	56 30	16N 3	1GE38	3S44
3/ 1	28TA 6	3S42	56 43	16N 8	1GE47	3S45
3/11	28TA26	3S41	57 2	16N13	1GE56	3S46
3/21	28TA51	3S39	57 27	16N20	2GE 5	3S47
3/31	29TA21	3S38	57 58	16N28	2GE14	3S48
4/10	29TA56	3S38	58 33	16N36	2GE23	3S49
4/20	0GE35	3S37	59 12	16N44	2GE31	3S49
4/30	1GE16	3S37	59 55	16N53	2GE40	3S50
5/10	1GE59	3S37	60 39	17N 1	2GE49	3S51
5/20	2GE44	3S37	61 25	17N 9	2GE58	3S52
5/30	3GE29	3S38	62 11	17N17	3GE 7	3S53
6/ 9	4GE13	3S40	62 57	17N24	3GE16	3S54
6/19	4GE57	3S41	63 42	17N30	3GE25	3S55
6/29	5GE38	3S43	64 25	17N35	3GE34	3S56
7/ 9	6GE17	3S45	65 5	17N40	3GE43	3S57
7/19	6GE52	3S48	65 42	17N43	3GE53	3S58
7/29	7GE23	3S51	66 14	17N45	4GE 2	3S58
8/ 8	7GE49	3S54	66 42	17N46	4GE11	3S59
8/18	8GE 9	3S57	67 3	17N46	4GE20	4S 0
8/28	8GE24	4S 1	67 19	17N45	4GE29	4S 1
9/ 7	8GE32	4S 4	67 28	17N42	4GE38	4S 2
9/17	8GE33	4S 8	67 30	17N39	4GE48	4S 3
9/27	8GE28	4S12	67 25	17N34	4GE57	4S 4
10/ 7	8GE16	4S15	67 13	17N29	5GE 6	4S 5
10/17	7GE58	4S18	66 55	17N23	5GE15	4S 6
10/27	7GE34	4S21	66 31	17N16	5GE25	4S 7
11/ 6	7GE 6	4S24	66 2	17N 9	5GE34	4S 7
11/16	6GE34	4S26	65 30	17N 2	5GE43	4S 8
11/26	6GE 1	4S27	64 56	16N55	5GE53	4S 9
12/ 6	5GE27	4S28	64 22	16N49	6GE 2	4S10
12/16	4GE55	4S28	63 49	16N43	6GE11	4S11
12/26	4GE25	4S28	63 18	16N38	6GE21	4S12

Stations	Date	Long.	Lat.
DIRECT	2/ 5.46	27TA46	3S46
RETROGRADE	9/14.02	8GE33	4S 7

Date	Long.	Lat.	R.A.		Dec.	HLong.	HLat.
1/ 5	3GE59	4S27	62	51	16N35	6GE30	4S13
1/15	3GE39	4S25	62	30	16N32	6GE40	4S14
1/25	3GE24	4S24	62	15	16N31	6GE49	4S15
2/ 4	3GE17	4S22	62	7	16N32	6GE59	4S16
2/14	3GE16	4S20	62	6	16N34	7GE 8	4S17
2/24	3GE23	4S17	62	13	16N37	7GE18	4S17
3/ 6	3GE36	4S15	62	26	16N42	7GE27	4S18
3/16	3GE57	4S13	62	46	16N47	7GE37	4S19
3/26	4GE23	4S12	63	13	16N54	7GE46	4S20
4/ 5	4GE54	4S10	63	45	17N 1	7GE56	4S21
4/15	5GE30	4S 9	64	21	17N 8	8GE 6	4S22
4/25	6GE10	4S 8	65	2	17N16	8GE15	4S23
5/ 5	6GE53	4S 8	65	47	17N23	8GE25	4S24
5/15	7GE38	4S 8	66	33	17N30	8GE35	4S25
5/25	8GE25	4S 8	67	21	17N37	8GE45	4S26
6/ 4	9GE12	4S 9	68	10	17N44	8GE54	4S27
6/14	9GE59	4S10	68	59	17N49	9GE 4	4S27
6/24	10GE44	4S12	69	46	17N54	9GE14	4S28
7/ 4	11GE28	4S14	70	32	17N58	9GE24	4S29
7/14	12GE 9	4S16	71	15	18N 1	9GE34	4S30
7/24	12GE47	4S19	71	54	18N 3	9GE44	4S31
8/ 3	13GE20	4S22	72	29	18N 4	9GE53	4S32
8/13	13GE48	4S26	72	59	18N 3	10GE 3	4S33
8/23	14GE11	4S30	73	23	18N 2	10GE13	4S34
9/ 2	14GE27	4S34	73	41	18N 0	10GE23	4S35
9/12	14GE37	4S38	73	52	17N57	10GE33	4S36
9/22	14GE40	4S42	73	55	17N53	10GE43	4S37
10/ 2	14GE36	4S46	73	51	17N49	10GE53	4S37
10/12	14GE25	4S50	73	40	17N43	11GE 3	4S38
10/22	14GE 7	4S54	73	23	17N38	11GE14	4S39
11/ 1	13GE44	4S57	72	58	17N32	11GE24	4S40
11/11	13GE15	5S 0	72	29	17N25	11GE34	4S41
11/21	12GE43	5S 3	71	56	17N19	11GE44	4S42
12/ 1	12GE 9	5S 4	71	21	17N13	11GE54	4S43
12/11	11GE34	5S 5	70	45	17N 8	12GE 4	4S44
12/21	11GE 0	5S 5	70	10	17N 3	12GE15	4S45
12/31	10GE29	5S 4	69	38	17N 0	12GE25	4S46

Stations	Date	Long.	Lat.
DIRECT	2/ 9.72	3GE16	4S21
RETROGRADE	9/21.09	14GE40	4S42

1986

Date	Long.	Lat.	R.A.	Dec.	HLong.	HLat.
1/10	10GE 1	5S 3	69 10	16N57	12GE35	4S46
1/20	9GE40	5S 1	68 47	16N56	12GE46	4S47
1/30	9GE24	4S59	68 31	16N56	12GE56	4S48
2/ 9	9GE16	4S57	68 22	16N57	13GE 6	4S49
2/19	9GE15	4S54	68 20	16N59	13GE17	4S50
3/ 1	9GE21	4S51	68 27	17N 3	13GE27	4S51
3/11	9GE35	4S49	68 40	17N 8	13GE38	4S52
3/21	9GE56	4S46	69 1	17N13	13GE48	4S53
3/31	10GE22	4S44	69 28	17N19	13GE59	4S54
4/10	10GE55	4S42	70 2	17N25	14GE 9	4S55
4/20	11GE32	4S41	70 40	17N32	14GE20	4S56
4/30	12GE14	4S40	71 23	17N38	14GE30	4S56
5/10	12GE59	4S39	72 10	17N45	14GE41	4S57
5/20	13GE46	4S39	72 59	17N51	14GE52	4S58
5/30	14GE35	4S39	73 49	17N56	15GE 2	4S59
6/ 9	15GE24	4S39	74 41	18N 1	15GE13	5S 0
6/19	16GE14	4S41	75 33	18N 5	15GE24	5S 1
6/29	17GE 2	4S42	76 23	18N 8	15GE35	5S 2
7/ 9	17GE49	4S44	77 12	18N10	15GE45	5S 3
7/19	18GE33	4S47	77 58	18N11	15GE56	5S 4
7/29	19GE13	4S50	78 41	18N11	16GE 7	5S 4
8/ 8	19GE49	4S54	79 19	18N10	16GE18	5S 5
8/18	20GE21	4S57	79 52	18N 9	16GE29	5S 6
8/28	20GE46	5S 2	80 19	18N 6	16GE40	5S 7
9/ 7	21GE 5	5S 6	80 40	18N 3	16GE51	5S 8
9/17	21GE18	5S11	80 53	17N59	17GE 2	5S 9
9/27	21GE23	5S16	80 58	17N55	17GE13	5S10
10/ 7	21GE20	5S20	80 56	17N50	17GE24	5S11
10/17	21GE11	5S25	80 47	17N45	17GE35	5S12
10/27	20GE54	5S29	80 29	17N39	17GE46	5S12
11/ 6	20GE31	5S33	80 6	17N34	17GE57	5S13
11/16	20GE 2	5S36	79 36	17N28	18GE 8	5S14
11/26	19GE30	5S39	79 3	17N23	18GE20	5S15
12/ 6	18GE54	5S41	78 26	17N19	18GE31	5S16
12/16	18GE18	5S42	77 48	17N15	18GE42	5S17
12/26	17GE43	5S42	77 12	17N12	18GE53	5S18

Stations	Date	Long.	Lat.
DIRECT	2/15.33	9GE15	4S55
RETROGRADE	9/28.89	21GE23	5S16

Date	Long.	Lat.	R.A.	Dec.	HLong.	HLat.
1/ 5	17GE10	5S41	76 37	17N10	19GE 5	5S19
1/15	16GE41	5S40	76 7	17N 8	19GE16	5S20
1/25	16GE17	5S38	75 43	17N 8	19GE28	5S20
2/ 4	16GE 1	5S35	75 25	17N 9	19GE39	5S21
2/14	15GE51	5S32	75 15	17N11	19GE50	5S22
2/24	15GE49	5S29	75 12	17N14	20GE 2	5S23
3/ 6	15GE55	5S25	75 18	17N18	20GE13	5S24
3/16	16GE 8	5S22	75 32	17N23	20GE25	5S25
3/26	16GE29	5S19	75 53	17N28	20GE37	5S26
4/ 5	16GE57	5S16	76 21	17N33	20GE48	5S27
4/15	17GE30	5S14	76 56	17N39	21GE 0	5S27
4/25	18GE 9	5S12	77 36	17N44	21GE12	5S28
5/ 5	18GE52	5S10	78 21	17N50	21GE23	5S29
5/15	19GE39	5S 9	79 9	17N54	21GE35	5S30
5/25	20GE28	5S 8	80 1	17N58	21GE47	5S31
6/ 4	21GE19	5S 8	80 55	18N 2	21GE59	5S32
6/14	22GE12	5S 9	81 49	18N 5	22GE11	5S33
6/24	23GE 4	5S10	82 44	18N 6	22GE22	5S33
7/ 4	23GE56	5S11	83 38	18N 7	22GE34	5S34
7/14	24GE46	5S13	84 31	18N 7	22GE46	5S35
7/24	25GE33	5S16	85 21	18N 6	22GE58	5S36
8/ 3	26GE18	5S19	86 7	18N 4	23GE10	5S37
8/13	26GE58	5S23	86 49	18N 1	23GE22	5S38
8/23	27GE33	5S27	87 26	17N58	23GE35	5S39
9/ 2	28GE 2	5S32	87 56	17N54	23GE47	5S39
9/12	28GE25	5S37	88 20	17N49	23GE59	5S40
9/22	28GE40	5S42	88 37	17N44	24GE11	5S41
10/ 2	28GE48	5S47	88 45	17N39	24GE23	5S42
10/12	28GE49	5S53	88 46	17N33	24GE36	5S43
10/22	28GE42	5S58	88 38	17N28	24GE48	5S44
11/ 1	28GE27	6S 3	88 23	17N23	25GE 0	5S44
11/11	28GE 5	6S 7	88 0	17N18	25GE13	5S45
11/21	27GE36	6S11	87 31	17N14	25GE25	5S46
12/ 1	27GE 4	6S14	86 56	17N10	25GE37	5S47
12/11	26GE27	6S17	86 19	17N 7	25GE50	5S48
12/21	25GE50	6S18	85 40	17N 5	26GE 2	5S49
12/31	25GE12	6S18	85 1	17N 4	26GE15	5S49

Stations		Date	Long.	Lat.
DIRECT		2/21.48	15GE49	5S29
RETROGRADE		10/ 7.53	28GE50	5S50

1988

Date	Long.	Lat.	R.A.	Dec.	HLong.	HLat.
1/10	24GE37	6S17	84 24	17N 3	26GE28	5S50
1/20	24GE 6	6S15	83 52	17N 4	26GE40	5S51
1/30	23GE41	6S13	83 25	17N 5	26GE53	5S52
2/ 9	23GE22	6S10	83 5	17N 7	27GE 6	5S53
2/19	23GE10	6S 6	82 53	17N10	27GE19	5S53
2/29	23GE 7	6S 2	82 50	17N14	27GE31	5S54
3/10	23GE11	5S58	82 54	17N18	27GE44	5S55
3/20	23GE24	5S54	83 7	17N23	27GE57	5S56
3/30	23GE45	5S50	83 29	17N28	28GE10	5S57
4/ 9	24GE12	5S47	83 57	17N33	28GE23	5S57
4/19	24GE47	5S43	84 33	17N37	28GE36	5S58
4/29	25GE26	5S41	85 14	17N41	28GE49	5S59
5/ 9	26GE11	5S39	86 1	17N45	29GE 2	6S 0
5/19	27GE 0	5S37	86 52	17N48	29GE15	6S 1
5/29	27GE52	5S36	87 46	17N50	29GE28	6S 1
6/ 8	28GE46	5S35	88 43	17N51	29GE42	6S 2
6/18	29GE41	5S36	89 41	17N51	29GE55	6S 3
6/28	0CN37	5S36	90 39	17N50	0CN 8	6S 4
7/ 8	1CN33	5S38	91 37	17N48	0CN21	6S 5
7/18	2CN27	5S40	92 33	17N45	0CN35	6S 5
7/28	3CN19	5S42	93 27	17N42	0CN48	6S 6
8/ 7	4CN 7	5S46	94 18	17N37	1CN 2	6S 7
8/17	4CN52	5S50	95 5	17N32	1CN15	6S 8
8/27	5CN32	5S54	95 46	17N26	1CN29	6S 8
9/ 6	6CN 6	5S59	96 21	17N20	1CN42	6S 9
9/16	6CN33	6S 4	96 49	17N13	1CN56	6S10
9/26	6CN53	6S10	97 10	17N 6	2CN 9	6S11
10/ 6	7CN 6	6S16	97 23	17N 0	2CN23	6S11
10/16	7CN10	6S22	97 27	16N54	2CN37	6S12
10/26	7CN 6	6S28	97 22	16N48	2CN51	6S13
11/ 5	6CN54	6S33	97 9	16N43	3CN 5	6S14
11/15	6CN34	6S38	96 48	16N39	3CN18	6S14
11/25	6CN 7	6S43	96 20	16N35	3CN32	6S15
12/ 5	5CN34	6S47	95 47	16N33	3CN46	6S16
12/15	4CN58	6S49	95 8	16N32	4CN 0	6S16
12/25	4CN19	6S51	94 28	16N32	4CN14	6S17

Uranus

Venus

Stations	Date	Long.	Lat.
DIRECT	2/28.20	23GE 7	6S 2
RETROGRADE	10/16.14	7CN10	6S22

1989

Venus

Date	Long.	Lat.	R.A.	Dec.	HLong.	HLat.
1/ 4	3CN40	6S51	93 47	16N33	4CN29	6S18
1/14	3CN 2	6S50	93 9	16N34	4CN43	6S19
1/24	2CN28	6S48	92 34	16N37	4CN57	6S19
2/ 3	2CN 0	6S45	92 4	16N40	5CN11	6S20
2/13	1CN38	6S42	91 41	16N44	5CN25	6S21
2/23	1CN24	6S37	91 27	16N49	5CN40	6S21
3/ 5	1CN18	6S33	91 21	16N53	5CN54	6S22
3/15	1CN21	6S28	91 24	16N58	6CN 9	6S23
3/25	1CN32	6S23	91 36	17N 3	6CN23	6S23
4/ 4	1CN52	6S19	91 56	17N 7	6CN38	6S24
4/14	2CN19	6S14	92 25	17N11	6CN52	6S25
4/24	2CN54	6S10	93 1	17N14	7CN 7	6S25
5/ 4	3CN34	6S 7	93 43	17N17	7CN21	6S26
5/14	4CN20	6S 4	94 31	17N19	7CN36	6S27
5/24	5CN11	6S 1	95 24	17N19	7CN51	6S27
6/ 3	6CN 5	6S 0	96 21	17N19	8CN 6	6S28
6/13	7CN 3	5S59	97 20	17N17	8CN21	6S29
6/23	8CN 1	5S58	98 22	17N14	8CN36	6S29
7/ 3	9CN 1	5S59	99 24	17N10	8CN51	6S30
7/13	10CN 1	6S 0	100 26	17N 5	9CN 6	6S31
7/23	11CN 0	6S 2	101 26	16N59	9CN21	6S31
8/ 2	11CN57	6S 4	102 25	16N52	9CN36	6S32
8/12	12CN51	6S 7	103 21	16N44	9CN51	6S32
8/22	13CN41	6S11	104 12	16N35	10CN 6	6S33
9/ 1	14CN27	6S15	104 59	16N26	10CN21	6S34
9/11	15CN 7	6S20	105 39	16N17	10CN37	6S34
9/21	15CN40	6S26	106 13	16N 8	10CN52	6S35
10/ 1	16CN 6	6S32	106 40	15N59	11CN 8	6S35
10/11	16CN24	6S38	106 57	15N51	11CN23	6S36
10/21	16CN34	6S45	107 7	15N43	11CN39	6S36
10/31	16CN35	6S51	107 7	15N37	11CN54	6S37
11/10	16CN27	6S57	106 58	15N31	12CN10	6S38
11/20	16CN10	7S 3	106 40	15N27	12CN25	6S38
11/30	15CN46	7S 8	106 14	15N25	12CN41	6S39
12/10	15CN15	7S13	105 42	15N24	12CN57	6S39
12/20	14CN38	7S16	105 4	15N25	13CN13	6S40
12/30	13CN59	7S18	104 24	15N27	13CN29	6S40

Stations	Date	Long.	Lat.
DIRECT	3/ 6.72	1CN18	6S32
RETROGRADE	10/26.98	16CN36	6S49

1990

Date	Long.	Lat.	R.A.	Dec.	HLong.	HLat.
1/ 9	13CN18	7S19	103 41	15N30	13CN45	6S41
1/19	12CN37	7S18	103 0	15N34	14CN 1	6S41
1/29	12CN 0	7S16	102 22	15N40	14CN17	6S42
2/ 8	11CN28	7S13	101 49	15N45	14CN33	6S42
2/18	11CN 2	7S 9	101 23	15N51	14CN49	6S43
2/28	10CN44	7S 4	101 5	15N58	15CN 5	6S43
3/10	10CN35	6S59	100 56	16N 4	15CN22	6S44
3/20	10CN35	6S53	100 57	16N 9	15CN38	6S44
3/30	10CN44	6S47	101 6	16N14	15CN54	6S45
4/ 9	11CN 2	6S42	101 25	16N19	16CN11	6S45
4/19	11CN28	6S36	101 53	16N22	16CN27	6S46
4/29	12CN 2	6S31	102 28	16N24	16CN44	6S46
5/ 9	12CN43	6S27	103 11	16N25	17CN 0	6S46
5/19	13CN30	6S23	104 0	16N24	17CN17	6S47
5/29	14CN22	6S20	104 54	16N22	17CN34	6S47
6/ 8	15CN19	6S17	105 53	16N19	17CN51	6S48
6/18	16CN19	6S16	106 55	16N14	18CN 8	6S48
6/28	17CN22	6S14	107 59	16N 7	18CN24	6S48
7/ 8	18CN26	6S14	109 5	16N 0	18CN41	6S49
7/18	19CN30	6S15	110 11	15N51	18CN58	6S49
7/28	20CN34	6S16	111 16	15N40	19CN16	6S49
8/ 7	21CN37	6S18	112 20	15N29	19CN33	6S50
8/17	22CN37	6S20	113 21	15N17	19CN50	6S50
8/27	23CN34	6S24	114 18	15N 5	20CN 7	6S51
9/ 6	24CN27	6S28	115 11	14N52	20CN25	6S51
9/16	25CN14	6S33	115 58	14N39	20CN42	6S51
9/26	25CN55	6S38	116 38	14N26	20CN59	6S51
10/ 6	26CN29	6S44	117 11	14N14	21CN17	6S52
10/16	26CN55	6S51	117 36	14N 3	21CN34	6S52
10/26	27CN12	6S58	117 51	13N53	21CN52	6S52
11/ 5	27CN19	7S 4	117 58	13N45	22CN10	6S53
11/15	27CN18	7S11	117 55	13N39	22CN28	6S53
11/25	27CN 6	7S18	117 42	13N35	22CN45	6S53
12/ 5	26CN46	7S24	117 21	13N33	23CN 3	6S53
12/15	26CN18	7S29	116 52	13N33	23CN21	6S54
12/25	25CN43	7S33	116 16	13N35	23CN39	6S54

Stations	Date	Long.	Lat.
DIRECT	3/15.21	10CN34	6S56
RETROGRADE	11/ 8.18	27CN20	7S 7

Date	Long.	Lat.	R.A.	Dec.	HLong.	HLat.
1/ 4	25CN 4	7S35	115 36	13N39	23CN57	6S54
1/14	24CN21	7S36	114 53	13N45	24CN15	6S54
1/24	23CN39	7S36	114 10	13N53	24CN34	6S54
2/ 3	22CN58	7S34	113 29	14N 1	24CN52	6S55
2/13	22CN21	7S31	112 53	14N10	25CN10	6S55
2/23	21CN51	7S27	112 23	14N19	25CN29	6S55
3/ 5	21CN28	7S22	112 1	14N27	25CN47	6S55
3/15	21CN14	7S16	111 47	14N35	26CN 6	6S55
3/25	21CN 9	7S 9	111 43	14N42	26CN24	6S55
4/ 4	21CN14	7S 2	111 49	14N48	26CN43	6S55
4/14	21CN28	6S56	112 5	14N53	27CN 2	6S55
4/24	21CN52	6S49	112 30	14N55	27CN20	6S55
5/ 4	22CN25	6S43	113 4	14N56	27CN39	6S56
5/14	23CN 5	6S38	113 46	14N55	27CN58	6S56
5/24	23CN52	6S33	114 35	14N53	28CN17	6S56
6/ 3	24CN45	6S29	115 29	14N48	28CN36	6S56
6/13	25CN44	6S25	116 29	14N41	28CN55	6S56
6/23	26CN46	6S22	117 33	14N33	29CN14	6S56
7/ 3	27CN52	6S20	118 40	14N23	29CN34	6S56
7/13	29CN 0	6S19	119 48	14N11	29CN53	6S56
7/23	0LE 9	6S18	120 58	13N57	0LE12	6S56
8/ 2	1LE19	6S19	122 8	13N42	0LE32	6S56
8/12	2LE28	6S20	123 16	13N27	0LE51	6S56
8/22	3LE35	6S22	124 23	13N10	1LE11	6S55
9/ 1	4LE40	6S24	125 26	12N52	1LE31	6S55
9/11	5LE40	6S28	126 25	12N35	1LE50	6S55
9/21	6LE36	6S32	127 20	12N17	2LE10	6S55
10/ 1	7LE26	6S37	128 8	12N 1	2LE30	6S55
10/11	8LE10	6S42	128 49	11N44	2LE50	6S55
10/21	8LE45	6S49	129 22	11N30	3LE10	6S55
10/31	9LE11	6S55	129 46	11N17	3LE30	6S55
11/10	9LE29	7S 2	130 1	11N 6	3LE50	6S54
11/20	9LE36	7S 9	130 6	10N57	4LE10	6S54
11/30	9LE33	7S16	130 1	10N51	4LE31	6S54
12/10	9LE19	7S22	129 47	10N49	4LE51	6S54
12/20	8LE57	7S27	129 23	10N49	5LE11	6S54
12/30	8LE26	7S32	128 52	10N52	5LE32	6S53

Stations	Date	Long.	Lat.
DIRECT	3/24.85	21CN 9	7S 9
RETROGRADE	11/21.96	9LE36	7S10

1992

Date	Long.	Lat.	R.A.		Dec.	HLong.	HLat.
1/ 9	7LE49	7S35	128	14	10N58	5LE52	6S53
1/19	7LE 6	7S37	127	33	11N 7	6LE13	6S53
1/29	6LE22	7S38	126	49	11N17	6LE34	6S52
2/ 8	5LE38	7S36	126	6	11N29	6LE54	6S52
2/18	4LE57	7S33	125	26	11N41	7LE15	6S52
2/28	4LE20	7S29	124	51	11N54	7LE36	6S51
3/ 9	3LE51	7S24	124	24	12N 6	7LE57	6S51
3/19	3LE30	7S17	124	5	12N16	8LE18	6S51
3/29	3LE19	7S10	123	56	12N26	8LE39	6S50
4/ 8	3LE18	7S 3	123	56	12N33	9LE 1	6S50
4/18	3LE28	6S55	124	7	12N39	9LE22	6S49
4/28	3LE47	6S48	124	28	12N41	9LE43	6S49
5/ 8	4LE15	6S41	124	58	12N42	10LE 5	6S48
5/18	4LE53	6S34	125	37	12N40	10LE26	6S48
5/28	5LE39	6S28	126	24	12N35	10LE48	6S47
6/ 7	6LE32	6S22	127	17	12N28	11LE 9	6S47
6/17	7LE30	6S18	128	16	12N18	11LE31	6S46
6/27	8LE35	6S14	129	21	12N 6	11LE53	6S46
7/ 7	9LE43	6S10	130	29	11N52	12LE15	6S45
7/17	10LE54	6S 8	131	39	11N36	12LE36	6S45
7/27	12LE 8	6S 6	132	52	11N18	12LE58	6S44
8/ 6	13LE23	6S 5	134	5	10N58	13LE20	6S43
8/16	14LE38	6S 5	135	18	10N37	13LE43	6S43
8/26	15LE52	6S 5	136	30	10N15	14LE 5	6S42
9/ 5	17LE 5	6S 7	137	39	9N53	14LE27	6S41
9/15	18LE14	6S 9	138	46	9N30	14LE49	6S41
9/25	19LE20	6S12	139	47	9N 7	15LE12	6S40
10/ 5	20LE20	6S16	140	44	8N45	15LE34	6S39
10/15	21LE14	6S20	141	34	8N24	15LE57	6S38
10/25	22LE 1	6S26	142	17	8N 5	16LE20	6S38
11/ 4	22LE39	6S31	142	51	7N48	16LE42	6S37
11/14	23LE 8	6S37	143	17	7N33	17LE 5	6S36
11/24	23LE26	6S44	143	33	7N21	17LE28	6S35
12/ 4	23LE34	6S50	143	38	7N12	17LE51	6S34
12/14	23LE32	6S56	143	34	7N 7	18LE14	6S33
12/24	23LE18	7S 2	143	19	7N 6	18LE37	6S32

Stations	Date	Long.	Lat.
DIRECT	4/ 4.00	3LE17	7S 6
RETROGRADE	12/ 6.39	23LE35	6S51

Date	Long.	Lat.	R.A.		Dec.	HLong.	HLat.
1/ 3	22LE55	7S 7	142	55	7N 9	19LE 0	6S32
1/13	22LE22	7S10	142	23	7N16	19LE23	6S31
1/23	21LE43	7S13	141	45	7N25	19LE46	6S30
2/ 2	21LE 0	7S14	141	3	7N38	20LE10	6S29
2/12	20LE14	7S13	140	20	7N53	20LE33	6S28
2/22	19LE28	7S11	139	37	8N 9	20LE57	6S27
3/ 4	18LE46	7S 7	138	58	8N25	21LE20	6S26
3/14	18LE10	7S 2	138	25	8N41	21LE44	6S25
3/24	17LE41	6S56	137	59	8N56	22LE 7	6S23
4/ 3	17LE21	6S49	137	43	9N 8	22LE31	6S22
4/13	17LE12	6S41	137	36	9N18	22LE55	6S21
4/23	17LE13	6S33	137	39	9N26	23LE19	6S20
5/ 3	17LE25	6S25	137	53	9N30	23LE43	6S19
5/13	17LE47	6S17	138	17	9N31	24LE 7	6S18
5/23	18LE20	6S 9	138	51	9N29	24LE31	6S16
6/ 2	19LE 1	6S 2	139	33	9N23	24LE55	6S15
6/12	19LE51	5S55	140	23	9N14	25LE20	6S14
6/22	20LE48	5S49	141	19	9N 2	25LE44	6S13
7/ 2	21LE52	5S44	142	22	8N48	26LE 8	6S11
7/12	23LE 1	5S39	143	29	8N30	26LE33	6S10
7/22	24LE14	5S35	144	40	8N10	26LE57	6S 9
8/ 1	25LE31	5S32	145	54	7N48	27LE22	6S 7
8/11	26LE50	5S30	147	9	7N24	27LE46	6S 6
8/21	28LE10	5S28	148	26	6N59	28LE11	6S 4
8/31	29LE30	5S27	149	42	6N32	28LE36	6S 3
9/10	0VI50	5S27	150	57	6N 5	29LE 1	6S 1
9/20	2VI 8	5S27	152	10	5N37	29LE26	6S 0
9/30	3VI23	5S29	153	19	5N 9	29LE51	5S58
10/10	4VI33	5S31	154	24	4N42	0VI16	5S57
10/20	5VI39	5S33	155	24	4N16	0VI41	5S55
10/30	6VI37	5S37	156	17	3N52	1VI 6	5S54
11/ 9	7VI29	5S41	157	4	3N29	1VI31	5S52
11/19	8VI11	5S45	157	41	3N10	1VI57	5S51
11/29	8VI44	5S50	158	10	2N53	2VI22	5S49
12/ 9	9VI 6	5S55	158	28	2N41	2VI47	5S47
12/19	9VI16	6S 0	158	36	2N32	3VI13	5S46
12/29	9VI16	6S 4	158	34	2N28	3VI38	5S44

Stations	Date	Long.	Lat.
DIRECT	4/16.89	17LE11	6S38
RETROGRADE	12/23.35	9VI17	6S 2

1994

Date	Long.	Lat.	R.A.	Dec.	HLong.	HLat.
1/ 8	9VI 4	6S 9	158 21	2N28	4VI 4	5S42
1/18	8VI41	6S12	157 59	2N33	4VI30	5S40
1/28	8VI 9	6S15	157 28	2N43	4VI55	5S38
2/ 7	7VI30	6S16	156 51	2N56	5VI21	5S37
2/17	6VI45	6S16	156 10	3N12	5VI47	5S35
2/27	5VI58	6S15	155 27	3N30	6VI13	5S33
3/ 9	5VI12	6S12	154 45	3N50	6VI39	5S31
3/19	4VI28	6S 7	154 6	4N10	7VI 5	5S29
3/29	3VI51	6S 2	153 34	4N28	7VI31	5S27
4/ 8	3VI21	5S55	153 8	4N45	7VI57	5S25
4/18	3VI 1	5S48	152 52	4N59	8VI23	5S23
4/28	2VI52	5S40	152 46	5N10	8VI50	5S21
5/ 8	2VI53	5S32	152 50	5N17	9VI16	5S19
5/18	3VI 6	5S23	153 5	5N20	9VI42	5S17
5/28	3VI29	5S15	153 30	5N19	10VI 9	5S15
6/ 7	4VI 3	5S 8	154 4	5N15	10VI35	5S13
6/17	4VI46	5S 0	154 47	5N 6	11VI 2	5S11
6/27	5VI38	4S54	155 38	4N54	11VI28	5S 9
7/ 7	6VI38	4S47	156 36	4N38	11VI55	5S 7
7/17	7VI44	4S42	157 40	4N19	12VI22	5S 4
7/27	8VI56	4S37	158 48	3N57	12VI48	5S 2
8/ 6	10VI13	4S32	160 1	3N32	13VI15	5S 0
8/16	11VI33	4S28	161 17	3N 5	13VI42	4S58
8/26	12VI56	4S25	162 35	2N37	14VI 9	4S56
9/ 5	14VI21	4S23	163 54	2N 7	14VI36	4S53
9/15	15VI46	4S21	165 13	1N36	15VI 3	4S51
9/25	17VI10	4S20	166 31	1N 5	15VI30	4S49
10/ 5	18VI33	4S19	167 47	0N33	15VI57	4S46
10/15	19VI52	4S19	169 0	0N 3	16VI24	4S44
10/25	21VI 8	4S19	170 9	0S27	16VI51	4S41
11/ 4	22VI18	4S20	171 13	0S56	17VI18	4S39
11/14	23VI22	4S22	172 11	1S23	17VI46	4S37
11/24	24VI18	4S24	173 2	1S46	18VI13	4S34
12/ 4	25VI 5	4S26	173 44	2S 7	18VI40	4S32
12/14	25VI42	4S29	174 17	2S24	19VI 7	4S29
12/24	26VI 8	4S31	174 40	2S37	19VI35	4S27

Stations	Date	Long.	Lat.
DIRECT	5/ 1.74	2VI51	5S37

Date	Long.	Lat.	R.A.	Dec.	HLong.	HLat.
1/ 3	26VI23	4S34	174 52	2S45	20VI 2	4S24
1/13	26VI26	4S37	174 54	2S49	20VI30	4S21
1/23	26VI17	4S39	174 45	2S47	20VI57	4S19
2/ 2	25VI57	4S41	174 26	2S41	21VI25	4S16
2/12	25VI27	4S41	173 58	2S30	21VI52	4S14
2/22	24VI49	4S41	173 23	2S15	22VI20	4S11
3/ 4	24VI 5	4S40	172 43	1S56	22VI48	4S 8
3/14	23VI18	4S38	172 1	1S35	23VI15	4S 6
3/24	22VI30	4S34	171 19	1S14	23VI43	4S 3
4/ 3	21VI46	4S30	170 40	0S52	24VI11	4S 0
4/13	21VI 7	4S24	170 6	0S32	24VI38	3S57
4/23	20VI35	4S18	169 39	0S13	25VI 6	3S55
5/ 3	20VI13	4S11	169 22	0N 2	25VI34	3S52
5/13	20VI 1	4S 4	169 14	0N13	26VI 2	3S49
5/23	20VI 0	3S57	169 16	0N20	26VI30	3S46
6/ 2	20VI11	3S49	169 29	0N22	26VI57	3S43
6/12	20VI33	3S42	169 52	0N20	27VI25	3S40
6/22	21VI 6	3S35	170 24	0N14	27VI53	3S38
7/ 2	21VI48	3S28	171 6	0N 4	28VI21	3S35
7/12	22VI40	3S22	171 56	0S11	28VI49	3S32
7/22	23VI39	3S16	172 53	0S29	29VI17	3S29
8/ 1	24VI46	3S11	173 56	0S51	29VI45	3S26
8/11	25VI59	3S 6	175 5	1S15	0LI13	3S23
8/21	27VI17	3S 2	176 18	1S42	0LI41	3S20
8/31	28VI39	2S58	177 35	2S11	1LI 9	3S17
9/10	0LI 4	2S54	178 54	2S41	1LI37	3S14
9/20	1LI30	2S51	180 15	3S13	2LI 5	3S11
9/30	2LI58	2S48	181 36	3S45	2LI34	3S 8
10/10	4LI25	2S46	182 57	4S17	3LI 2	3S 5
10/20	5LI50	2S44	184 16	4S50	3LI30	3S 2
10/30	7LI13	2S42	185 33	5S21	3LI58	2S59
11/ 9	8LI32	2S41	186 46	5S51	4LI26	2S56
11/19	9LI46	2S40	187 55	6S19	4LI54	2S53
11/29	10LI53	2S40	188 57	6S45	5LI22	2S50
12/ 9	11LI53	2S39	189 53	7S 9	5LI50	2S46
12/19	12LI44	2S39	190 40	7S28	6LI19	2S43
12/29	13LI25	2S39	191 19	7S44	6LI47	2S40

Stations	Date	Long.	Lat.
RETROGRADE	1/10.38	26VI26	4S36
DIRECT	5/18.52	19VI59	4S 0

1996

Date	Long.	Lat.	R.A.		Dec.	HLong.	HLat.
1/ 8	13LI55	2S39	191	47	7S56	7LI15	2S37
1/18	14LI14	2S39	192	4	8S 3	7LI43	2S34
1/28	14LI21	2S39	192	10	8S 6	8LI11	2S31
2/ 7	14LI16	2S38	192	6	8S 3	8LI39	2S27
2/17	13LI59	2S37	191	51	7S56	9LI 8	2S24
2/27	13LI32	2S36	191	26	7S44	9LI36	2S21
3/ 8	12LI56	2S34	190	53	7S29	10LI 4	2S18
3/18	12LI14	2S32	190	15	7S10	10LI32	2S15
3/28	11LI28	2S29	189	33	6S49	11LI 0	2S11
4/ 7	10LI40	2S25	188	51	6S27	11LI28	2S 8
4/17	9LI55	2S21	188	11	6S 5	11LI56	2S 5
4/27	9LI14	2S16	187	35	5S44	12LI25	2S 2
5/ 7	8LI39	2S11	187	5	5S26	12LI53	1S58
5/17	8LI14	2S 6	186	44	5S11	13LI21	1S55
5/27	7LI59	2S 0	186	32	5S 0	13LI49	1S52
6/ 6	7LI55	1S54	186	31	4S53	14LI17	1S48
6/16	8LI 2	1S49	186	39	4S51	14LI45	1S45
6/26	8LI20	1S43	186	58	4S53	15LI13	1S42
7/ 6	8LI49	1S38	187	27	5S 0	15LI41	1S39
7/16	9LI28	1S33	188	5	5S11	16LI 9	1S35
7/26	10LI17	1S28	188	52	5S26	16LI37	1S32
8/ 5	11LI14	1S24	189	47	5S44	17LI 5	1S29
8/15	12LI19	1S20	190	48	6S 5	17LI33	1S25
8/25	13LI30	1S15	191	55	6S29	18LI 1	1S22
9/ 4	14LI46	1S12	193	8	6S55	18LI29	1S19
9/14	16LI 7	1S 8	194	24	7S23	18LI57	1S15
9/24	17LI31	1S 5	195	44	7S52	19LI25	1S12
10/ 4	18LI57	1S 2	197	5	8S22	19LI52	1S 9
10/14	20LI24	0S58	198	28	8S52	20LI20	1S 5
10/24	21LI51	0S56	199	51	9S22	20LI48	1S 2
11/ 3	23LI17	0S53	201	13	9S52	21LI16	0S59
11/13	24LI40	0S50	202	32	10S20	21LI44	0S55
11/23	26LI 0	0S48	203	49	10S47	22LI11	0S52
12/ 3	27LI15	0S45	205	1	11S12	22LI39	0S49
12/13	28LI24	0S43	206	7	11S34	23LI 7	0S45
12/23	29LI25	0S40	207	7	11S53	23LI34	0S42

Stations	Date	Long.	Lat.
RETROGRADE	1/28.62	14LI21	2S39
DIRECT	6/ 4.75	7LI55	1S55

Date	Long.	Lat.	R.A.	Dec.	HLong.	HLat.
1/ 2	0SC18	0S37	207 58	12S10	24LI 2	0S39
1/12	1SC 1	0S35	208 41	12S22	24LI29	0S35
1/22	1SC34	0S32	209 13	12S31	24LI57	0S32
2/ 1	1SC55	0S29	209 34	12S36	25LI24	0S29
2/11	2SC 5	0S27	209 45	12S37	25LI52	0S25
2/21	2SC 2	0S23	209 44	12S33	26LI19	0S22
3/ 3	1SC49	0S20	209 32	12S25	26LI47	0S19
3/13	1SC25	0S17	209 10	12S14	27LI14	0S15
3/23	0SC52	0S13	208 39	11S59	27LI41	0S12
4/ 2	0SC12	0S10	208 2	11S42	28LI 9	0S 9
4/12	29LI27	0S 6	207 21	11S22	28LI36	0S 5
4/22	28LI40	0S 2	206 38	11S 2	29LI 3	0S 2
5/ 2	27LI54	0N 1	205 55	10S43	29LI30	0N 1
5/12	27LI12	0N 5	205 17	10S24	29LI57	0N 4
5/22	26LI36	0N 9	204 44	10S 8	0SC24	0N 8
6/ 1	26LI 8	0N12	204 18	9S54	0SC51	0N11
6/11	25LI49	0N15	204 2	9S44	1SC18	0N14
6/21	25LI41	0N19	203 55	9S38	1SC45	0N18
7/ 1	25LI44	0N22	203 59	9S36	2SC12	0N21
7/11	25LI57	0N25	204 13	9S39	2SC39	0N24
7/21	26LI22	0N27	204 37	9S45	3SC 5	0N27
7/31	26LI56	0N30	205 11	9S55	3SC32	0N31
8/10	27LI40	0N33	205 53	10S 8	3SC59	0N34
8/20	28LI33	0N35	206 44	10S25	4SC25	0N37
8/30	29LI33	0N38	207 43	10S44	4SC52	0N40
9/ 9	0SC40	0N40	208 48	11S 5	5SC19	0N43
9/19	1SC53	0N43	209 58	11S28	5SC45	0N47
9/29	3SC10	0N45	211 13	11S52	6SC11	0N50
10/ 9	4SC31	0N48	212 32	12S17	6SC38	0N53
10/19	5SC54	0N51	213 53	12S42	7SC 4	0N56
10/29	7SC19	0N53	215 16	13S 7	7SC30	0N59
11/ 8	8SC43	0N56	216 39	13S31	7SC57	1N 2
11/18	10SC 7	0N59	218 1	13S55	8SC23	1N 6
11/28	11SC28	1N 2	219 22	14S17	8SC49	1N 9
12/ 8	12SC46	1N 6	220 40	14S37	9SC15	1N12
12/18	13SC59	1N 9	221 53	14S56	9SC41	1N15
12/28	15SC 6	1N13	223 1	15S12	10SC 7	1N18

Stations	Date	Long.	Lat.
RETROGRADE	2/14.12	2SC 5	0S26
DIRECT	6/23.60	25LI41	0N19

1998

Date	Long.	Lat.	R.A.	Dec.	HLong.	HLat.
1/ 7	16SC 6	1N17	224 2	15S25	10SC33	1N21
1/17	16SC58	1N22	224 54	15S36	10SC58	1N24
1/27	17SC41	1N26	225 38	15S44	11SC24	1N27
2/ 6	18SC14	1N31	226 12	15S48	11SC50	1N30
2/16	18SC35	1N36	226 35	15S50	12SC15	1N33
2/26	18SC46	1N41	226 47	15S48	12SC41	1N36
3/ 8	18SC45	1N46	226 48	15S43	13SC 6	1N39
3/18	18SC33	1N51	226 37	15S34	13SC32	1N42
3/28	18SC11	1N55	226 16	15S24	13SC57	1N45
4/ 7	17SC40	2N 0	225 47	15S11	14SC23	1N48
4/17	17SC 2	2N 5	225 10	14S56	14SC48	1N51
4/27	16SC19	2N 9	224 29	14S40	15SC13	1N54
5/ 7	15SC33	2N12	223 45	14S23	15SC38	1N57
5/17	14SC48	2N15	223 2	14S 8	16SC 3	2N 0
5/27	14SC 6	2N18	222 21	13S53	16SC28	2N 3
6/ 6	13SC29	2N20	221 45	13S40	16SC53	2N 6
6/16	12SC59	2N21	221 16	13S30	17SC18	2N 9
6/26	12SC38	2N22	220 56	13S22	17SC43	2N12
7/ 6	12SC27	2N23	220 45	13S18	18SC 8	2N14
7/16	12SC26	2N23	220 44	13S17	18SC32	2N17
7/26	12SC35	2N24	220 53	13S20	18SC57	2N20
8/ 5	12SC55	2N24	221 13	13S26	19SC21	2N23
8/15	13SC25	2N24	221 42	13S34	19SC46	2N26
8/25	14SC 4	2N24	222 21	13S46	20SC10	2N29
9/ 4	14SC52	2N25	223 8	13S59	20SC35	2N31
9/14	15SC48	2N25	224 3	14S15	20SC59	2N34
9/24	16SC50	2N26	225 5	14S32	21SC23	2N37
10/ 4	17SC58	2N27	226 13	14S50	21SC47	2N39
10/14	19SC11	2N28	227 25	15S 9	22SC11	2N42
10/24	20SC27	2N30	228 42	15S27	22SC35	2N45
11/ 3	21SC46	2N31	230 1	15S46	22SC59	2N47
11/13	23SC 6	2N34	231 22	16S 4	23SC23	2N50
11/23	24SC26	2N36	232 44	16S21	23SC47	2N53
12/ 3	25SC45	2N39	234 5	16S37	24SC11	2N55
12/13	27SC 2	2N42	235 24	16S52	24SC34	2N58
12/23	28SC16	2N46	236 40	17S 5	24SC58	3N 1

Stations	Date	Long.	Lat.
RETROGRADE	3/ 2.15	18SC47	1N43
DIRECT	7/12.00	12SC25	2N23

Date	Long.	Lat.	R.A.	Dec.	HLong.	HLat.
1/ 2	29SC25	2N50	237 51	17S15	25SC22	3N 3
1/12	0SA29	2N55	238 57	17S24	25SC45	3N 6
1/22	1SA25	3N 0	239 56	17S31	26SC 8	3N 8
2/ 1	2SA14	3N 5	240 47	17S35	26SC32	3N11
2/11	2SA54	3N10	241 29	17S37	26SC55	3N13
2/21	3SA24	3N16	242 2	17S37	27SC18	3N16
3/ 3	3SA44	3N22	242 23	17S35	27SC41	3N18
3/13	3SA53	3N29	242 34	17S31	28SC 4	3N21
3/23	3SA51	3N35	242 33	17S24	28SC27	3N23
4/ 2	3SA39	3N41	242 22	17S16	28SC50	3N26
4/12	3SA17	3N47	242 1	17S 6	29SC13	3N28
4/22	2SA47	3N52	241 31	16S56	29SC36	3N30
5/ 2	2SA10	3N56	240 54	16S44	29SC58	3N33
5/12	1SA29	4N 0	240 13	16S32	0SA21	3N35
5/22	0SA45	4N 3	239 29	16S20	0SA44	3N37
6/ 1	0SA 2	4N 6	238 45	16S 9	1SA 6	3N40
6/11	29SC20	4N 7	238 3	15S59	1SA29	3N42
6/21	28SC44	4N 7	237 26	15S51	1SA51	3N44
7/ 1	28SC14	4N 7	236 56	15S45	2SA13	3N47
7/11	27SC52	4N 6	236 34	15S41	2SA35	3N49
7/21	27SC39	4N 5	236 20	15S39	2SA57	3N51
7/31	27SC36	4N 3	236 17	15S40	3SA20	3N53
8/10	27SC43	4N 2	236 23	15S44	3SA41	3N55
8/20	27SC59	4N 0	236 40	15S49	4SA 3	3N58
8/30	28SC26	3N58	237 6	15S57	4SA25	4N 0
9/ 9	29SC 1	3N56	237 42	16S 6	4SA47	4N 2
9/19	29SC45	3N55	238 26	16S17	5SA 9	4N 4
9/29	0SA37	3N53	239 18	16S28	5SA30	4N 6
10/ 9	1SA34	3N52	240 17	16S41	5SA52	4N 8
10/19	2SA38	3N52	241 21	16S54	6SA13	4N10
10/29	3SA46	3N52	242 31	17S 6	6SA35	4N13
11/ 8	4SA57	3N52	243 44	17S19	6SA56	4N15
11/18	6SA11	3N53	245 1	17S30	7SA18	4N17
11/28	7SA26	3N55	246 18	17S41	7SA39	4N19
12/ 8	8SA41	3N57	247 36	17S51	8SA 0	4N21
12/18	9SA55	4N 0	248 53	17S59	8SA21	4N23
12/28	11SA 6	4N 3	250 8	18S 6	8SA42	4N25

Stations	Date	Long.	Lat.
RETROGRADE	3/16.42	3SA53	3N31
DIRECT	7/29.14	27SC36	4N 4

2000

Date	Long.	Lat.	R.A.	Dec.	HLong.	HLat.
1/ 7	12SA15	4N 6	251 20	18S11	9SA 3	4N27
1/17	13SA18	4N11	252 27	18S15	9SA24	4N28
1/27	14SA17	4N16	253 28	18S17	9SA45	4N30
2/ 6	15SA 8	4N21	254 22	18S17	10SA 5	4N32
2/16	15SA52	4N27	255 8	18S16	10SA26	4N34
2/26	16SA27	4N33	255 46	18S14	10SA47	4N36
3/ 7	16SA53	4N39	256 13	18S10	11SA 7	4N38
3/17	17SA 8	4N46	256 31	18S 4	11SA28	4N40
3/27	17SA14	4N53	256 37	17S58	11SA48	4N42
4/ 6	17SA10	4N59	256 34	17S51	12SA 8	4N43
4/16	16SA57	5N 6	256 20	17S44	12SA29	4N45
4/26	16SA34	5N11	255 57	17S36	12SA49	4N47
5/ 6	16SA 4	5N17	255 26	17S28	13SA 9	4N49
5/16	15SA28	5N21	254 49	17S20	13SA29	4N50
5/26	14SA48	5N24	254 8	17S12	13SA49	4N52
6/ 5	14SA 5	5N27	253 25	17S 5	14SA 9	4N54
6/15	13SA23	5N28	252 41	16S59	14SA29	4N56
6/25	12SA44	5N28	252 1	16S54	14SA48	4N57
7/ 5	12SA 9	5N27	251 25	16S50	15SA 8	4N59
7/15	11SA40	5N26	250 55	16S48	15SA28	5N 1
7/25	11SA19	5N23	250 32	16S48	15SA47	5N 2
8/ 4	11SA 6	5N21	250 19	16S49	16SA 7	5N 4
8/14	11SA 3	5N17	250 15	16S52	16SA26	5N 5
8/24	11SA 9	5N14	250 21	16S56	16SA46	5N 7
9/ 3	11SA24	5N10	250 36	17S 1	17SA 5	5N 9
9/13	11SA49	5N 7	251 1	17S 8	17SA24	5N10
9/23	12SA22	5N 4	251 35	17S15	17SA43	5N12
10/ 3	13SA 3	5N 1	252 17	17S23	18SA 3	5N13
10/13	13SA51	4N59	253 7	17S31	18SA22	5N15
10/23	14SA46	4N57	254 3	17S39	18SA41	5N16
11/ 2	15SA45	4N55	255 5	17S47	18SA59	5N18
11/12	16SA49	4N54	256 11	17S54	19SA18	5N19
11/22	17SA56	4N54	257 21	18S 0	19SA37	5N21
12/ 2	19SA 5	4N55	258 33	18S 6	19SA56	5N22
12/12	20SA15	4N56	259 46	18S10	20SA15	5N24
12/22	21SA24	4N57	260 59	18S13	20SA33	5N25

Stations	Date	Long.	Lat.
RETROGRADE	3/27.90	17SA14	4N53
DIRECT	8/12.60	11SA 3	5N18

Longitudes of
CHIRON
1686-1889

by
Mark Pottenger

0h Ephemeris Time
Equinox of Date

© Copyright by Phenomena Publications, 1980

Mo/Dy   Long

```
1686
1/22     7Ta43        5/31      5Gm14      10/ 7    15Cn33       4/18.5  19Le59D
2/21     8   23       6/30      7   36     11/ 6    15   45R    12/27.5  13Vi25R
3/23     9   50       7/30      9   33     12/ 6    14   38
4/22    11   47       8/29     10   45                          1699
5/22    13   51       9/28     10   54R    3/ 3.7   29Gm27D     1/14    13Vi 7R
6/21    15   43      10/28     10    1    10/26.5   15Cn51R     2/13    11   26
7/21    17    3      11/27      8   22                          3/15     9    4
8/20    17   35      12/27      6   39     1695                 4/14     7   17
9/19    17   12R                           1/ 5    12Cn38R      5/14     6   58D
10/19   16    1      2/ 4.5    28Ta57D     2/ 4    10   41      6/13     8   19
11/18   14   27      9/17.4    10Gm58R     3/ 6     9   41      7/13    11    6
12/18   13    6                            4/ 5    10    4D     8/12    14   52
                     1691                  5/ 5    11   46      9/11    19   10
8/22.4  17Ta35R      1/26      5Gm33R      6/ 4    14   27     10/11    23   29
                     2/25      5   32D     7/ 4    17   43     11/10    27   19
1687                 3/27      6   37      8/ 3    21    7     12/10     0Li 7
1/17    12Ta30R      4/26      8   35      9/ 2    24   12
2/16    12   52D     5/26     11    2     10/ 2    26   31      5/ 4.8   6Vi53D
3/18    14    8      6/25     13   37     11/ 1    27   37
4/17    16    0      7/25     15   55     12/ 1    27   16R     1700
5/17    18    9      8/24     17   34     12/31    25   38      1/ 9     1Li23
6/16    20   12      9/23     18   15                           2/ 8     0   51R
7/16    21   48     10/23     17   47R     3/13.1    9Cn39D     3/10    28Vi54
8/15    22   41     11/22     16   20     11/ 8.8   27Cn41R     4/ 9    26   34
9/14    22   38R    12/22     14   29                           5/ 9    25    4
10/14   21   40                            1696                 6/ 8    25    8D
11/13   20    8      2/10.5    5Gm24D      1/30    23Cn26R      7/ 8    26   52
12/13   18   36      9/25.8   18Gm15R      2/29    21   46      8/ 7    29   56
                                           3/30    21   23D     9/ 6     3Li54
1/20.7  12Ta29D      1692                  4/29    22   29     10/ 6     8   17
8/28.4  22Ta47R      1/21     13Gm 1R      5/29    24   51     11/ 5    12   35
                     2/20     12   32D     6/28    28    4     12/ 5    16   15
1688                 3/21     13   14      7/28     1Le43
1/12    17Ta41R      4/20     14   59      8/27     5   19      1/14.9   1Li25R
2/11    17   44D     5/20     17   25      9/26     8   24      5/22.8  24Vi53D
3/12    18   45      6/19     20    9     10/26    10   30
4/11    20   31      7/19     22   47     11/25    11   11R     1701
5/11    22   41      8/18     24   55     12/25    10   18      1/ 4    18Li44
6/10    24   54      9/17     26    9                           2/ 3    19   35R
7/10    26   47     10/17     26   15      3/22.7   21Cn20D     3/ 5    18   41
8/ 9    28    0     11/16     25   10     11/22.8   11Le12R     4/ 4    16   34
9/ 8    28   20R    12/16     23   20                           5/ 4    14   21
10/ 8   27   41                            1697                 6/ 3    13    9
11/ 7   26   15      2/17.2   12Gm32D      1/24     8Le16R      7/ 3    13   33D
12/ 7   24   36     10/ 4.2   26Gm21R      2/23     6    6      8/ 2    15   32
                                           3/25     4   50      9/ 1    18   46
1/25.6  17Ta35D      1693                  4/24     5    6D    10/ 1    22   48
9/ 2.8  28Ta21R      1/15     21Gm32R      5/24     6   52     10/31    27    7
                     2/14     20   33      6/23     9   49     11/30     1Sc13
1689                 3/16     20   47D     7/23    13   30     12/30     4   32
1/ 6    23Ta22R      4/15     22   12      8/22    17   27
2/ 5    23    3D     5/15     24   32      9/21    21   13      2/ 2.1  19Li35R
3/ 7    23   47      6/14     27   21     10/21    24   17      6/10.8  13Li 5D
4/ 6    25   24      7/14      0Cn16     11/20     26    8
5/ 6    27   33      8/13      2   52     12/20    26   24R     1702
6/ 5    29   53      9/12      4   43                           1/29     6Sc34
7/ 5     2Gm 1     10/12      5   29      4/ 4.2    4Le45D      2/28     6   55R
8/ 4     3   37     11/11      4   57R    12/ 9.5   26Le30R     3/30     5   39
9/ 3     4   21     12/11      3   20                           4/29     3   26
10/ 3    4    4R                           1698                 5/29     1   24
11/ 2    2   51      2/23.5   20Gm29D      1/19    25Le 3R      6/28     0   32
12/ 2    1    9     10/14.6    5Cn29R      2/18    22   47      7/28     1   15D
                                           3/20    20   46      8/27     3   27
1/29.9  23Ta 2D      1694                  4/19    19   59D     9/26     6   45
9/ 9.8   4Gm23R      1/10      1Cn20R      5/19    20   51     10/26    10   43
                     2/ 9     29Gm50       6/18    23   11     11/25    14   50
1690                 3/11     29   29D     7/18    26   36     12/25    18   34
1/ 1    29Ta39R      4/10      0Cn28       8/17     0Vi39
1/31    28   57      5/10      2   33      9/16     4   51      2/18.9   6Sc60R
3/ 2    29   20D     6/ 9      5   23     10/16     8   42      6/29.8   0Sc32D
4/ 1     0Gm43      7/ 9      8   31     11/15    11   41
5/ 1     2   49      8/ 8     11   33     12/15    13   16
                     9/ 7     14    2
```

Mo/Dy Long

1703

Mo/Dy	Long
1/24	21Sc24
2/23	22 49
3/25	22 37R
4/24	21 1
5/24	18 48
6/23	17 3
7/23	16 34D
8/22	17 36
9/21	19 59
10/21	23 19
11/20	27 9
12/20	0Sa56
3/ 6.1	22Sc56R
7/17.7	16Sc32D

1704

Mo/Dy	Long
1/19	4Sa11
2/18	6 22
3/19	7 7R
4/18	6 22
5/18	4 29
6/17	2 24
7/17	1 1
8/16	0 59D
9/15	2 21
10/15	4 55
11/14	8 15
12/14	11 51
3/18.4	7Sa 7R
8/ 2.0	0Sa49D

1705

Mo/Dy	Long
1/13	15Sa14
2/12	17 53
3/14	19 22
4/13	19 25R
5/13	18 10
6/12	16 10
7/12	14 19
8/11	13 25
9/10	13 51D
10/10	15 35
11/ 9	18 18
12/ 9	21 33
3/30.0	19Sa35R
8/16.5	13Sa23D

1706

Mo/Dy	Long
1/ 8	24Sa53
2/ 7	27 45
3/ 9	29 44
4/ 8	0Cp29
5/ 8	29Sa53R
6/ 7	28 15
7/ 7	26 17
8/ 6	24 49
9/ 5	24 28D
10/ 5	25 23
11/ 4	27 27
12/ 4	0Cp16
4/ 9.2	0Cp29R
8/29.4	24Sa26D

1707

Mo/Dy	Long
1/ 3	3Cp23
2/ 2	6 20
3/ 4	8 38
4/ 3	9 53
5/ 3	9Cp54R
6/ 2	8 45
7/ 2	6 56
8/ 1	5 11
8/31	4 13
9/30	4 26D
10/30	5 50
11/29	8 10
12/29	11 0
4/18.1	10Cp 3R
9/ 9.7	4Cp 9D

1708

Mo/Dy	Long
1/28	13Cp53
2/27	16 22
3/28	18 1
4/27	18 32R
5/27	17 54
6/26	16 22
7/26	14 33
8/25	13 11
9/24	12 48D
10/24	13 36
11/23	15 24
12/23	17 54
4/25.2	18Cp32R
9/18.7	12Cp47D

1709

Mo/Dy	Long
1/22	20Cp39
2/21	23 12
3/23	25 7
4/22	26 4
5/22	25 54R
6/21	24 43
7/21	23 0
8/20	21 25
9/19	20 34
10/19	20 48D
11/18	22 7
12/18	24 14
5/ 2.4	26Cp 8R
9/27.7	20Cp31D

1710

Mo/Dy	Long
1/17	26Cp47
2/16	29 19
3/18	1Aq24
4/17	2 42
5/17	2 57R
6/16	2 10
7/16	0 39
8/15	28Cp59
9/14	27 48
10/14	27 33D
11/13	28 23
12/13	0Aq 7
5/ 8.9	2Aq59R
10/ 5.8	27Cp31D

1711

Mo/Dy	Long
1/12	2Aq25
2/11	4 53
3/13	7 4
4/12	8 37
5/12	9 14
6/11	8 51R
7/11	7 36
8/10	5 57
9/ 9	4Aq33
10/ 9	3 55
11/ 8	4 17D
12/ 8	5 38
5/15.1	9Aq15R
10/13.2	3Aq54D

1712

Mo/Dy	Long
1/ 7	7Aq39
2/ 6	9 60
3/ 7	12 14
4/ 6	13 58
5/ 6	14 54
6/ 5	14 52R
7/ 5	13 55
8/ 4	12 24
9/ 3	10 53
10/ 3	9 55
11/ 2	9 53D
12/ 2	10 50
5/19.7	15Aq 1R
10/18.9	9Aq47D

1713

Mo/Dy	Long
1/ 1	12Aq35
1/31	14 46
3/ 2	16 59
4/ 1	18 52
5/ 1	20 3
5/31	20 21R
6/30	19 43
7/30	18 23
8/29	16 49
9/28	15 38
10/28	15 14D
11/27	15 49
12/27	17 15
5/25.0	20Aq22R
10/25.2	15Aq14D

1714

Mo/Dy	Long
1/26	19Aq15
2/25	21 25
3/27	23 23
4/26	24 47
5/26	25 22
6/25	25 3R
7/25	23 56
8/24	22 26
9/23	21 4
10/23	20 23
11/22	20 36D
12/22	21 43
5/30.1	25Aq23R
10/31.0	20Aq21D

1715

Mo/Dy	Long
1/21	23Aq30
2/20	25 35
3/22	27 36
4/21	29 10
5/21	0Pi 1
6/20	29Aq59R
7/20	29 7
8/19	27 43
9/18	26 17
10/18	25 20
11/17	25 13D
12/17	26 2
6/ 3.8	0Pi 7R
11/ 5.5	25Aq 9D

1716

Mo/Dy	Long
1/16	27Aq35
2/15	29 33
3/16	1Pi34
4/15	3 16
5/15	4 21
6/14	4 36R
7/14	3 59
8/13	2 44
9/12	1 16
10/12	0 8
11/11	29Aq43D
12/11	0Pi13
6/ 7.5	4Pi37R
11/ 9.6	29Aq43D

1717

Mo/Dy	Long
1/10	1Pi31
2/ 9	3 21
3/11	5 20
4/10	7 8
5/10	8 24
6/ 9	8 55
7/ 9	8 35R
8/ 8	7 31
9/ 7	6 5
10/ 7	4 48
11/ 6	4 7
12/ 6	4 19D
6/11.9	8Pi55R
11/14.5	4Pi 5D

1718

Mo/Dy	Long
1/ 5	5Pi21
2/ 4	7 1
3/ 6	8 57
4/ 5	10 48
5/ 5	12 14
6/ 4	12 59
7/ 4	12 55R
8/ 3	12 4
9/ 2	10 43
10/ 2	9 20
11/ 1	8 27
12/ 1	8 21D
12/31	9 7
6/16.2	13Pi 4R
11/19.2	8Pi17D

1719

Mo/Dy	Long
1/30	10Pi35
3/ 1	12 26
3/31	14 19
4/30	15 54
5/30	16 52
6/29	17 3R
7/29	16 25
8/28	15 12
9/27	13 47
10/27	12 42
11/26	12 20D
12/26	12 51
6/20.5	17Pi 5R
11/23.6	12Pi20D

Mo/Dy Long

Mo/Dy	Long		Mo/Dy	Long		Mo/Dy	Long		Mo/Dy	Long	
1720			5/ 3	4Ar16		9/ 9	20Ar29		1/ 8.8	28Ar49D	
1/25	14Pi	6	6/ 2	5	31	10/ 9	19	10	8/12.0	8Ta	4R
2/24	15	51	7/ 2	6	6	11/ 8	17	47			
3/25	17	44	8/ 1	5	54R	12/ 8	16	52	**1733**		
4/24	19	24	8/31	4	58				1/16	3Ta	9D
5/24	20	34	9/30	3	38	7/25.1	21Ar23R		2/15	3	44
6/23	20	60	10/30	2	21	12/27.4	16Ar41D		3/17	5	6
7/23	20	37R	11/29	1	35				4/16	6	58
8/22	19	33	12/29	1	38D	**1729**			5/16	8	59
9/21	18	9				1/ 7	16Ar44D		6/15	10	48
10/21	16	55	7/ 9.1	6Ar	8R	2/ 6	17	28	7/15	12	7
11/20	16	19	12/12.5	1Ar30D		3/ 8	18	53	8/14	12	39
12/20	16	33D				4/ 7	20	41	9/13	12	18R
			1725			5/ 7	22	32	10/13	11	10
6/23.6	20Pi60R		1/28	2Ar29		6/ 6	24	6	11/12	9	39
11/27.0	16Pi17D		2/27	3	58	7/ 6	25	6	12/12	8	19
			3/29	5	46	8/ 5	25	21R			
1721			4/28	7	32	9/ 4	24	46	1/12.2	3Ta	8D
1/19	17Pi35		5/28	8	57	10/ 4	23	34	8/17.3	12Ta39R	
2/18	19	11	6/27	9	46	11/ 3	22	8			
3/20	21	3	7/27	9	48R	12/ 3	21	1	**1734**		
4/19	22	48	8/26	9	4				1/11	7Ta41R	
5/19	24	8	9/25	7	49	7/29.5	25Ar22R		2/10	7	58D
6/18	24	47	10/25	6	27	12/31.5	20Ar37D		3/12	9	9
7/18	24	39R	11/24	5	29				4/11	10	56
8/17	23	46	12/24	5	17D	**1730**			5/11	13	0
9/16	22	26				1/ 2	20Ar37D		6/10	14	59
10/16	21	7	7/13.3	9Ar53R		2/ 1	21	6	7/10	16	33
11/15	20	17	12/16.4	5Ar15D		3/ 3	22	21	8/ 9	17	24
12/15	20	15D				4/ 2	24	6	9/ 8	17	22R
			1726			5/ 2	25	59	10/ 8	16	28
6/27.7	24Pi50R		1/23	5Ar55		6/ 1	27	42	11/ 7	14	59
12/ 1.3	20Pi10D		2/22	7	14	7/ 1	28	56	12/ 7	13	29
			3/24	8	59	7/31	29	27			
1722			4/23	10	48	8/30	29	7R	1/16.6	7Ta39D	
1/14	21Pi	3	5/23	12	21	9/29	28	3	8/22.8	17Ta30R	
2/13	22	30	6/22	13	23	10/29	26	37			
3/15	24	18	7/22	13	40R	11/28	25	20	**1735**		
4/14	26	6	8/21	13	9	12/28	24	41	1/ 6	12Ta33R	
5/14	27	35	9/20	12	0				2/ 5	12	32D
6/13	28	28	10/20	10	37	8/ 3.2	29Ar27R		3/ 7	13	29
7/13	28	34R	11/19	9	29				4/ 6	15	9
8/12	27	54	12/19	9	1	**1731**			5/ 6	17	14
9/11	26	40				1/27	24Ar54D		6/ 5	19	21
10/11	25	17	7/17.5	13Ar40R		2/26	25	58	7/ 5	21	9
11/10	24	16	12/20.4	9Ar	1D	3/28	27	37	8/ 4	22	20
12/10	23	59D				4/27	29	32	9/ 3	22	39R
			1727			5/27	1Ta22		10/ 3	22	1
7/ 1.8	28Pi37R		1/18	9Ar24D		6/26	2	49	11/ 2	20	39
12/ 5.4	23Pi58D		2/17	10	34	7/26	3	35	12/ 2	19	3
			3/19	12	13	8/25	3	32R			
1723			4/18	14	3	9/24	2	40	1/21.3	12Ta25D	
1/ 9	24Pi32		5/18	15	44	10/24	1	17	8/28.8	22Ta40R	
2/ 8	25	49	6/17	16	57	11/23	29Ar52				
3/10	27	32	7/17	17	29	12/23	28	58	**1736**		
4/ 9	29	21	8/16	17	13R				1/ 1	17Ta50R	
5/ 9	0Ar57		9/15	16	14	1/ 4.6	24Ar39D		1/31	17	29D
6/ 8	2	2	10/15	14	51	8/ 7.9	3Ta40R		3/ 1	18	9
7/ 8	2	23R	11/14	13	34				3/31	19	40
8/ 7	1	56	12/14	12	53	**1732**			4/30	21	43
9/ 6	0	50				1/22	28Ar54D		5/30	23	56
10/ 6	29Pi28		7/21.7	17Ar30R		2/21	29	44	6/29	25	58
11/ 5	28	17	12/24.4	12Ar49R		3/22	1Ta16		7/29	27	29
12/ 5	27	45				4/21	3	10	8/28	28	10
			1728			5/21	5	7	9/27	27	53R
7/ 5.9	2Ar23R		1/13	13Ar 1D		6/20	6	45	10/27	26	42
12/ 9.5	27Pi45D		2/12	13	58	7/20	7	48	11/26	25	4
			3/13	15	31	8/19	8	2R	12/26	23	37
1724			4/12	17	21	9/18	7	25			
1/ 4	28Pi	3D	5/12	19	7	10/18	6	7	1/26.3	17Ta29D	
2/ 3	29	8	6/11	20	32	11/17	4	38	9/ 3.2	28Ta12R	
3/ 4	0Ar45		7/11	21	18	12/17	3	29			
4/ 3	2	34	8/10	21	16R						

	Mo/Dy	Long

1737
1/25	22Ta55R
2/24	23 15D
3/26	24 33
4/25	26 31
5/25	28 49
6/24	1Gm 4
7/24	2 54
8/23	3 59
9/22	4 5R
10/22	3 12
11/21	1 37
12/21	29Ta58

| 1/30.5 | 22Ta54D |
| 9/10.2 | 4Gm10R |

1738
1/20	28Ta55R
2/19	28 52D
3/21	29 54
4/20	1Gm45
5/20	4 4
6/19	6 30
7/19	8 38
8/18	10 8
9/17	10 42
10/17	10 11R
11/16	8 46
12/16	7 0

| 2/ 5.0 | 28Ta45D |
| 9/17.7 | 10Gm42R |

1739
1/15	5Gm36R
2/14	5 9D
3/16	5 50
4/15	7 29
5/15	9 47
6/14	12 21
7/14	14 47
8/13	16 42
9/12	17 46
10/12	17 44R
11/11	16 37
12/11	14 50

| 2/11.0 | 5Gm 9D |
| 9/26.0 | 17Gm53R |

1740
1/10	13Gm 9R
2/ 9	12 14
3/10	12 30D
4/ 9	13 52
5/ 9	16 5
6/ 8	18 44
7/ 8	21 25
8/ 7	23 46
9/ 6	25 22
10/ 6	25 54R
11/ 5	25 14
12/ 5	23 37

| 2/17.5 | 12Gm11D |
| 10/ 4.3 | 25Gm54R |

1741
1/ 4	21Gm42R
2/ 3	20 21
3/ 5	20 6D
4/ 4	21 6

5/ 4	23Gm 7
6/ 3	25 47
7/ 3	28 41
8/ 2	1Cn25
9/ 1	3 34
10/ 1	4 45
10/31	4 42R
11/30	3 26
12/30	1 29

| 2/23.8 | 20Gm 2D |
| 10/14.6 | 4Cn53R |

1742
1/29	29Gm42R
2/28	28 53
3/30	29 23D
4/29	1Cn 5
5/29	3 40
6/28	6 43
7/28	9 48
8/27	12 30
9/26	14 24
10/26	15 5
11/25	14 25R
12/25	12 40

| 3/ 3.9 | 28Gm52D |
| 10/26.2 | 15Cn 5R |

1743
1/24	10Cn36R
2/23	9 10
3/25	9 2D
4/24	10 16
5/24	12 37
6/23	15 42
7/23	19 4
8/22	22 16
9/21	24 53
10/21	26 27
11/20	26 37R
12/20	25 23

| 3/13.1 | 8Cn55D |
| 11/ 8.4 | 26Cn44R |

1744
1/19	23Cn17R
2/18	21 19
3/19	20 25
4/18	20 59D
5/18	22 55
6/17	25 52
7/17	29 22
8/16	2Le60
9/15	6 17
10/15	8 46
11/14	9 58
12/14	9 36R

| 3/22.6 | 20Cn25D |
| 11/22.2 | 10Le 1R |

1745
1/13	7Le53R
2/12	5 38
3/14	3 58
4/13	3 40D
5/13	4 55
6/12	7 29
7/12	10 55
8/11	14 48

9/10	18Le38
10/10	21 58
11/ 9	24 16
12/ 9	25 5R

| 4/ 3.7 | 3Le35D |
| 12/ 8.5 | 25Le 5R |

1746
1/ 8	24Le15R
2/ 7	22 11
3/ 9	19 57
4/ 8	18 40
5/ 8	18 57D
6/ 7	20 49
7/ 7	23 53
8/ 6	27 45
9/ 5	1Vi55
10/ 5	5 54
11/ 4	9 12
12/ 4	11 17

| 4/17.8 | 18Le35D |
| 12/26.4 | 11Vi47R |

1747
1/ 3	11Vi44R
2/ 2	10 29
3/ 4	8 13
4/ 3	6 7
5/ 3	5 15
6/ 2	6 3D
7/ 2	8 23
8/ 1	11 52
8/31	16 1
9/30	20 21
10/30	24 24
11/29	27 35
12/29	29 23

| 5/ 3.9 | 5Vi15D |

1748
1/28	29Vi26R
2/27	27 52
3/28	25 31
4/27	23 38
5/27	23 9D
6/26	24 21
7/26	27 1
8/25	0Li44
9/24	5 2
10/24	9 25
11/23	13 21
12/23	16 16

| 1/13.8 | 29Vi38R |
| 5/20.7 | 23Vi 7D |

1749
1/22	17Li42
2/21	17 21R
3/23	15 32
4/22	13 12
5/22	11 34
6/21	11 25D
7/21	12 56
8/20	15 49
9/19	19 38
10/19	23 56
11/18	28 10
12/18	1Sc49

| 1/30.9 | 17Li47R |
| 6/ 8.6 | 11Li17D |

1750
1/17	4Sc20
2/16	5 16
3/18	4 30R
4/17	2 29
5/17	0 15
6/16	28Li56
7/16	29 7D
8/15	0Sc52
9/14	3 53
10/14	7 42
11/13	11 51
12/13	15 47

| 2/16.9 | 5Sc16R |
| 6/27.5 | 28Li48D |

1751
1/12	18Sc60
2/11	20 57
3/13	21 18R
4/12	20 6
5/12	17 58
6/11	15 57
7/11	14 60
8/10	15 32D
9/ 9	17 31
10/ 9	20 37
11/ 8	24 21
12/ 8	28 15

| 3/ 4.3 | 21Sc22R |
| 7/15.5 | 14Sc59D |

1752
1/ 7	1Sa46
2/ 6	4 23
3/ 7	5 40
4/ 6	5 25R
5/ 6	3 50
6/ 5	1 42
7/ 5	29Sc59
8/ 4	29 28D
9/ 3	0Sa23
10/ 3	2 36
11/ 2	5 45
12/ 2	9 20

| 3/16.8 | 5Sa45R |
| 7/31.0 | 29Sc27D |

1753
1/ 1	12Sa53
1/31	15 52
3/ 2	17 49
4/ 1	18 24R
5/ 1	17 33
5/31	15 43
6/30	13 42
7/30	12 25
8/29	12 23D
9/28	13 42
10/28	16 8
11/27	19 17
12/27	22 40

| 3/28.6 | 18Sa24R |
| 8/14.7 | 12Sa13D |

Mo/Dy　Long

1754	5/ 5 2Aq26	9/11 21Aq 7	6/15.4 12Pi38R
1/26 25Sa47	6/ 4 2 1R	10/11 20 8	11/18.4 7Pi52D
2/25 28 9	7/ 4 0 43	11/10 20 0D	
3/27 29 22	8/ 3 29Cp 1	12/10 20 48	**1767**
4/26 29 14R	9/ 2 27 35		1/18 9Pi33
5/26 27 54	10/ 2 26 58	5/29.3 24Aq58R	2/17 11 18
6/25 25 57	11/ 1 27 25D	10/30.2 19Aq57D	3/19 13 12
7/25 24 14	12/ 1 28 51		4/18 14 55
8/24 23 27	12/31 0Aq60	**1763**	5/18 16 8
9/23 23 56D		1/ 9 22Aq23	6/17 16 37
10/23 25 38	5/ 8.1 2Aq26R	2/ 8 24 24	7/17 16 17R
11/22 28 15	10/ 4.8 26Cp58D	3/10 26 29	8/16 15 15
12/22 1Cp21		4/ 9 28 15	9/15 13 51
	1759	5/ 9 29 24	10/15 12 36
4/ 7.9 29Sa29R	1/30 3Aq27	6/ 8 29 42R	11/14 11 56
8/27.8 23Sa26D	3/ 1 5 48	7/ 8 29 8	12/14 12 7D
	3/31 7 38	8/ 7 27 53	
1755	4/30 8 38	9/ 6 26 23	6/19.5 16Pi37R
1/21 4Cp26	5/30 8 37R	10/ 6 25 12	11/22.9 11Pi54D
2/20 7 2	6/29 7 38	11/ 5 24 46D	
3/22 8 43	7/29 6 4	12/ 5 25 14	**1768**
4/21 9 12R	8/28 4 31		1/13 13Pi 7
5/21 8 26	9/27 3 33	6/ 3.1 29Aq43R	2/12 14 42
6/20 6 46	10/27 3 32D	11/ 4.7 24Aq46D	3/13 16 34
7/20 4 54	11/26 4 33		4/12 18 21
8/19 3 35	12/26 6 22	**1764**	5/12 19 43
9/18 3 22D		1/ 4 26Aq32	6/11 20 26
10/18 4 23	5/14.3 8Aq45R	2/ 3 28 23	7/11 20 21R
11/17 6 26	10/12.3 3Aq24D	3/ 4 0Pi26	8/10 19 31
12/17 9 9		4/ 3 2 17	9/ 9 18 12
	1760	5/ 3 3 37	10/ 9 16 51
4/17.1 9Cp12R	1/25 8Aq39	6/ 2 4 12	11/ 8 15 59
9/ 8.3 3Cp18D	2/24 10 58	7/ 2 3 54R	12/ 8 15 54D
	3/25 12 56	8/ 1 2 51	
1756	4/24 14 12	8/31 1 25	6/22.7 20Pi30R
1/16 12Cp 6	5/24 14 32R	9/30 0 6	11/26.2 15Pi50D
2/15 14 47	6/23 13 54	10/30 29Aq23	
3/16 16 47	7/23 12 33	11/29 29 32D	**1769**
4/15 17 45	8/22 10 57	12/29 0Pi33	1/ 7 16Pi39
5/15 17 32R	9/21 9 44		2/ 6 18 4
6/14 16 16	10/21 9 20D	6/ 6.6 4Pi12R	3/ 8 19 51
7/14 14 28	11/20 9 56	11/ 8.8 29Aq20D	4/ 7 21 40
8/13 12 51	12/20 11 25		5/ 7 23 11
9/12 12 5		**1765**	6/ 6 24 6
10/12 12 28D	5/18.9 14Aq33R	1/28 2Pi13	7/ 6 24 16R
11/11 13 56	10/18.1 9Aq20D	2/27 4 11	8/ 5 23 39
12/11 16 15		3/29 6 6	9/ 4 22 26
	1761	4/28 7 35	10/ 4 21 4
4/24.2 17Cp49R	1/19 13Aq29	5/28 8 24	11/ 3 20 0
9/17.5 12Cp 4D	2/18 15 45	6/27 8 23R	12/ 3 19 40D
	3/20 17 48	7/27 7 34	
1757	4/19 19 17	8/26 6 13	6/26.7 24Pi18R
1/10 18Cp58	5/19 19 55	9/25 4 49	11/30.4 19Pi39D
2/ 9 21 39	6/18 19 37R	10/25 3 53	
3/11 23 52	7/18 18 30	11/24 3 44D	**1770**
4/10 25 12	8/17 16 58	12/24 4 29	1/ 2 20Pi 9
5/10 25 27R	9/16 15 35		2/ 1 21 23
6/ 9 24 37	10/16 14 51	6/11.1 8Pi30R	3/ 3 23 5
7/ 9 23 2	11/15 15 4D	11/13.7 3Pi41D	4/ 2 24 55
8/ 8 21 18	12/15 16 13		5/ 2 26 32
9/ 7 20 8		**1766**	6/ 1 27 39
10/ 7 19 58D	5/24.3 19Aq56R	1/23 5Pi56	7/ 1 28 3R
11/ 6 20 54	10/24.4 14Aq49D	2/22 7 48	7/31 27 39
12/ 6 22 47		3/24 9 43	8/30 26 35
	1762	4/23 11 20	9/29 25 13
5/ 1.5 25Cp30R	1/14 18Aq 3	5/23 12 22	10/29 24 2
9/26.6 19Cp54D	2/13 20 12	6/22 12 36R	11/28 23 27
	3/15 22 17	7/22 12 2	12/28 23 41D
1758	4/14 23 56	8/21 10 49	
1/ 5 25Cp14	5/14 24 51	9/20 9 24	6/30.8 28Pi 3R
2/ 4 27 50	6/13 24 52R	10/20 8 17	12/ 4.5 23Pi25D
3/ 6 0Aq 9	7/13 24 1	11/19 7 52D	
4/ 5 1 46	8/12 22 36	12/19 8 19	

Mo/Dy   Long

1771

Mo/Dy	Long
1/27	24Pi43
2/26	26 17
3/28	28 6
4/27	29 48
5/27	1Ar 5
6/26	1 43
7/26	1 33R
8/25	0 40
9/24	29Pi21
10/24	28 3
11/23	27 15
12/23	27 14D
7/ 4.8	1Ar45R
12/ 8.5	27Pi 8D

1772

Mo/Dy	Long
1/22	28Pi 3
2/21	29 29
3/22	1Ar15
4/21	3 1
5/21	4 27
6/20	5 17
7/20	5 22R
8/19	4 41
9/18	3 27
10/18	2 6
11/17	1 7
12/17	0 51D
7/ 7.9	5Ar26R
12/11.5	0Ar50D

1773

Mo/Dy	Long
1/16	1Ar25
2/15	2 41
3/17	4 23
4/16	6 11
5/16	7 45
6/15	8 47
7/15	9 6R
8/14	8 38
9/13	7 32
10/13	6 10
11/12	5 1
12/12	4 31
7/11.9	9Ar 7R
12/15.4	4Ar31D

1774

Mo/Dy	Long
1/11	4Ar50D
2/10	5 56
3/12	7 32
4/11	9 21
5/11	11 0
6/10	12 14
7/10	12 47
8/ 9	12 33R
9/ 8	11 37
10/ 8	10 16
11/ 7	8 60
12/ 7	8 16
7/16.1	12Ar48R
12/19.4	8Ar12D

1775

Mo/Dy	Long
1/ 6	8Ar21D
2/ 5	9 14
3/ 7	10 43
4/ 6	12 30
5/ 6	14Ar15
6/ 5	15 39
7/ 5	16 26
8/ 4	16 26R
9/ 3	15 41
10/ 3	14 24
11/ 2	13 3
12/ 2	12 7
7/20.2	16Ar32R
12/23.3	11Ar54D

1776

Mo/Dy	Long
1/ 1	11Ar56D
1/31	12 36
3/ 1	13 57
3/31	15 41
4/30	17 30
5/30	19 2
6/29	20 2
7/29	20 18R
8/28	19 45
9/27	18 36
10/27	17 12
11/26	16 5
12/26	15 39
7/23.4	20Ar18R
12/26.2	15Ar39D

1777

Mo/Dy	Long
1/25	16Ar 5D
2/24	17 15
3/26	18 56
4/25	20 46
5/25	22 26
6/24	23 38
7/24	24 9
8/23	23 51R
9/22	22 50
10/22	21 27
11/21	20 11
12/21	19 30
7/27.7	24Ar 9R
12/30.2	19Ar28D

1778

Mo/Dy	Long
1/20	19Ar41D
2/19	20 40
3/21	22 14
4/20	24 5
5/20	25 52
6/19	27 15
7/19	28 1
8/18	27 58R
9/17	27 8
10/17	25 48
11/16	24 25
12/16	23 31
8/ 1.2	28Ar 6R

1779

Mo/Dy	Long
1/15	23Ar26D
2/14	24 12
3/16	25 39
4/15	27 28
5/15	29 20
6/14	0Ta55
7/14	1 54
8/13	2 8R
9/12	1 32
10/12	0Ta17
11/11	28Ar51
12/11	27 44
1/ 3.2	23Ar22D
8/ 5.8	2Ta 9R

1780

Mo/Dy	Long
1/10	27Ar22D
2/ 9	27 54
3/10	29 11
4/ 9	0Ta58
5/ 9	2 53
6/ 8	4 37
7/ 8	5 51
8/ 7	6 21
9/ 6	6 0R
10/ 6	4 55
11/ 5	3 27
12/ 5	2 10
1/ 7.3	27Ar22D
8/ 9.6	6Ta22R

1781

Mo/Dy	Long
1/ 4	1Ta32R
2/ 3	1 48D
3/ 5	2 54
4/ 4	4 36
5/ 4	6 33
6/ 3	8 25
7/ 3	9 53
8/ 2	10 40
9/ 1	10 36R
10/ 1	9 43
10/31	8 17
11/30	6 51
12/30	5 58
1/10.4	1Ta31D
8/14.6	10Ta45R

1782

Mo/Dy	Long
1/29	5Ta56D
2/28	6 49
3/30	8 24
4/29	10 21
5/29	12 21
6/28	14 1
7/28	15 6
8/27	15 20R
9/26	14 41
10/26	13 22
11/25	11 51
12/25	10 42
1/14.7	5Ta50D
8/19.9	15Ta21R

1783

Mo/Dy	Long
1/24	10Ta23D
2/23	11 0
3/25	12 25
4/24	14 21
5/24	16 26
6/23	18 18
7/23	19 40
8/22	20 14
9/21	19 53R
10/21	18 43
11/20	17 10
12/20	15 48

1784

Mo/Dy	Long
1/19.2	10Ta22D
8/25.5	20Ta14R
1/19	15Ta10R
2/18	15 30D
3/19	16 44
4/18	18 35
5/18	20 43
6/17	22 46
7/17	24 24
8/16	25 19
9/15	25 18R
10/15	24 23
11/14	22 52
12/14	21 19
1/23.8	15Ta 9D
8/30.6	25Ta26R

1785

Mo/Dy	Long
1/13	20Ta22R
2/12	20 23D
3/14	21 22
4/13	23 6
5/13	25 16
6/12	27 29
7/12	29 23
8/11	0Gm39
9/10	1 1R
10/10	0 24
11/ 9	28Ta60
12/ 9	27 20
1/27.8	20Ta15D
9/ 6.1	1Gm 1R

1786

Mo/Dy	Long
1/ 8	26Ta 5R
2/ 7	25 44D
3/ 9	26 26
4/ 8	28 0
5/ 8	0Gm 9
6/ 7	2 29
7/ 7	4 38
8/ 6	6 15
9/ 5	7 2
10/ 5	6 48R
11/ 4	5 37
12/ 4	3 55
2/ 2.1	25Ta43D
9/13.1	7Gm 4R

1787

Mo/Dy	Long
1/ 3	2Gm24R
2/ 2	1 40
3/ 4	2 1D
4/ 3	3 21
5/ 3	5 25
6/ 2	7 50
7/ 2	10 14
8/ 1	12 12
8/31	13 26
9/30	13 38R
10/30	12 47
11/29	11 10
12/29	9 26
2/ 7.6	1Gm39D
9/20.7	13Gm41R

Mo/Dy   Long

Mo/Dy	Long		Mo/Dy	Long		Mo/Dy	Long		Mo/Dy	Long
1788			5/ 6	14Cn32		9/12	21Vi45		3/ 7.6	25Sc 3R
1/28	8Gm19R		6/ 5	17 12		10/12	26 4		7/19.5	18Sc41D
2/27	8 15D		7/ 5	20 26		11/11	29 54			
3/28	9 17		8/ 4	23 51		12/11	2Li45		**1801**	
4/27	11 13		9/ 3	26 57					1/20	6Sa 7
5/27	13 40		10/ 3	29 19		5/ 7.2	9Vi44D		2/19	8 18
6/26	16 15		11/ 2	0Le30					3/21	9 4R
7/26	18 34		12/ 2	0 13R		**1797**			4/20	8 20
8/25	20 16					1/10	4Li 4		5/20	6 29
9/24	20 59		3/15.4	12Cn31D		2/ 9	3 36R		6/19	4 24
10/24	20 34R		11/11.3	0Le34R		3/11	1 42		7/19	3 2
11/23	19 10					4/10	29Vi22		8/18	2 57D
12/23	17 19		**1793**			5/10	27 49·		9/17	4 18
			1/ 1	28Cn37R		6/ 9	27 49D		10/17	6 49
2/13.7	8Gm 8D		1/31	26 27		7/ 9	29 28		11/16	10 7
9/28.2	20Gm60R		3/ 2	24 44		8/ 8	2Li28		12/16	13 41
			4/ 1	24 17D		9/ 7	6 23			
1789			5/ 1	25 19		10/ 7	10 44		3/20.8	9Sa 4R
1/22	15Gm49R		5/31	27 37		11/ 6	15 1		8/ 4.5	2Sa48D
2/21	15 17D		6/30	0Le49		12/ 6	18 41			
3/23	15 57		7/30	4 27					**1802**	
4/22	17 39		8/29	8 4		1/17.1	4Li 7R		1/15	17Sa 3
5/22	20 4		9/28	11 11		5/25.2	27Vi36D		2/14	19 42
6/21	22 48		10/28	13 21					3/16	21 10
7/21	25 27		11/27	14 7R		**1798**			4/15	21 15R
8/20	27 37		12/27	13 18		1/ 5	21Li12		5/15	20 0
9/19	28 54					2/ 4	22 6		6/14	18 1
10/19	29 3R		3/26.2	24Cn15D		3/ 6	21 16R		7/14	16 11
11/18	28 1		11/26.3	14Le 7R		4/ 5	19 11		8/13	15 16
12/18	26 12					5/ 5	16 57		9/12	15 41D
			1794			6/ 4	15 42		10/12	17 23
2/19.4	15Gm17D		1/26	11Le18R		7/ 4	16 2D		11/11	20 4
10/ 7.5	29Gm 8R		2/25	9 7		8/ 3	17 57		12/11	23 18
			3/27	7 48		9/ 2	21 8			
1790			4/26	7 59D		10/ 2	25 6		4/ 1.3	21Sa23R
1/17	24Gm23R		5/26	9 41		11/ 1	29 24		8/18.9	15Sa15D
2/16	23 21		6/25	12 35		12/ 1	3Sc28			
3/18	23 32D		7/25	16 14		12/31	6 48		**1803**	
4/17	24 55		8/24	20 11					1/10	26Sa36
5/17	27 12		9/23	23 57		2/ 4.1	22Li 6R		2/ 9	29 28
6/16	0Cn 2		10/23	27 4		6/13.1	15Li38D		3/11	1Cp26
7/16	2 57		11/22	28 59					4/10	2 11
8/15	5 34		12/22	29 19R		**1799**			5/10	1 35R
9/14	7 29					1/30	8Sc51		6/ 9	29Sa58
10/14	8 18		4/ 7.5	7Le41D		3/ 1	9 14R		7/ 9	28 1
11/13	7 49R		12/12.9	29Le24R		3/31	8 1		8/ 8	26 34
12/13	6 15					4/30	5 50		9/ 7	26 12D
			1795			5/30	3 47		10/ 7	27 7
2/26.7	23Gm16D		1/21	28Le 3R		6/29	2 53		11/ 6	29 9
10/18.1	8Cn18R		2/20	25 49		7/29	3 32D		12/ 6	1Cp56
			3/22	23 45		8/28	5 40			
1791			4/21	22 54		9/27	8 56		4/11.4	2Cp11R
1/12	4Cn14R		5/21	23 41D		10/27	12 51		8/31.6	26Sa10D
2/11	2 42		6/20	25 57		11/26	16 56			
3/13	2 18D		7/20	29 19		12/26	20 40		**1804**	
4/12	3 13		8/19	3Vi20					1/ 5	5Cp 2
5/12	5 17		9/18	7 32		2/20.7	9Sc18R		2/ 4	7 57
6/11	8 5		10/18	11 24		7/ 1.7	2Sc52D		3/ 5	10 14
7/11	11 13		11/17	14 25					4/ 4	11 30
8/10	14 16		12/17	16 4		**1800**			5/ 4	11 31R
9/ 9	16 48					1/25	23Sc29		6/ 3	10 23
10/ 9	18 22		4/21.9	22Le54D		2/24	24 55		7/ 3	8 34
11/ 8	18 38R		12/30.7	16Vi15R		3/26	24 45R		8/ 2	6 50
12/ 8	17 34					4/25	23 11		9/ 1	5 52
			1796			5/25	20 59		10/ 1	6 5D
3/ 7.0	2Cn16D		1/16	15Vi60R		6/24	19 13		10/31	7 28
10/29.9	18Cn42R		2/15	14 22		7/24	18 42D		11/30	9 46
			3/16	12 1		8/23	19 42		12/30	12 35
1792			4/15	10 12		9/22	22 2			
1/ 7	15Cn36R		5/15	9 48D		10/22	25 20		4/19.3	11Cp40R
2/ 6	13 38		6/14	11 4		11/21	29 7		9/10.9	5Cp48D
3/ 7	12 34		7/14	13 46		12/21	2Sa53			
4/ 6	12 53D		8/13	17 29						

Mo/Dy   Long

1805
```
1/29   15Cp27
2/28   17  54
3/30   19  32
4/29   20   4R
5/29   19  26
6/28   17  55
7/28   16   7
8/27   14  45
9/26   14  23D
10/26  15   9
11/25  16  57
12/25  19  26

4/27.2  20Cp 4R
9/20.8  14Cp22D
```

1806
```
1/24   22Cp 9
2/23   24  41
3/25   26  35
4/24   27  31
5/24   27  21R
6/23   26  11
7/23   24  29
8/22   22  54
9/21   22   4
10/21  22  18D
11/20  23  36
12/20  25  42

5/ 4.3  27Cp35R
9/29.8  22Cp 1D
```

1807
```
1/19   28Cp14
2/18    0Aq45
3/20    2  49
4/19    4   6
5/19    4  21R
6/18    3  34
7/18    2   4
8/17    0  24
9/16   29Cp14
10/16  28  59D
11/15  29  48
12/15   1Aq32

5/10.8   4Aq23R
10/ 7.8 28Cp57D
```

1808
```
1/14    3Aq49
2/13    6  15
3/14    8  26
4/13    9  58
5/13   10  34
6/12   10  10R
7/12    8  56
8/11    7  18
9/10    5  54
10/10   5  16
11/ 9   5  39D
12/ 9   6  59

5/15.8  10Aq35R
10/14.1  5Aq16D
```

1809
```
1/ 8    8Aq60
2/ 7   11  19
3/ 9   13  32
4/ 8   15  16
```

```
5/ 8   16Aq11
6/ 7   16   8R
7/ 7   15  11
8/ 6   13  40
9/ 5   12  10
10/ 5  11  13
11/ 4  11  11D
12/ 4  12   8

5/21.5  16Aq17R
10/20.8 11Aq 5D
```

1810
```
1/ 3   13Aq52
2/ 2   16   2
3/ 4   18  14
4/ 3   20   6
5/ 3   21  16
6/ 2   21  33R
7/ 2   20  54
8/ 1   19  35
8/31   18   2
9/30   16  51
10/30  16  28D
11/29  17   3
12/29  18  29

5/26.6  21Aq34R
10/27.0 16Aq28D
```

1811
```
1/28   20Aq28
2/27   22  37
3/29   24  34
4/28   25  57
5/28   26  31
6/27   26  11R
7/27   25   4
8/26   23  34
9/25   22  14
10/25  21  33
11/24  21  46D
12/24  22  53

5/31.6  26Aq31R
11/ 1.7 21Aq31D
```

1812
```
1/23   24Aq40
2/22   26  44
3/23   28  43
4/22    0Pi16
5/22    1   6
6/21    1   3R
7/21    0  11
8/20   28Aq47
9/19   27  22
10/19  26  26
11/18  26  20D
12/18  27   8

6/ 4.4   1Pi11R
11/ 6.2 26Aq16D
```

1813
```
1/17   28Aq41
2/16    0Pi38
3/18    2  38
4/17    4  19
5/17    5  22
6/16    5  36R
7/16    4  59
8/15    3  44
```

```
9/14    2Pi17
10/14   1   9
11/13   0  46D
12/13   1  16

6/ 8.9   5Pi38R
11/11.3  0Pi46D
```

1814
```
1/12    2Pi34
2/11    4  23
3/13    6  21
4/12    8   7
5/12    9  22
6/11    9  52
7/11    9  31R
8/10    8  27
9/ 9    7   1
10/ 9   5  45
11/ 8   5   6
12/ 8   5  19D

6/13.3   9Pi52R
11/16.1  5Pi 4D
```

1815
```
1/ 7    6Pi21
2/ 6    7  60
3/ 8    9  55
4/ 7   11  45
5/ 7   13  10
6/ 6   13  53
7/ 6   13  48R
8/ 5   12  56
9/ 4   11  36
10/ 4  10  14
11/ 3   9  22
12/ 3   9  17D

6/17.5  13Pi57R
11/20.6  9Pi13D
```

1816
```
1/ 2   10Pi 4
2/ 1   11  31
3/ 2   13  22
4/ 1   15  13
5/ 1   16  46
5/31   17  43
6/30   17  52R
7/30   17  14
8/29   16   1
9/28   14  37
10/28  13  34
11/27  13  13D
12/27  13  44

6/20.7  17Pi55R
11/24.1 13Pi13D
```

1817
```
1/26   14Pi59
2/25   16  43
3/27   18  35
4/26   20  14
5/26   21  22
6/25   21  46R
7/25   21  22
8/24   20  18
9/23   18  55
10/23  17  43
11/22  17   8
12/22  17  23D
```

```
6/24.8  21Pi46R
11/28.4 17Pi 7D
```

1818
```
1/21   18Pi25
2/20   20   1
3/22   21  51
4/21   23  35
5/21   24  53
6/20   25  31
7/20   25  21R
8/19   24  28
9/18   23   9
10/18  21  51
11/17  21   2
12/17  21   1D

6/28.9  25Pi33R
12/ 2.5 20Pi55D
```

1819
```
1/16   21Pi50
2/15   23  17
3/17   25   4
4/16   26  50
5/16   28  17
6/15   29   8
7/15   29  13R
8/14   28  32
9/13   27  18
10/13  25  57
11/12  24  57
12/12  24  41D

7/ 2.9  29Pi17R
12/ 6.6 24Pi40D
```

1820
```
1/11   25Pi15
2/10   26  32
3/11   28  14
4/10    0Ar 2
5/10    1  36
6/ 9    2  39
7/ 9    2  58R
8/ 8    2  30
9/ 7    1  24
10/ 7   0   2
11/ 6  28Pi54
12/ 6  28  23

7/ 5.9   2Ar58R
12/ 9.6 28Pi23D
```

1821
```
1/ 5   28Pi42D
2/ 4   29  47
3/ 6    1Ar23
4/ 5    3  12
5/ 5    4  51
6/ 4    6   5
7/ 4    6  38
8/ 3    6  24R
9/ 2    5  27
10/ 2   4   7
11/ 1   2  52
12/ 1   2   8
12/31   2  12D

7/10.0   6Ar39R
12/13.6  2Ar 3D
```

Mo/Dy　Long

```
1822
 1/30    3Ar 4
 3/ 1    4  33
 3/31    6  19
 4/30    8   4
 5/30    9  26
 6/29   10  13
 7/29   10  13R
 8/28    9  28
 9/27    8  12
10/27    6  52
11/26    5  56
12/26    5  45D

 7/14.0  10Ar19R
12/17.5   5Ar43D

1823
 1/25    6Ar24
 2/24    7  44
 3/26    9  27
 4/25   11  14
 5/25   12  46
 6/24   13  44
 7/24   13  59R
 8/23   13  27
 9/22   12  18
10/22   10  55
11/21    9  49
12/21    9  24

 7/18.1  13Ar60R
12/21.5   9Ar24D

1824
 1/20    9Ar48D
 2/19   10  58
 3/20   12  36
 4/19   14  25
 5/19   16   3
 6/18   17  13
 7/18   17  42
 8/17   17  24R
 9/16   16  24
10/16   15   2
11/15   13  48
12/15   13   8

 7/21.3  17Ar43R
12/24.3  13Ar 5D

1825
 1/14   13Ar18D
 2/13   14  15
 3/15   15  48
 4/14   17  36
 5/14   19  20
 6/13   20  41
 7/13   21  24
 8/12   21  21R
 9/11   20  31
10/11   19  13
11/10   17  52
12/10   16  59

 7/25.5  21Ar29R
12/28.3  16Ar50D

1826
 1/ 9   16Ar54D
 2/ 8   17  38
 3/10   19   3
 4/ 9   20  50

 5/ 9   22Ar38
 6/ 8   24   9
 7/ 8   25   6
 8/ 7   25  17R
 9/ 6   24  41
10/ 6   23  28
11/ 5   22   4
12/ 5   20  59

 7/29.7  25Ar19R

1827
 1/ 4   20Ar38D
 2/ 3   21   9
 3/ 5   22  24
 4/ 4   24   7
 5/ 4   25  59
 6/ 3   27  38
 7/ 3   28  48
 8/ 2   29  15
 9/ 1   28  53R
10/ 1   27  48
10/31   26  23
11/30   25   9
12/30   24  32

 1/ 1.2  20Ar38D
 8/ 3.3  29Ar15R

1828
 1/29   24Ar48D
 2/28   25  52
 3/29   27  30
 4/28   29  23
 5/28    1Ta10
 6/27    2  33
 7/27    3  15
 8/26    3   8R
 9/25    2  52
10/25    0  52
11/24   29Ar29
12/24   28  39

 1/ 5.2  24Ar31D
 8/ 6.8   3Ta19R

1829
 1/23   28Ar38D
 2/22   29  30
 3/24    1Ta 1
 4/23    2  53
 5/23    4  47
 6/22    6  21
 7/22    7  19
 8/21    7  29R
 9/20    6  48
10/20    5  31
11/19    4   3
12/19    2  59

 1/ 8.3  28Ar32D
 8/11.6   7Ta31R

1830
 1/18    2Ta41D
 2/17    3  18
 3/19    4  41
 4/18    6  31
 5/18    8  29
 6/17   10  14
 7/17   11  27
 8/16   11  55
 9/15   11  30R

10/15   10Ta21
11/14    8  51
12/14    7  35

 1/12.5   2Ta41D
 8/16.7  11Ta55R

1831
 1/13    7Ta 0R
 2/12    7  21D
 3/14    8  33
 4/13   10  19
 5/13   12  20
 6/12   14  14
 7/12   15  43
 8/11   16  28
 9/10   16  21R
10/10   15  24
11/ 9   13  56
12/ 9   12  29

 1/16.7   7Ta 0D
 8/22.1  16Ta32R

1832
 1/ 8   11Ta38R
 2/ 7   11  42D
 3/ 8   12  40
 4/ 7   14  20
 5/ 7   16  22
 6/ 6   18  24
 7/ 6   20   7
 8/ 5   21  11
 9/ 4   21  23R
10/ 4   20  41
11/ 3   19  19
12/ 3   17  45

 1/21.2  11Ta32D
 8/26.7  21Ta25R

1833
 1/ 2   16Ta38R
 2/ 1   16  22D
 3/ 3   17   5
 4/ 2   18  36
 5/ 2   20  37
 6/ 1   22  46
 7/ 1   24  42
 7/31   26   5
 8/30   26  38
 9/29   26  15R
10/29   25   2
11/28   23  26
12/28   22   3

 1/24.9  16Ta21D
 9/ 1.7  26Ta39R

1834
 1/27   21Ta28R
 2/26   21  53D
 3/28   23  12
 4/27   25   9
 5/27   27  23
 6/26   29  31
 7/26    1Gm12
 8/25    2   8
 9/24    2   7R
10/24    1   9
11/23   29Ta34
12/23   27  60

 1/29.8  21Ta28D
 9/ 8.3   2Gm15R

1835
 1/22   27Ta 3R
 2/21   27   7D
 3/23   28  12
 4/22    0Gm 3
 5/22    2  19
 6/21    4  37
 7/21    6  37
 8/20    7  56
 9/19    8  20R
10/19    7  42
11/18    6  14
12/18    4  31

 2/ 4.1  26Ta57D
 9/15.3   8Gm20R

1836
 1/17    3Gm15R
 2/16    2  56D
 3/17    3  42
 4/16    5  23
 5/16    7  38
 6/15   10   5
 7/15   12  22
 8/14   14   5
 9/13   14  57
10/13   14  43R
11/12   13  31
12/12   11  45

 2/ 9.7   2Gm55D
 9/21.9  14Gm60R

1837
 1/11   10Gm11R
 2/10    9  26
 3/12    9  49D
 4/11   11  16
 5/11   13  27
 6/10   16   0
 7/10   18  32
 8/ 9   20  40
 9/ 8   22   1
10/ 8   22  18R
11/ 7   21  28
12/ 7   19  48

 2/14.9   9Gm25D
 9/30.5  22Gm20R

1838
 1/ 6   17Gm59R
 2/ 5   16  48
 3/ 7   16  44D
 4/ 6   17  51
 5/ 6   19  53
 6/ 5   22  29
 7/ 5   25  15
 8/ 4   27  45
 9/ 3   29  38
10/ 3    0Cn30
11/ 2    0  10R
12/ 2   28Gm46

 2/21.6  16Gm37D
10/ 9.9   0Cn32R
```

Mo/Dy	Long
1839	
1/ 1	26Gm50R
1/31	25 14
3/ 2	24 39D
4/ 1	25 20
5/ 1	27 7
5/31	29 41
6/30	2Cn36
7/30	5 28
8/29	7 52
9/28	9 24
10/28	9 44R
11/27	8 47
12/27	6 56
3/ 1.0	24Gm39D
10/20.5	9Cn46R
1840	
1/26	4Cn59R
2/25	3 50
3/26	3 57D
4/25	5 22
5/25	7 46
6/24	10 46
7/24	13 56
8/23	16 51
9/22	19 4
10/22	20 11
11/21	19 55R
12/21	18 25
3/ 8.3	3Cn43D
10/31.4	20Cn15R
1841	
1/20	16Cn19R
2/19	14 36
3/21	14 3D
4/20	14 55
5/20	17 1
6/19	19 58
7/19	23 20
8/18	26 42
9/17	29 36
10/17	1Le34
11/16	2 13R
12/16	1 23
3/17.7	14Cn 3D
11/13.8	2Le13R
1842	
1/15	29Cn26R
2/14	27 18
3/16	26 0
4/15	26 8D
5/15	27 42
6/14	0Le25
7/14	3 51
8/13	7 33
9/12	11 3
10/12	13 53
11/11	15 34
12/11	15 44R
3/28.6	25Cn52D
11/29.0	15Le52R
1843	
1/10	14Le23R
2/ 9	12 11
3/11	10 12
4/10	9Le25
5/10	10 12D
6/ 9	12 25
7/ 9	15 40
8/ 8	19 30
9/ 7	23 28
10/ 7	27 4
11/ 6	29 48
12/ 6	1Vi10
4/10.1	9Le25D
12/15.7	1Vi16R
1844	
1/ 5	0Vi53R
2/ 4	29Le 8
3/ 5	26 49
4/ 4	25 7
5/ 4	24 52D
6/ 3	26 15
7/ 3	28 59
8/ 2	2Vi40
9/ 1	6 49
10/ 1	10 58
10/31	14 36
11/30	17 10
12/30	18 13
4/23.5	24Le46D
1845	
1/29	17Vi31R
2/28	15 29
3/30	13 11
4/29	11 49
5/29	12 3D
6/28	13 54
7/28	17 3
8/27	21 2
9/26	25 22
10/26	29 35
11/25	3Li 8
12/25	5 28
1/ 1.6	18Vi13R
5/10.0	11Vi42D
1846	
1/24	6Li 8R
2/23	5 4
3/25	2 51
4/24	0 41
5/24	29Vi39
6/23	0Li17D
7/23	2 28
8/22	5 52
9/21	10 0
10/21	14 24
11/20	18 31
12/20	21 49
1/20.1	6Li 9R
5/28.1	29Vi38D
1847	
1/19	23Li47
2/18	24 1R
3/20	22 38
4/19	20 21
5/19	18 22
6/18	17 40D
7/18	18 37
8/17	21 3
9/16	24Li34
10/16	28 42
11/15	2Sc58
12/15	6 50
2/ 6.9	24Li 9R
6/16.0	17Li40D
1848	
1/14	9Sc44
2/13	11 11
3/14	10 56R
4/13	9 15
5/13	6 59
6/12	5 17
7/12	4 56D
8/11	6 10
9/10	8 45
10/10	12 18
11/ 9	16 20
12/ 9	20 20
2/23.5	11Sc17R
7/ 3.7	4Sc52D
1849	
1/ 8	23Sc46
2/ 7	26 7
3/ 9	26 57
4/ 8	26 12R
5/ 8	24 17
6/ 7	22 8
7/ 7	20 46
8/ 6	20 49D
9/ 5	22 20
10/ 5	25 4
11/ 4	28 35
12/ 4	2Sa25
3/ 9.4	26Sc57R
7/21.4	20Sc36D
1850	
1/ 3	6Sa 1
2/ 2	8 54
3/ 4	10 35
4/ 3	10 46R
5/ 3	9 32
6/ 2	7 29
7/ 2	5 34
8/ 1	4 39
8/31	5 6D
9/30	6 55
10/30	9 46
11/29	13 13
12/29	16 45
3/22.5	10Sa52R
8/ 6.4	4Sa37D
1851	
1/28	19Sa53
2/27	22 7
3/29	23 4
4/28	22 36R
5/28	20 60
6/27	18 58
7/27	17 24
8/26	16 59D
9/25	17 54
10/25	19 60
11/24	22 56
12/24	26 14
4/ 2.8	23Sa 5R
8/20.6	16Sa57D
1852	
1/23	29Sa24
2/22	1Cp58
3/23	3 29
4/22	3 42R
5/22	2 40
6/21	0 50
7/21	28Sa59
8/20	27 53
9/19	28 1D
10/19	29 23
11/18	1Cp44
12/18	4 41
4/11.8	3Cp47R
9/ 1.3	27Sa47D
1853	
1/17	7Cp46
2/16	10 28
3/18	12 23
4/17	13 10
5/17	12 43R
6/16	11 14
7/16	9 22
8/15	7 52
9/14	7 20D
10/14	8 0
11/13	9 47
12/13	12 19
4/20.5	13Cp11R
9/12.4	7Cp20D
1854	
1/12	15Cp12
2/11	17 56
3/13	20 7
4/12	21 20
5/12	21 24R
6/11	20 22
7/11	18 39
8/10	16 57
9/ 9	15 55
10/ 9	15 59D
11/ 8	17 11
12/ 8	19 17
4/28.5	21Cp31R
9/22.3	15Cp49D
1855	
1/ 7	21Cp54
2/ 6	24 35
3/ 8	26 54
4/ 7	28 27
5/ 7	28 58R
6/ 6	28 23
7/ 6	26 56
8/ 5	25 12
9/ 4	23 51
10/ 4	23 25D
11/ 3	24 4
12/ 3	25 43
5/ 5.5	28Cp58R
10/ 1.2	23Cp24D

Mo/Dy   Long

Mo/Dy	Long
1856	
1/ 2	28Cp 2
2/ 1	0Aq36
3/ 2	2 58
4/ 1	4 46
5/ 1	5 39
5/31	5 29R
6/30	4 22
7/30	2 43
8/29	1 11
9/28	0 20
10/28	0 31D
11/27	1 43
12/27	3 42
5/11.0	5Aq43R
10/ 8.1	0Aq17D
1857	
1/26	6Aq 5
2/25	8 28
3/27	10 25
4/26	11 36
5/26	11 49R
6/25	11 2
7/25	9 35
8/24	7 58
9/23	6 50
10/23	6 35D
11/22	7 21
12/22	8 59
5/16.9	11Aq51R
10/15.4	6Aq33D
1858	
1/21	11Aq10
2/20	13 29
3/22	15 33
4/21	16 58
5/21	17 31
6/20	17 5R
7/20	15 52
8/19	14 17
9/18	12 56
10/18	12 19
11/17	12 41D
12/17	13 59
5/22.5	17Aq31R
10/22.0	12Aq19D
1859	
1/16	15Aq55
2/15	18 9
3/17	20 15
4/16	21 52
5/16	22 42
6/15	22 36R
7/15	21 38
8/14	20 9
9/13	18 42
10/13	17 48
11/12	17 47D
12/12	18 44
5/27.7	22Aq46R
10/28.2	17Aq40D
1860	
1/11	20Aq25
2/10	22 30
3/11	24 37

Mo/Dy	Long
4/10	26Aq22
5/10	27 27
6/ 9	27 39R
7/ 9	26 59
8/ 8	25 39
9/ 7	24 9
10/ 7	23 2
11/ 6	22 41D
12/ 6	23 17
5/31.6	27Aq42R
11/ 1.8	22Aq41D
1861	
1/ 5	24Aq42
2/ 4	26 38
3/ 6	28 43
4/ 5	0Pi34
5/ 5	1 51
6/ 4	2 20
7/ 4	1 57R
8/ 3	0 49
9/ 2	29Aq20
10/ 2	28 3
11/ 1	27 26
12/ 1	27 42D
12/31	28 50
6/ 5.4	2Pi20R
11/ 7.2	27Aq24D
1862	
1/30	0Pi34
3/ 1	2 35
3/31	4 30
4/30	5 57
5/30	6 42
6/29	6 35R
7/29	5 40
8/28	4 17
9/27	2 54
10/27	2 2
11/26	1 59D
12/26	2 50
6/ 9.8	6Pi45R
11/12.3	1Pi54D
1863	
1/25	4Pi22
2/24	6 18
3/26	8 14
4/25	9 49
5/25	10 47
6/24	10 56R
7/24	10 16
8/23	9 0
9/22	7 35
10/22	6 31
11/21	6 12D
12/21	6 45
6/14.3	10Pi59R
11/17.1	6Pi11D
1864	
1/20	8Pi 4
2/19	9 52
3/20	11 48
4/19	13 29
5/19	14 39
6/18	15 3R
7/18	14 38

Mo/Dy	Long
8/17	13Pi32
9/16	12 8
10/16	10 55
11/15	10 20
12/15	10 36D
6/17.5	15Pi 3R
11/20.6	10Pi19D-
1865	
1/14	11Pi41
2/13	13 20
3/15	15 14
4/14	16 60
5/14	18 20
6/13	18 58
7/13	18 48R
8/12	17 54
9/11	16 33
10/11	15 14
11/10	14 26
12/10	14 25D
6/21.7	19Pi 1R
11/25.1	14Pi19D
1866	
1/ 9	15Pi15
2/ 8	16 45
3/10	18 34
4/ 9	20 23
5/ 9	21 51
6/ 8	22 43
7/ 8	22 48R
8/ 7	22 6
9/ 6	20 51
10/ 6	19 29
11/ 5	18 29
12/ 5	18 13D
6/25.8	22Pi52R
11/29.4	18Pi12D
1867	
1/ 4	18Pi48
2/ 3	20 6
3/ 5	21 50
4/ 4	23 40
5/ 4	25 16
6/ 3	26 19
7/ 3	26 38R
8/ 2	26 10
9/ 1	25 4
10/ 1	23 41
10/31	22 32
11/30	22 1
12/30	22 21D
6/29.9	26Pi39R
12/ 3.5	22Pi 1D
1868	
1/29	23Pi26
2/28	25 4
3/29	26 53
4/28	28 34
5/28	29 48
6/27	0Ar21
7/27	0 7R
8/26	29Pi10
9/25	27 50
10/25	26 34
11/24	25 50

Mo/Dy	Long
12/24	25Pi54D
7/ 2.9	0Ar22R
12/ 6.6	25Pi46D
1869	
1/23	26Pi47
2/22	28 16
3/24	0Ar 3
4/23	1 48
5/23	3 11
6/22	3 57
7/22	3 57R
8/21	3 12
9/20	1 57
10/20	0 37
11/19	29Pi41
12/19	29 30D
7/ 6.9	4Ar 3R
12/10.6	29Pi28D
1870	
1/18	0Ar 8
2/17	1 28
3/19	3 11
4/18	4 58
5/18	6 30
6/17	7 28
7/17	7 43R
8/16	7 10
9/15	6 2
10/15	4 40
11/14	3 34
12/14	3 8
7/10.9	7Ar43R
12/14.6	3Ar 8D
1871	
1/13	3Ar32D
2/12	4 41
3/14	6 19
4/13	8 7
5/13	9 45
6/12	10 55
7/12	11 23
8/11	11 5R
9/10	10 5
10/10	8 44
11/ 9	7 30
12/ 9	6 50
7/14.9	11Ar23R
12/18.5	6Ar48D
1872	
1/ 8	6Ar60D
2/ 7	7 56
3/ 8	9 28
4/ 7	11 15
5/ 7	12 58
6/ 6	14 18
7/ 6	15 0
8/ 5	14 56R
9/ 4	14 7
10/ 4	12 49
11/ 3	11 30
12/ 3	10 37
7/18.1	15Ar 4R
12/21.4	10Ar28D

Mo/Dy	Long
1873	
1/ 2	10Ar32
2/ 1	11 16
3/ 3	12 39
4/ 2	14 24
5/ 2	16 11
6/ 1	17 40
7/ 1	18 35
7/31	18 45R
8/30	18 9
9/29	16 57
10/29	15 34
11/28	14 31
12/28	14 10D
7/22.2	18Ar47R
12/25.3	14Ar10D
1874	
1/27	14Ar40
2/26	15 54
3/28	17 35
4/27	19 24
5/27	21 1
6/26	22 9
7/26	22 34
8/25	22 11R
9/24	21 7
10/24	19 44
11/23	18 31
12/23	17 55
7/26.5	22Ar34R
12/29.2	17Ar54D
1875	
1/22	18Ar11D
2/21	19 13
3/23	20 49
4/22	22 39
5/22	24 23
6/21	25 42
7/21	26 22
8/20	26 14R
9/19	25 20
10/19	23 59
11/18	22 39
12/18	21 50
7/30.7	26Ar25R
1876	
1/17	21Ar50D
2/16	22 40
3/17	24 9
4/16	25 58
5/16	27 47
6/15	29 17
7/15	0Ta11
8/14	0 19R
9/13	29Ar38
10/13	28 22
11/12	26 57
12/12	25 55
1/ 2.2	21Ar43D
8/ 3.3	0Ta22R
1877	
1/11	25Ar39D
2/10	26 15
3/12	27 35
4/11	29 22
5/11	1Ta15
6/10	2 55
7/10	4 3
8/ 9	4 26R
9/ 8	3 60
10/ 8	2 52
11/ 7	1 25
12/ 7	0 12
1/ 5.2	25Ar38D
8/ 7.9	4Ta27R
1878	
1/ 6	29Ar40R
2/ 5	0Ta 1D
3/ 7	1 10
4/ 6	2 53
5/ 6	4 48
6/ 5	6 37
7/ 5	7 58
8/ 4	8 38
9/ 3	8 28R
10/ 3	7 30
11/ 2	6 5
12/ 2	4 42
1/ 9.3	29Ar39D
8/12.7	8Ta41R
1879	
1/ 1	3Ta55R
1/31	3 60D
3/ 2	4 57
4/ 1	6 33
5/ 1	8 29
5/31	10 24
6/30	11 59
7/30	12 56
8/29	13 3R
9/28	12 19
10/28	10 57
11/27	9 29
12/27	8 26
1/13.4	3Ta50D
8/17.8	13Ta 6R
1880	
1/26	8Ta14D
2/25	8 56
3/26	10 24
4/25	12 19
5/25	14 20
6/24	16 7
7/24	17 20
8/23	17 46R
9/22	17 18
10/22	16 5
11/21	14 33
12/21	13 17
1/17.7	8Ta12D
8/22.2	17Ta46R
1881	
1/20	12Ta46R
2/19	13 12D
3/21	14 30
4/20	16 21
5/20	18 26
6/19	20 24
7/19	21 54
8/18	22 39
9/17	22Ta30R
10/17	21 29
11/16	19 57
12/16	18 30
1/21.3	12Ta46D
8/27.9	22Ta42R
1882	
1/15	17Ta41R
2/14	17 49D
3/16	18 53
4/15	20 38
5/15	22 46
6/14	24 53
7/14	26 38
8/13	27 44
9/12	27 55R
10/12	27 11
11/11	25 44
12/11	24 8
1/26.0	17Ta37D
9/ 3.0	27Ta58R
1883	
1/10	23Ta 1R
2/ 9	22 49D
3/11	23 37
4/10	25 14
5/10	27 21
6/ 9	29 36
7/ 9	1Gm36
8/ 8	3 3
9/ 7	3 37
10/ 7	3 13R
11/ 6	1 56
12/ 6	0 16
1/31.0	22Ta46D
9/ 9.5	3Gm38R
1884	
1/ 5	28Ta53R
2/ 4	28 19
3/ 5	28 48D
4/ 4	0Gm13
5/ 4	2 17
6/ 3	4 37
7/ 3	6 52
8/ 2	8 39
9/ 1	9 39
10/ 1	9 38R
10/31	8 38
11/30	6 59
12/30	5 21
2/ 5.3	28Ta19D
9/15.6	9Gm46R
1885	
1/29	4Gm25R
2/28	4 31D
3/30	5 41
4/29	7 39
5/29	10 2
6/28	12 29
7/28	14 36
8/27	16 2
9/26	16 29R
10/26	15 51
11/25	14 21
12/25	12 34
2/10.0	4Gm19D
9/23.5	16Gm30R
1886	
1/24	11Gm15R
2/23	10 56D
3/25	11 46
4/24	13 33
5/24	15 56
6/23	18 33
7/23	20 59
8/22	22 52
9/21	23 51
10/21	23 42R
11/20	22 28
12/20	20 39
2/16.2	10Gm54D
10/ 2.1	23Gm56R
1887	
1/19	18Gm59R
2/18	18 12
3/20	18 37D
4/19	20 8
5/19	22 27
6/18	25 10
7/18	27 54
8/17	0Cn15
9/16	1 47
10/16	2 14R
11/15	1 27
12/15	29Gm44
2/22.9	18Gm11D
10/11.6	2Cn14R
1888	
1/14	27Gm50R
2/13	26 33
3/14	26 27D
4/13	27 35
5/13	29 44
6/12	2Cn30
7/12	5 29
8/11	8 15
9/10	10 24
10/10	11 31
11/ 9	11 21R
12/ 9	9 59
3/ 1.5	26Gm20D
10/21.4	11Cn37R
1889	
1/ 8	7Cn59R
2/ 7	6 15
3/ 9	5 32
4/ 8	6 11D
5/ 8	8 1
6/ 7	10 44
7/ 7	13 52
8/ 6	17 2
9/ 5	19 46
10/ 5	21 38
11/ 4	22 16R
12/ 4	21 30
3/ 9.8	5Cn32D
11/ 2.5	22Cn16R

Orbital Data

Chiron was initially identified as 1977UB, and was subsequently assigned the official asteroid number 2060 by the Minor Planet Center of the International Astronomical Union. The following orbital elements by Dr. Brian Marsden, as published in IAU Circular 3151, were used to generate this ephemeris. They satisfy observations of Chiron in 1895, 1941, 1952, 1969, 1976 and 1977 to within 2" of arc. Perturbations by Jupiter through Pluto were taken into account, although subsequent discoveries have revealed Pluto's mass to be so small as to have far less effect than it had been given in the calculations.

Mean daily motion:	1'10".0/day
Maximum daily motion:	2'47".8
Minimum daily motion:	0'34".1
Maximum yearly motion:	16°59'36"
Minimum yearly motion:	3°27'35"
Perihelion distance:	8.5099 AU
Aphelion distance:	18.8805 AU
Sidereal period:	50.68 yrs
Synodic period:	372.6 days

T = 1996 Feb 19.5345 ET	Epoch = 1977 Sept 14.0 ET
ω = 339°.1051	e = 0.378623
N = 208°.7141 {1950.0	a = 13.695195 AU
i = 6°.9229	(n° = 0.01944702)
q = 8°.509883	p = 50.68 yrs

Osculating Elements

Date	North Node	Perihelion
12 Dec. 1899	208° 48'	186° 40'
30 Dec. 1949	208° 46'	188° 40'
17 Jan. 2000	209° 29'	188° 32'

Data ± 30'

Notes